This book is lovingly dedicated to our grandchildren:

Sierra, Alexander, Zachary, and Savannah and to our beloved friend and colleague, Al Segrist

Eighth Edition

COUNSELING STRATEGIES AND INTERVENTIONS

Sherry Cormier
West Virginia University

Harold Hackney
Syracuse University

Boston   Columbus   Indianapolis   New York   San Francisco   Upper Saddle River
Amsterdam   Cape Town   Dubai   London   Madrid   Milan   Munich   Paris   Montreal   Toronto
Delhi   Mexico City   São Paulo   Sydney   Hong Kong   Seoul   Singapore   Taipei   Tokyo

Vice President and Editor in Chief: Jeffery W. Johnston
Senior Acquisitions Editor: Meredith D. Fossel
Editorial Assistant: Nancy Holstein
Senior Marketing Manager: Christopher Barry
Senior Managing Editor: Pamela Bennett
Senior Project Manager: Mary M. Irvin
Operations Supervisor: Central Publishing
Operations Specialist: Laura Messerly
Senior Art Director: Jayne Conte
Cover Designer: Karen Salzbach
Cover Art: Fotolia/compass © fox17
Full-Service Project Management: Chitra Ganesan/PreMediaGlobal
Composition: PreMediaGlobal
Printer/Binder: Courier/Stoughton
Cover Printer: Courier/Stoughton
Text Font: Times 10/12

Every effort has been made to provide accurate and current Internet information in this book. However, the Internet and information posted on it are constantly changing, so it is inevitable that some of the Internet addresses listed in this textbook will change.

Library of Congress Cataloging-in-Publication Data

Cormier, L. Sherilyn (Louise Sherilyn),
    Counseling strategies and interventions / Sherry Cormier, Harold Hackney. — 8th ed.
        p. cm.
    Includes bibliographical references and index.
    ISBN-13: 978-0-13-707018-3
    ISBN-10: 0-13-707018-7
    1. Counseling psychology—Textbooks. I. Hackney, Harold, II. Title.

    BF636.6.C67 2012
    158'.3—dc22   2010038135

10 9 8 7 6 5 4 3 2 1

www.pearsonhighered.com

ISBN 10:   0-13-707018-7
ISBN 13: 978-0-13-707018-3

ABOUT THE AUTHORS

Sherry Cormier is Professor Emerita of counseling, rehabilitation counseling, and counseling psychology at West Virginia University, a licensed psychologist in the state of West Virginia, and a long-standing member of the American Counseling Association. Her areas of expertise include counseling training, counseling interventions, cognitive-behavioral therapy, clinical supervision, and health and wellness. Currently, Sherry is affiliated with Transformational Practices, an endeavor in which she provides clinical and consultation services and training to a variety of individuals and organizations. Prior to her appointment at West Virginia University, she was a faculty member at the University of Tennessee.

Harold Hackney is Professor Emeritus of counseling at Syracuse University, is a national certified counselor, licensed professional counselor, and approved clinical supervisor, and is a fellow of the American Counseling Association. Harold is a past president of the Association for Counselor Education and Supervision, member of the ACA Governing Council, and a board member of the Center for Credentialing in Education. His writings draw from his experiences as a school counselor, a marriage and family counselor, and his research on counseling processes and spirituality in counseling. Prior to his appointment at Syracuse University, Harold was a professor at Fairfield University and Purdue University.

BRIEF CONTENTS

CONTENTS

APPLICATION EXERCISES

PREFACE

Since the seventh edition of *Counseling Strategies and Interventions*, the helping professions have continued to expand and evolve. In writing the eighth edition, we have kept several well-grounded features from the previous editions. First, we have tried to be comprehensive yet concise. Second, the book has been written with upper-class undergraduates or beginning-level graduate students in mind in a variety of helping disciplines. Third, we have included a variety of learning exercises to help students apply and review what they have learned.

NEW TO THIS EDITION

An overall goal in this edition is the elimination of out-of-date material and the addition of content that reflects new sources and new thinking about the field. Many recently published sources are included.

A perusal of new content infused throughout the chapters includes the following topics:

- Cultural and racial microaggressions in the helping process
- The advocacy role for helpers
- Neurobiology and mindfulness
- Communication with clients with disabilities
- Notice and informed consent
- Focusing in depth in helping interviews
- Ethical issues in termination
- Stages of change model
- Ethical issues in web counseling, technology, and social networking
- Interpersonal therapy model
- Anxiety and shame in supervision
- Preparing for supervision
- New and additional cases and application exercises focusing on ethical issues and cultural issues, such as religious minorities and clients with disabilities

In addition, at the end of each of the ten chapters, we have now included activities from My Helping Lab (http://www.myhelpinglab.com), the online destination designed to help students make the transition from academic coursework to professional practice. This online content consists of video clips of authentic practitioner/client sessions with some well-known clinicians, video interviews with professionals in the field, an interactive case archive, and a licensing center with valuable information for students who are beginning their careers as helpers. Instructors can package access to My Helping Lab with this text by contacting their Pearson sales representative.

OVERVIEW OF THE BOOK

Chapter 1 identifies the context of the helping professions—who the helping professional is; what kinds of activities he or she performs; and the qualities and skills of helpers, such as cultural competence, resilience, and virtue. In addition, Chapter 1 describes issues related to professionalism, such as identity, training, and credentialing of professional helpers. The context of helping includes a wide variety of roles and functions. It might even seem to the untrained eye that the differences among helpers are greater than the similarities. We attempt to dispel that impression in Chapter 2, in which we discuss the helping relationship. It is this helping relationship that proves to be the unifying force for disparate roles and functions.

Although the helping relationship connotes a sense of shared purpose, there is an added expectation for the helper—the expectation that he or she be both responsible and responsive in exploring the client's needs and concerns. In Chapters 3 through 9, we identify the skills and interventions expected of a beginning professional helper. Some of these skills are rudimentary; others are more advanced and require coaching and practice. Chapters 3 and 4 define the helper's responsibility to be aware of and attentive to the client's communication patterns, especially silence. This responsibility is examined in Chapter 5, which deals with session management, including strategies for opening and terminating helping interviews as well as managing subsequent interviews. We also discuss ethical issues affecting initial sessions, such as confidentiality, informed consent, and privacy, and we also discuss ethical and pragmatic issues in terminating the helping relationship.

Chapters 6 and 7 delineate the basic helping strategies designed to elicit, support, or direct client change. Whether the focus is the client's thoughts or feelings or, more likely, a combination of both, the helper has certain tools or skills that facilitate the client's growth. Often, these skills enable the helper to understand the client's concerns or the client's world.

Chapter 8 is a pivotal point in the book. It builds on the fundamentals of the early chapters and is the foundation for the remaining chapters of the book. Although the helper is instrumental in conceptualizing issues (usually with the assistance of a particular theoretical orientation), the goal-setting process inherently depends on mutual discussion and agreement between helper and client. Drawing on mutually accepted goals, the helper begins the most crucial portion of the relationship: the focus on overt change. This calls for more than relationship skills and more than active listening. There are many helping interventions—derived both from theory and practice and supported by research—that are synonymous with effective helping practices. In Chapters 8 and 9, we explain and suggest classroom activities that will help the helper understand and begin practicing these interventions. In Chapter 9, we offer a variety of different helping strategies that are integrative in focus and purpose and reflect a host of theoretical orientations to helping, ranging from experiential and interpersonal to cognitive and behavioral as well as from individual, systemic, and collective approaches.

Finally, Chapter 10 includes several areas pertinent to beginning helpers. We explore common concerns of beginning helpers, such as managing personal issues, bridging the gulf between theory and practice, and managing all types and combinations of anxiety. This chapter also discusses preparing for ethical challenges, such as confidentiality, informed consent, privacy, and multiple relationships. Finally, the chapter focuses on the process of clinical supervision and how beginning helpers may use it to enhance their personal and professional development.

INSTRUCTOR SUPPLEMENTS

With this edition, we offer a revised online Instructor's Manual/Test Bank, authored by Beth Robinson, Ph.D., assistant professor of counseling, Acadia University. The manual contains test questions, chapter summaries, recommended readings, and additional classroom and homework activities. To download the Instructor's Manual go to the Pearson Instructor Resource Center at http://www.pearsonhighered.com.

ACKNOWLEDGMENTS

We extend our thanks and appreciation to several people who have helped make this eighth edition possible. We thank our editor, Meredith Fossel; our project manager, Mary Irvin; and editorial assistant Nancy Holstein, whose timely and expert help made our jobs so much easier. We gratefully acknowledge the reviewers of our manuscript for their insights and comments: Lisa D. Hines, San Francisco State University; Laura J. Perry, University of Florida; and Judith Slater, Kennesaw State University. We also gratefully acknowledge Beth Robinson for her wonderful work on the Instructor's Manual.

The Helping Profession

A woman goes into a beauty salon, and as she is getting her hair cut, she whispers to her hairdresser something about her marriage disintegrating.

A man goes into a sports bar and watches a game and says something to the bartender about losing his job.

A couple seeks the counsel of a rabbi about the declining health of their elderly parents.

A child confides in a school counselor about the big bruise that shows up on his leg.

A young adult refers herself to a community mental health center because she thought about killing herself after disclosing to her parents that she is a lesbian. There, she is seen by a social worker and a case manager.

An older man seeks the services of a psychologist for sexual dysfunction issues following prostate surgery.

A person who has been hospitalized following an accident in which his back was broken decides to talk with a rehabilitation counselor.

It could be argued that helping occurs in all the above examples. Certainly, the woman whose hair is being cut probably feels helped by her hairdresser in much the same way that the man feels helped by telling the bartender about his job loss. And the couple that seeks the wisdom of a rabbi would not be doing so without some sort of implicit trust and respect for this person. And the clients who are seen respectively by a counselor, social worker, case manager, psychologist, and so on, are also both seeking and, in all likelihood, receiving help. Yet, there are differences— hopefully, positive ones. The hairdresser and the bartender—despite possibly providing help— would be referred to as nonprofessional helpers, whereas the rabbi, social worker, case manager, psychologist, and counselor would be called professional helpers. And even among these kinds of professional helpers, there are differences; the helping profession includes a broadly knit collection of professionals, each fitting a particular need or segment of society. Some are directly identified as helping professionals, such as psychiatrists, psychologists, professional helpers, marriage and family therapists, and social workers. Others are professionals from other disciplines who enter the helping network on a temporary basis. Most notable among these are ministers, physicians, nurses, and teachers.

Professional helpers can be distinguished from nonprofessional helpers by their identification with a professional organization, their use of an ethical code and standards of practice, and their acknowledgment of an accrediting body that governs training, credentialing, and licensing of practice (Gale & Austin, 2003, p. 3). These are important ways in which a professional helper develops a sense of professional identity. *Professional identity* is defined as the identity assumed by a practitioner of a particular discipline; it is reflected in the title, role, and intention of the profession and results from a cohesive decision of the members of the profession (Myers, Sweeney & White, 2002, p. 396). As noted, one way that helping professionals achieve a sense of professional identity is by membership in a professional organization. As Vacc and Loesch (2000) pointed out, there are a number of relevant professional organizations for helping professionals, such as the American Counseling Association (ACA) for helpers, the American Psychological Association (APA) for psychologists, the National Association of Social Workers (NASW) for social workers, and the National Organization for Human Services (NOHS) for human service professionals. (See Appendix A for a list of websites for these and other organizations.)

Finally, professional helpers distinguish themselves from nonprofessional helpers by their sense of vocation and mission—the public promise (the meaning of the word *profess*) to act for the good of the public (Ponton & Duba, 2009, p. 117).

In this chapter, we examine the many facets of the helping professions. We also explore what constitutes differences among laypersons, such as the beautician who may help in the context of the job and professional helpers whose job is defined primarily by the focus of the helping process.

WHAT IS HELPING?

The process of helping has several dimensions, each of which contributes to the definition of *helping*. One dimension specifies the conditions under which helping occurs. Another dimension specifies the preconditions that lead one person to seek help and another to provide help. A third dimension relates to the results of the interaction between these two persons.

Helping Conditions

The conditions under which helping occurs are quite complex but in their simplest terms may be described as involving four components: (1) someone seeking help and (2) someone willing to give help who is (3) capable of or trained to help (4) in a setting that permits help to be given and received. The first of these conditions is obvious; one cannot help without the presence of someone seeking help. If I do not want to be helped, nothing you can do will be helpful. If I am not sure I want to be helped, then perhaps you will be helpful, provided you can enjoin me to make a commitment to accept help. The second condition requires the willingness or intention to be helpful. Here, it would be good to differentiate between the intention to be helpful and the need to be helpful. Many would-be helpers are driven by the need to be helpful and use the helping relationship for their own needs. This is rarely a conscious act. Neediness has a way of camouflaging itself in more respectable attire. But when the relationship is dictated by the helper's needs, the possibilities for helping are minimal. The third condition reflects the helper's skills, either learned or natural. It is not enough to be well-intentioned if your awareness and behaviors drive people away. Indeed, the primary purpose of pursuing training in the field of helping is to develop, expand, and refine your therapeutic skills. The fourth condition refers to the physical surroundings in which the helper and client meet. Privacy, comfort, aesthetic character of the room, and timing of the encounter all contribute to the setting in which helping transpires.

All four conditions occur within a cultural and environmental context in which individual clients may present with a variety of concerns and individual differences, including such dimensions as race, ethnicity, socioeconomic level, gender, religious and spiritual affiliation, ability status, sexual orientation, age, developmental stage of life, and so on. Naturally, such differences affect the help-giving and help-receiving processes in various ways. For example, some clients' cultural affiliations greatly impact even the decision to seek or not seek help from a helping professional. Instead, they may turn to family or tribal elders, religious and spiritual advisors, or close family confidants for guidance. Cultural variables also affect the setting in which help giving occurs. For some clients, the idea of going to see a helper in a professional office is too foreign to consider as a viable option. These clients may prefer a more informal and less structured setting. Also, even your best intentions to be helpful are influenced by your own cultural affiliations and may affect the degree to which some clients perceive you as able and qualified to help. If you do not understand your clients' expressions, the subtle nuances of their communication patterns, their cultural values, or their culturally related views of their problems, your best intentions may not be enough.

What Do Professional Helpers Do?

Having discussed the process of helping, we now turn our attention to what professional helpers actually do. Perhaps this is best illustrated by a story:

> Irina came to see Sherry because, she said, "Even though I am 50 years old, I don't think for myself, and I have trouble making any decision." Earlier in her life, Irina had once seen a professional helper with her now ex-husband. Initially, Sherry educated Irina about the helping process and specifically about issues related to privacy and confidentiality. This educational process was followed by an exploration process in which Irina told her story while Sherry created a safe therapeutic environment for self-disclosure and listened carefully. At different times, Sherry gently probed to move Irina's narrative along, to obtain historical information about Irina's life, and to explore Irina's cultural background. As Irina continued to tell her story, with Sherry's help, it became clearer what Irina wanted from the helping process. She wanted to develop greater reliance on herself so she could trust herself and her decision-making process. Sherry helped Irina develop this goal for change more specifically and then initiated several intervention strategies for Irina to use in working toward this desired outcome, including problem-solving training, cultural genogram work, modeling, and role-playing and behavioral rehearsal. As the sessions continued, Sherry helped Irina expand her story to include a newer version of herself—someone she saw as competent, confident, and capable. As Irina moved toward this point, Sherry helped her explore her readiness to terminate the helping process and continue the gains begun in counseling on her own.

As you read over this sample case, note how it generally illustrates the kinds of things that professional helpers do with clients:

- They help clients identify and explore life concerns and issues.
- They help clients identify and pursue culturally relevant expectations, wishes, or goals.

- They help clients identify, assess, and implement culturally relevant strategies for change.
- They help clients identify and assess results and plan for self-directed change in the client's own environment.

Professional helpers are trained in the general functions we just described of creating a helping relationship—communication, conceptualization, assessment, and intervention. In addition, some professionals—such *counselors,* social workers, and psychologists—provide more specialized services based on their training and work setting. For example, some practitioners may work specifically with minority clients, whereas others may work solely with children or adolescents or the elderly. Others may focus on couples and family systems or adults or even adults with particular kinds of issues, such as anxiety or depression or career counseling. Some clinicians may work primarily in group modalities; others may work in crisis intervention. And depending on the setting, professional helpers may focus on prevention, remediation, change, and/or life enhancement. Professional helpers use both theory and research to support best practices for working most effectively with particular kinds of clients in particular kinds of settings. Although there are differences within and between settings in which helping professionals work, they all honor the following principles:

- Professional helping involves responding to feelings, thoughts, actions, and social systems of clients.
- Professional helping is based on a stance or frame that involves a basic acceptance of clients.
- Professional helping is characterized by confidentiality and privacy.
- Professional helping is noncoercive.
- Professional helping focuses on the needs and disclosure of the client rather than the counselor.
- A skill underlying effective helping is communication.
- Professional helping is a multicultural experience (Hackney & Cormier, 2009, pp. 6–7).

SETTINGS IN WHICH HELPERS WORK

As we mentioned at the beginning of this chapter, there are a variety of trained persons and specializations in the helping professions. It is estimated that in the years between 2006–2016, the employment outlook for professional helpers is especially strong as emerging settings and needs continue to grow. Helpers in various disciplines are forging new paths all the time. Some helpers are working with persons with trauma, some are helping veterans, many others are working with older populations, and still others are working with residential youth schools and programs, parenting programs, and sports settings. The following discussion of representative settings and the services helpers working in them will offer some sense of the helping spectrum.

School Settings

School counselors are found in elementary, middle or junior high, and high schools. Elementary school counselors do provide some individual counseling with children, but they are more likely to work with the total school environment. Much of the elementary school counselor's focus is on preventive and developmental guidance programs and activities, such as classroom guidance units, small-group counseling, and parent-teacher conferences (Baker, 2000). Middle school and junior high school counselors share this total school perspective but tend to spend more time with students—individually and in groups—and somewhat less time with teachers and parents.

This slight shift in focus reflects the developmental changes that occur with preteens, who find themselves involved in self-exploration and identity crises. Two common programs in middle schools include peer facilitation and teacher-as-advisor programs (Vacc & Loesch, 2000). Counseling in the high school reflects a noticeable shift to the students as individuals. Career and college planning, interpersonal concerns, family matters, substance use, and personal identity issues tend to dominate the students' awareness, and the counseling process attempts to provide an environment in which to address these issues. The counselor's day is therefore much more task-oriented. Some students are referred by teachers, but many are self-referrals. The high school counselor often works with student groups on career and college issues, although counseling focuses on all types of secondary students, not just those who are college-bound. Secondary school counselors also engage in much consultation with teachers and administrators (Vacc & Loesch, 2000).

Regardless of the level of a school, school counselors work collaboratively with students, parents, teachers, administrators, and the community. Recent developments in school counseling focus on the use of school counseling programs that facilitate student achievement as well as student development. To help answer the question "How students are different as a result of what school helpers do?" the American School Counselor Association (ASCA, 2005) has developed the *ASCA National Model: A Framework for School Counseling Programs*. This document describes the competencies students obtain as a result of participating in school counseling programs and also defines both appropriate and inappropriate functions of school counselors. It also describes the mission statement of school counselors as supporting all facets of the educational environment in three domains: personal/social, academic, and career development. (For more on this model, see http://www.schoolcounselor.org.) This national model highlights the dramatic transformation of school counseling in the last decade. While individual counseling, small group work, and classroom guidance are still components of school counseling programs, the new initiatives in school counseling stress the importance of consultation and collaboration between school counselors and teachers, parents, and administrators, with the goal of promoting effective systemic wide change that offers access to opportunities and better achievement for all students (Clark & Breman, 2009, p. 7).

What will your future look like if you want to be a school counselor? First, you will need to be able and equipped to focus on the issues of the school as a system, in addition to the issues of individual students. An emerging role for school helpers is that of advocacy. This focus on systemic change and advocacy is central to the American School Counselor Association National Model (2005) that we previously identified. This might mean speaking "with teachers who intentionally or unintentionally discriminate against students in marginalized or devalued groups or challenging administrators to address various forms of institutionalized educational inequities" (Bemak & Chung, 2008, p. 375). Second, although responsive services to individuals will probably never "go out of style," there will be an increasing emphasis on developing programs that focus on prevention. Third, you will be heavily involved in the facilitation of groups, teams, or communities and on the achievement and educational needs of all students, making sure that minority students are as well-served as other students (Colbert, Vernon-Jones & Pransky, 2006).

College Settings

Although much college counseling occurs in counseling centers or psychological services centers, some helpers in higher education settings also work in offices related to student affairs, such as residence halls, career services, academic advising, and so on. A wide variety of problems are addressed, including career counseling, personal adjustment counseling, crisis counseling, and substance abuse counseling. College counselors also see students with mild to severe pathological problems, such as anxiety, depression, suicidal gestures, eating disorders, and trauma. Boyd and colleagues (2003) observed that the recent past has seen a huge increase in the number of college counseling services and in the functions they provide. Emerging issue in college settings include financial issues, immigration status concerns, date rape, and domestic and relationship violence.

In addition to individual counseling, much reliance is placed on group counseling and on the needs of special student populations and student retention. For example, most college counseling centers have a special focus and staff person to engage in counseling-related services for students with disabilities. Rollins (2005) described three special populations that are increasing on college campuses in the 21st century: domestic minorities and multiracial students, international students, and TCK, or third-culture kids. Students who belong to these groups may be more reluctant than others to seek the services of a college counselor.

What does the future look like for you should you decide to become a college counselor? First, you will be heavily involved in working with students representing special populations. This work involves outreach programming and consultation with other student offices, such as the Disability office, the International Students office, and the Multicultural Affairs office as well as with the residence halls. Second, you can expect to see clients who arrive on campus with more severe psychological issues. Some of these students may already be on psychotropic medications to manage such conditions as depression, anxiety, eating disorders, substance abuse, and even chronic mental illness. Unfortunately, some students who are severely distressed may be less likely to walk through the counseling center's doors (Faqrrell, 2005). In addition to reaching these students through psychological education, support groups, and outreach programming, you also can expect to become involved in technology, as college counseling centers are adding on-line counseling resources to more traditional in-office services (Faqrrell, 2005). An excellent example of a recent technological advance in college counseling (as cited by Kennedy, 2004) is the *Career CyberGuide* offered by York University in Toronto, Canada (available online at http://www.yorku.ca/careers/cyberguide). As technological services grow, so do issues surrounding confidentiality and privacy. An ethical intention checklist surrounding online counseling services is available from Shaw and Shaw (2006).

Community Settings

Helpers working in community settings usually are social workers, mental health helpers, and other human service professionals, such as case managers, mental health aides, crisis intervention helpers, and community outreach workers. Their places of employment are the most diverse of all helping settings. Family service agencies, youth service bureaus, satellite mental health centers, YWCA counseling services, homeless shelters, and substance abuse centers are examples of community settings. Much of what is done is psychotherapy, whether with individuals, families, or groups. In addition, the community practitioner may become involved in community advocacy efforts and direct community intervention. The types of problems seen by community practitioners encompass the spectrum of mental health issues. Clients include children, adolescents, adults, couples, families, and the elderly. In other words, community-based helpers see an enormous variety of clients and problems in a typical month. The work demands are often heavy, with caseloads ranging from 20 to 40 clients per week.

Currently, mental health helpers are concerned with the delivery and implementation of services that are both therapeutic and cost-effective and are based on developmental notions as much as remediation. Couples and family helpers as well as addiction specialists also offer services through a variety of community agencies.

What can you expect should you choose to work as a practitioner in some sort of a community setting? One issue you will have to grapple with is the effects of managed health care, created by the reimbursement system of third-party payees of health insurance. You may engage in brief and short-term counseling in these settings because managed care usually only covers the cost of a certain number of counseling sessions a year. Moreover, you will probably be required to provide a fair amount of written documentation and accountability, often in the form of client treatment plans to "justify" the sessions for a given client with a particular diagnosis. Overall, you may be challenged to do more work with fewer available resources. Although at times this can be a test of your patience and resilience, working in a community setting provides the satisfaction of knowing that you are giving something back to the community in which you live.

Religious Settings

Vacc and Loesch (2000) noted that "an interesting mixture of professions is evident in the growing number of clerics (e.g., rabbis, priests, ministers, sisters) who have completed counselor-in-preparation programs" (p. 344). Despite many similarities, helping in religious settings is different in some ways from that in other settings. The similarities include the range of individual and family problems seen, the types and quality of therapy provided, and the helpers' professional qualifications. The differences reflect the reasons that some religious groups establish their own counseling services. There is at least some acknowledgment of the role of religion or spirituality in the individual's life problems. Many religious helpers believe that human problems must be examined and changes introduced within a context of spiritual and religious beliefs and values. The religious counseling center is undeniably attractive for many clients who, because of their backgrounds, place greater trust in the helper who works within a religious affiliation. According to Vacc and Loesch (2000), the three major counseling activities engaged in by clerics are bereavement counseling, marriage and family counseling, and referrals to other professionals.

Helpers in religious settings are often ordained ministers who have obtained postgraduate training in counseling. However, increasing numbers of the laity are also entering religious counseling settings or are receiving training in pastoral counseling and working in nonreligious settings, such as private practice, hospitals, and hospices. The number of academic programs granting degrees in pastoral counseling has increased substantially in recent years, as has the number of helpers who integrate a faith-based worldview with their academic training and subsequent licensure. This is important because regulation and oversight of unlicensed religious helpers involve substantial ethical and legal issues.

What can you anticipate if you decide to work in a religious setting or offer faith-based counseling? You may end up seeing well-known people who prefer to deal with issues or lapses in judgment by seeing someone in a religious setting. You also may work with people who cannot afford counseling services in other kinds of settings. You will also probably see clients who want to incorporate their faith heritage, spiritual beliefs, or spiritual modalities, such as prayer, in the counseling sessions. You also may work fairly often with people in crisis, so brushing up on your crisis intervention skills is a good idea.

Industrial and Employment Settings

Many professionals consider the private sector to be the new frontier for helping services. Such services occur primarily in the form of employee assistance programs (EAPs) that are administered either within the employment setting or through a private contract with a counseling agency. These programs are occurring with increasing frequency in business, industry, governmental units, hospitals, and schools. Many EAPs focus on the treatment of substance abuse issues, whereas others have expanded services to include individual, couple, and family concerns. To make the workplace a psychologically healthy environment, EAPs also deal with counterproductive workplace behaviors and stress management issues. Some research has found a connection between work stress and infectious disease (Hewlett, 2001).

Another type of counseling service that has appeared in industry settings is the outplacement counseling service. Outplacement refers to the process of facilitating the transition from employment to unemployment or from employment in one corporation to employment in another. The need for outplacement counseling has increased as corporations downsize their operations to cut costs or to address new goals and objectives. The client may be a top executive, middle manager, line supervisor, or laborer. Counseling takes the form of career counseling and includes the administration of career and personality inventories. The objectives for management clients are to provide data and counseling that will help executives assess their career options and develop plans for obtaining new positions as well as to support clients through that transition period. The objectives for employees who may be affected by plant closings are to identify career alternatives and to assist the company in designing retraining programs that will help unemployed workers obtain new jobs. The outplacement clinician has often worked in an industry setting and understands the characteristics of this clientele from firsthand experience. Practitioners in employment settings also focus on career issues and the interaction between the individuals and their work roles (Power & Rothausen, 2003).

What can you expect should you choose to work in industrial and employment settings? As job-related stress increases due to downsizing and outsourcing, you will see more clients who take advantage of employer-assisted counseling plans. Some clients may turn to substances such as prescription drugs and alcohol to self-medicate the anxiety and stress resulting from increased job demands. Having an excellent toolkit of substance abuse intervention skills is important. Also, as job stress increases, so too will the need and demand for employee wellness programs. Workplace violence and the prevention of it is also a focus area for helpers who serve in these settings.

Health Care and Rehabilitation Settings

An increasing number of practitioners are finding employment in health care settings such as hospitals, hospices, vocational rehabilitation centers, departments of behavioral medicine, rehabilitation clinics, and so on. Responsibilities of helpers in these settings are diverse and include such tasks as providing counseling to patients and/or patients' families, crisis management, grief work with the terminally ill, and the implementation of psychological and educational interventions for patients with chronic illnesses, people with physical challenges, and so on. More addictions specialists are also working in health care settings. Wellness programs are also increasing in numbers in these settings. It is believed that the number of helpers in health care and rehabilitation settings will continue to rise with increasing human service needs and advances in medicine. For example, the need for rehabilitation helpers now exceeds the supply by over 25 percent across the United States.

Your future as a helper in health care settings is constantly being defined and redefined. Generally, in these settings, you need a repertoire of skills to work effectively with both individuals and families and both illness and wellness. You are also likely to be functioning in a health care delivery setting that integrates both physical and behavioral/mental functioning because the two are so interrelated. You may become involved in teaching patients responsibility for medication compliance and pain management. And you will probably be heavily invested in prevention. For example, while providing informational and psycho-educational programs to patients whose disease processes are from unhealthy lifestyle factors, the future looks more and more promising for the implementation of programs to prevent disease processes in the first place by teaching patients effective self-care—proper nutrition, exercise, and reduction of negative thoughts and feelings.

APPLICATION EXERCISE 1.1
Work Settings and Job Functions

Think about a helping setting that interests you. Interview a person employed as a helper in this setting. Explore the job responsibilities, types of clients served, unique aspects of the setting, and joys and frustrations of the helper. Your instructor may have you either present to your class an oral summary on your visit or write a summary of your interview. In constructing this summary, note whether your findings about this setting are consistent with your expectations. If so, how? If not, why?

HELPER QUALITIES AND SKILLS

We have described six settings in which helping and counseling occur. Of course, there are many others, including couples and family therapy, correctional institution counseling, geriatric counseling, and even sports counseling. In all these settings—and with the variety of presenting issues that are seen—there is a common core of characteristics and skills of effective helpers. Over the years, a number of writers have described this core. Qualities such as self-awareness and understanding, open-mindedness and flexibility, objectivity, trustworthiness, interpersonally sensitivity and emotional intelligence, curiosity, and caring are supported by the literature. We concur with all these. We also believe that these are general enough characteristics and skills that you can deduce what they mean on your own and decide if they describe you or not. In this section of the chapter, we want to focus on four qualities that are not as transparent in meaning and implication as the ones just mentioned but in our opinion have tremendous importance for practitioners in the 21st century: virtue, cultural competence, neural integration, and resilience.

Virtue

A simple definition of *virtue* has to do with goodness (Kleist & Bitter, 2009). Virtue addresses the character traits of the individual helper and asks the question "What kind of person are you?" (Kleist & Bitter, 2009). Aristotle spoke about virtue as a way of being in the world or a basic disposition toward the world. For example, are you a person who is kind? Are you someone with integrity? Part of being a virtuous helper involves the capacity to put the well-being of your clients at the top of your list of priorities. To do so, helpers in all fields are guided by various codes of ethical behavior (American Association for Marriage and Family Therapy, 2001; American Counseling Association, 2005; American Psychological Association, 2003; National Association of Social Workers, 1999: National Organization for Human Services, 1996). A major guiding principle of these ethical codes is the recognition of the importance of being committed to the client's well-being. We think virtue is important today because much of our world seems to be morally compromised and fractured. Ethical codes of conduct do not just convey information; they also help inform a particular way of being in the world. Sullivan (2004)—who has designed an undergraduate mentorship for developing wise and effective habits of character—describes ethics as a particular worldview that incorporates virtue and aspiration. This ethical model assists us in learning to discern what helps persons and communities flourish and what does not (p. 69). For example, when it comes to choosing between the well-being of your client and your own pocketbook, how do you make this decision by using the ethical codes to guide you? What kind of character underlies this decision? What kind of "self" are you bringing to the ethical decisions you will inevitably need to make about clients? Some of you undoubtedly are reading this book while holding views that may label you as leaning toward the "left," while other readers hold views characterized as leaning toward the "right." Yet, despite differing views and values, both liberals and conservatives can share the characteristic of virtue. You may hold opposing views on politics or religion yet share something virtuous about your way of being in the world and the goodness that you bring to the ethical decisions you make about your clients. Virtue is also an important foundational quality in being a culturally competent helper.

Cultural Competence Skills

Helping professionals are seeing an increasingly diverse group of clients. It is expected that such increasing diversity will continue in the 21st century and beyond. As the dimensions of client diversity expand, the competence of helpers to deal with complex cultural issues must also grow. As Robinson (1997) noted, diversity and multiculturalism are not synonymous. *Diversity* describes clients who are different across dimensions such as age, gender, race, religion, ethnicity, sexual orientation, health status, social class, and so on. *Multiculturalism* involves an awareness and understanding of the principles of power and privilege. Power and privilege can be defined in many ways, but we especially like the definitions that Lott (2002, p. 101) has offered: *Power* is "access to resources" and *privilege* is "unearned advantage" and, thereby, "dominance." As you can see from these definitions, power and privilege are linked together in important ways. Those who have unearned privilege often use or abuse their power to dominate and subordinate (or oppress) those who do not have privilege and power. Multiculturalism is "willingly sharing power with those who have less power" and using "unearned privilege to empower others" (Robinson, 1997, p. 6). People who hold unearned privilege and power often seek to maintain their power by labeling, judging, and discriminating against those who do not. This discrimination usually occurs on the basis of various dimensions of diversity, such as race, social class, religion, age, gender, sexual orientation, health status, and so on. Those who are discriminated against on the basis of these dimensions not only feel excluded and disempowered, but they also have, in reality, fewer resources. For example, people living in poverty have less access to employment, decent housing, health care, pay and benefits, and even such resources as technology.

Another unfortunate result of power and privilege is the possibility that someone could have a professional commitment to diversity without a corresponding commitment to multiculturalism. When this occurs, differences usually pull people apart rather than bring them together—and the excluded person often feels like a scapegoat, and alienation results. As an example, consider the client who comes to see you after a particularly volatile staff meeting at her worksite. Her colleagues are primarily white men, with the exception of one African-American woman. Your client reports that during the meeting, one of the men (not the boss) publicly shamed her female colleague in front of the group for a particular way that this woman had handled a situation. Your client has also been publicly criticized by this same man. The man who has done this also publicly professes a strong commitment to diversity, yet his behavior suggests he has no commitment to multiculturalism. Moreover, he has engaged in "pulling rank" on the basis of his unearned privilege (race and gender) to maintain his power and privilege as well as to disempower the female worker, and as a result, he has engaged in both racism and sexism. Your client feels so intimidated and abused by this male colleague that she said nothing in the meeting after the public attack (nor did any of the other men, including the male boss). She is in a quandary about what she should now do: Should she attempt to talk to her boss, speak with her female colleague, or file some sort of complaint? In spite of her intimidation, your client feels strongly that she must do something, not just on behalf of herself but also on behalf of her female colleague and to protest the values reflected in this organizational behavior that has been permitted to continue over time.

This scenario reflects an emerging trend in the development of cultural competence that is referred to as *social justice*—or "how advantages and disadvantages are distributed to individuals in a society" (Miller, 1999, p. 11). Vera and Speight (2003, p. 254) have suggested that "social justice is at the heart of multiculturalism" because the existence of institutionalized discrimination, such as racism, sexism, religious persecution, homophobia, and so on, is what accounts for the unfair experiences for diverse groups of persons." We return to this concept throughout this book (see also the Social Justice ACA Division at http://www.counselors forsocialjustice.org).

In 1992, Sue, Arredondo, and McDavis developed a set of multicultural competencies that focused on attitudes, knowledge, and skill areas for the development of culturally sensitive practitioners. These competencies were updated in a 2002 guidebook (Roysircar, Arredondo, Fuertes, Ponterotto, Coleman, Israel & Toporek, 2002) and more recently summarized by Arredondo and Perez (2006). There are many other ideas of what it means to be a culturally competent helper. Montalvo (as cited in Daw, 1997) stated that *cultural competence* "is the business of spotting obstacles and facilitators to treatments" within a client's culture (p. 9). He illustrated this definition with the following story of a client who was a Vietnam veteran suffering from post-traumatic stress disorder (PTSD):

> The man was shunned by his family because they saw the spirits of the people he had killed in Vietnam. His therapist did some checking around in the man's ethnic group and discovered that the Navajos had a ritual dance for warriors dealing with the spirits of those they had harmed. Rather than EMDR [eye movement desensitization and reprocessing] or another treatment that had probably already been tried, the therapist connected the veteran to a medicine man. When the man opened up to his culture it was helpful to him and also to his family. The family opened their doors to him again. (p. 9)

Although Montalvo offered his definition a few years ago, there is still no universal agreement about what constitutes cultural competence (Sanchez-Hucles & Jones, 2005). However, there is general agreement that counseling/clinical competence is not the same as multicultural counseling competence (Sue & Sue, 2008). From the perspective of these authors, many helping professionals "have seldom functioned in a culturally competent manner" (p. 35).

An even more recent development in the area of cultural competence has to do with the role of helpers as advocates. Advocacy, which has its roots in both the social justice and multicultural competencies we described above, involves acting with or on behalf of clients at three different levels of intervention: client/individual, school/community, and the public arena (Toporek, Lewis & Cretha, 2009, p. 262). For example, these authors described the case of Mila, a 7th-grade student in a wheelchair attending a public school that had not been fully equipped for students with disabilities. Among other issues this posed for Mila, a major one was inaccessibility to the restroom and harassment from fellow students. At the individual level, the school counselor worked with Mila to empower her within her school and peer environment. However, as Mila's situation also reflected a picture of systemic problems within the school environment, the counselor also met with school administrators to address the issues of a lack of resources for appropriate accommodations as well as a lack of peer understanding and support. Ultimately, the counselor also addressed social/political advocacy efforts in the public arena by focusing on the community surrounding the school and on the implications of the Americans with Disabilities Act (ADA, 1991). Without such advocacy, the best efforts at helping may be limited, as oppression and systemic barriers that interfere with clients' well-being remain unaddressed (Toporek et al., 2009). (For a summary of more specific advocacy competencies, see those delineated by the American Counseling Association in Ratts, Toporek & Lewis, 2010).

How do helpers develop cultural competence and skills associated with social justice and advocacy? The answers to this question are not always simple. Moreover, developing cultural competence does not happen overnight. Indeed, it is most likely a lifelong process. However, we can make the following recommendations:

- Become aware of your own cultural heritage and affiliations and of the impact your culture has on the counseling relationship. Remember that culture affects both you and your clients. No one—regardless of race or ethnicity—is devoid of culture.
- Become immersed in the cultures of people who differ from you (Sue & Sue, 2008). Seek opportunities to interact with people who represent different cultural dimensions, and be open to what they have to say. Create opportunities rather than waiting for them to come to you. Hansen and colleagues (2006) suggest seizing such opportunities as getting culture-specific case consultation and learning about indigenous resources (p. 72).
- Be realistic and honest about your own range of experiences as well as issues of power, privilege, and poverty. Become aware of the great impact that poverty has on ethnicity. Think about the positions you have or hold that contribute to oppression, power, and privilege. In the United States or European-American countries, being White, able-bodied, young, intelligent, male, Christian, heterosexual, middle or upper class, and English-speaking all convey aspects of privilege. Individuals who do not share these privileged attributes are disempowered in significant ways, and the inequities between privileged and nonprivileged persons contribute to much injustice and oppression *especially when privilege is ignored by those who hold it* (Crethar, Rivera & Nash, 2008). Hardy (as cited in Daw, 1997) observed, "It's easier to talk about one's culture than one's power, one's ethnicity than one's privilege" (p. 9).
- Remember that as a helper, it is incumbent on you, not your clients, to educate yourself about various dimensions of culture. For example, if you feel uninformed about the background and cultural and religious heritage of your new client who is Muslim and you ask your client to inform you, this essentially constitutes a role reversal, and the client is likely to feel frustrated. A similar misuse of culture would be to tell your Latino client about your new Latino/a friends. A facet of cultural competence that emerges consistently from the literature is how important it is for helpers to demonstrate an interest in a client's culture and to seek out opportunities to educate yourself about cultures different from your own. At the same time, being a false "know it all" and pretending to have all the knowledge and answers about a client's varying dimensions of culture is also misguided.
- Become aware of your own biases and prejudices, of which racism is the most problematic (although not the only -*ism* that impacts practice). Remember that racism is not restricted to

overt behaviors but also includes everyday opinions, attitudes, and ideologies (Casas, 2005, p. 502). Recent literature has attested to covert racism in the form of what is known as racial microaggressions (Sue et al., 2007). Racial microaggressions are more insidious forms of racism, often committed by a well-intentioned person but still deeply wounding, that are "brief, commonplace, and subtle indignities (whether verbal, behavioral, or environmental) that communicate negative or denigrating messages to people of color" (Constantine, Smith, Redington & Owens, 2008, p. 349). As an example of this, consider the way that language is used. Watts-Jones (2004) points out the power conveyed by words and phrases such as "black sheep," "black mark," "white lie," and "Indian giver" and suggests that from a social justice perspective, practitioners need to pause and query when such language is used in the counseling room. Too often, we do not recognize such language, let alone challenge it. For example, in working with persons with disabilities, the use of first-person language is empowering. Group designations such as "the disabled" or "the blind" are inappropriate because they do not convey respect and equality. First-person language such as "persons with disabilities" or "individuals with visual impairments" is preferred (Daughtry, Abels & Gibson, 2009, p. 204). All helpers need to be aware of potential racist origins and implications of their actions and to also be sensitive to potential racist origins and implications of the actions of colleagues. Saying to a client of color "You are so light-skinned that you really don't look Black" or telling a client of color not to worry about getting racially profiled because "it happens to a lot of people all the time" are examples of very wounding racial microaggressions that drive clients away from the helping process. Sue (2010) has recently written a groundbreaking book—suitable for both helpers and clients on the insidious effects of microaggressions—that is based on 5 years of research he and his students have conducted. We list this book in the "Recommended Readings" at the end of the chapter, and we consider it to be essential reading for all helping professionals because many microaggressions are committed by people like you and me—well-meaning, well-intended, decent folks who lapse into states of unawareness that produce various categories of microaggressions that are devastating to the recipients of such slurs, insults, or invalidations.

• It is the responsibility of the helper, not the client, to get issues related to culture "out on the counseling table," so to speak. This responsibility has been defined by Day-Vines et al. (2007) as *broaching*—that is, the helper's "ability to consider the relationship of racial and cultural factors to the client's presenting problem, especially because these issues might otherwise remain unexamined during the counseling process" (p. 401). Broaching is important because the acknowledgment of cultural factors enhances the credibility of the helper, establishes trust, fosters greater client satisfaction, and influences the clients' decisions about returning for further sessions. Broaching behaviors essentially "refers to a consistent and ongoing attitude of openness with a genuine commitment by the counselor to continually invite the client to explore issues of diversity" (Day-Vines, 2007, p. 402). An example of a broaching behavior would be for the practitioner to say at the beginning of an initial counseling session something like the following: "I notice that we are from different ethnic backgrounds. I am wondering how you are feeling about working with someone like me who is a White European American woman . . ." (Day-Vines, 2007, p. 402).

In recent years, all major professional organizations for helping professionals have offered descriptions of various multicultural competencies required for helpers. (These are usually available from the organization's website, many of which we list in Appendix A.) We strongly encourage you to familiarize yourself with these competencies and to identify areas in which you need to develop greater awareness, sensitivity, and proficiency.

Neural Integration and Mindful Awareness

Earlier, we said that virtue was important in the development of cultural effectiveness. It is also likely that the development of cultural competence is impacted by the therapist's own level of neural integration. *Neural integration,* although complicated as a process, can be simply stated as describing what occurs when separate parts of the brain (hence the word *neural*) are connected together into a functional whole (hence the word *integration*) (Siegel, 2007). What does the counselor's level of neural integration have to do with being an effective helper? The recently emerging field of interpersonal neurobiology (Siegel, 1999, 2007) asserts that neural integration allows clinicians to enter a state of mind in which their ability to think clearly and maintain an emotional connection with clients is enhanced. When helpers do not have it "together," their capacity to think clearly during counseling and develop effective connections with clients is diminished. Siegel and Hartzell (2003) made the analogy between having neural integration as the "high road" or not having it as the "low road" (p. 154). When taking the "high road," neurally integrated practitioners are able to process information with clients that involves rational and reflective thought processes, mindfulness, and self-awareness. These neural processes occur in the prefrontal cortex of the brain, located in the front part of the brain behind the forehead. When the opposite occurs, the "low road"—or being in a nonintegrated brain state—helpers are governed more by emotions, impulsive reactions, and rigid rather than thoughtful responses to clients. In this nonintegrated state, the prefrontal cortex shuts down and disconnects from other parts of the brain that need its signals to function well.

Why is it so important for helping professionals to be neurally well-integrated? We now know from a decade or so of brain research that neural integration aids practitioners in developing empathy as well as having reflective conversations with clients that help them process information and regulate emotions. Moreover, the helper's own level of neural integration helps to foster new neural connections in the brains of clients, a process referred to as neural or brain plasticity. It is now believed that neural plasticity may be the path by which psychotherapy alters the brain (Siegel, 2006).

At this point, perhaps you are thinking how in the world can you integrate yourself "neurally"? What is the process? What does it mean? How does it happen? One major way that neural integration occurs for helpers is through "mindful awareness." Siegel (2006) stated that mindful awareness invokes receptivity to what arises within the mind's eye on a moment-to-moment basis. In other words, being mindful is simply paying attention to what is happening as it is happening. It is being aware of what we are doing *while* we are doing it. This morning, when I watered the outdoor plants, I caught myself doing it mindlessly—on "automatic pilot," so to speak—until I noticed a hummingbird and a beautiful coral-colored zinnia popping its head up through the yellow black-eyed susan patch. Immediately, I became mindful or aware and stopped to notice and pay attention and to appreciate. One way to develop mindful awareness is through a daily practice of some form of meditation. Meditation involves the focusing of our nonjudgmental attention on our own internal states—intentions, thoughts, feelings, and bodily functions (Siegel, 2006, p. 15). Although there are various forms of meditation, in its most elemental form, meditation simply means becoming still and quiet for a period of time and sitting with yourself and focusing on a mantra (such as "I am peaceful") or on your breath.

Two noted clinicians—Marsha Linehan and Carl Thoresen—have provided tips for cultivating mindfulness (Reiser, 2008; Harris, 2009). Among these tips are the following:

- Cultivate the practice of mindfulness on a daily basis. One way to do so is to take mindful breaks during the day. For example, set a timer or use a clock that chimes on the quarter hour. Each time the timer goes off or the clock chimes, stop, turn your attention to your breath, and observe your in-breath and out-breath for three cycles or more if feeling stressed. You can even install a bell of mindfulness on your computer; download it at http://www.mindfulnessdc.org/mindfulclock.html.

- Develop one or more of what Thoresen (in Harris, 2009) refers to as the "mindfulness-based spiritual practices." These include the following:
  - *Passage meditation:* Use a memorized passage or prayer from any religious or spiritual tradition that you repeat silently—once daily; preferably in the morning—to set a positive intention for the day.
  - *Mantra meditation:* Use a mantram or sacred word or phrase from any tradition you prefer—basically, a word or phrase that is meaningful to you, such as "peace" or "love."
  - *Slowing down:* Make conscious efforts to slow down your pace of daily life; drive more slowly, eat more slowly, type on the computer more slowly, talk more slowly.
  - *One-pointed attention:* Become more focused on one single thing and less preoccupied with trying to cram everything you can do into a short period of time. One-pointed attention is the opposite of multi-tasking, which is extremely stress-inducing.
  - *Train the senses:* With the acceleration of technology, we are bombarded with an onslaught of nonstop sensory information. Designate a time during the day in which you turn off the cell phone, the landline, the computer, and so on.

New research has discovered that having clinicians who meditated prior to counseling sessions resulted in better treatment outcomes for clients (Grepmair et al., 2007). Mediation also promotes integration of various parts of the brain that are associated with a secure and safe attachment relationship between helper and client. This in turn helps to promote resiliency in clients and helpers.

Resiliency

As important as resiliency is for clients, it is equally important for practitioners. *Resiliency* is defined as the capacity to bounce back from challenges or adversity. Resiliency is derived from the emerging strengths perspective. Always a cornerstone of human services and social work practice, this perspective is also becoming stronger in both psychology and counseling. The strengths perspective also has important implications for virtue and cultural competence. Smith (2006) noted that the *strengths-based perspective* is important because "it represents a dramatic paradigm shift" from focusing on pathology to developing assets (p. 16). She asserts that a strengths perspective seeks to understand human virtue and to answer the question of what strengths a person has used and continues to use to deal effectively with life. As you can see, this question impacts clients and helpers alike. Smith (2006) also observed the connection between a strengths perspective and cultural competence, noting that "a core component of the strength-based theory is that culture has a major impact on how people view and evaluate human strengths" (p. 17).

Why do a strengths perspective and resiliency matter for helpers? Today, helpers are expected to do more with less and to cope with such different global challenges as terrorism and natural disasters as well as everyday stressors and hassles. As clinicians share their sense of hope and optimism with clients, this perspective begins to be transferred to clients and informs the helping relationship (Smith, 2006, p. 42). How do we as helpers hold up during the stressful work that we do while offering support and help to our clients? The answers to this question come from the strengths-based perspective and the resiliency literature. Resiliency means that helpers are able to:

- Use an active, positive, proactive approach to challenges and issues.
- Perceive pain and frustration constructively, seeing a glass as half full rather than half empty.
- Make decisions based on our own strengths of character, such as virtue, integrity, and courage.
- Identify and use the protective factors present in our own cultural and ethnic group as well as our environment (Smith, 2006).

In general, clinicians develop resilience by replenishing the well that gets drained in doing therapeutic work with clients (Wicks, 2007). This is accomplished by acute care and sensitivity to one's own ongoing reflective process, such as daily journaling, and by strengthening one's own self-care protocol with tools such as exercise, solitude, and mindfulness.

An interesting extension of the resilience literature is provided by Osborn (2004), who describes helper resilience as stamina—the endurance and capacity to withstand or hold up under challenging conditions. Osborn gave seven suggestions for both off-the-job and on-the-job activities as well as ways of thinking to enhance our resilience and stamina. Based on the acronym of STAMINA (Selectivity, Temporal sensitivity, Accountability, Measurement and management, Inquisitiveness, Negotiation, Acknowledgment of agency), these ways of being in the world and with our work are setting limits, honoring the rhythms and cycles of time, respecting our ethical standards and employing virtue to make ethical decisions, conserving and protecting our resources, looking for the uniqueness of our clients, engaging in a give-and-take, and attending to the life force within ourselves. Note that this last skill in particular involves neural integration; when we are in a state of mindful awareness, we engage our energy and our life force in a way that flows and plays. On especially stressful days, can you imagine yourself dancing into your work setting?

APPLICATION EXERCISE 1.2
Skills of Helpers

Observe the day-to-day work of helping professionals or even the helper you observed for Application Exercise 1.1. What do you conclude about their skills? Were you aware of particular personal qualities that stood out for you? What did you notice about the way they interacted with other people in their work setting? Did anything about the interventions they used seem especially useful? From your observations, could you draw any conclusions about their cultural competence and commitment to social justice? What kinds of diverse clients do they serve? Did you obtain any information that would provide you with conclusions about their virtue? How did they promote the well-being of their clients? What challenges did they face in their work? Did they appear to be resilient in the face of such challenges or not? In their interactions with others, did they seem mindful and centered or were they frazzled and responding rigidly and/or emotionally?

TRAINING AND CREDENTIALING OF PROFESSIONAL HELPERS

Credentialing of professional helpers usually involves three activities:

1. Graduation from an accredited program
2. Certification
3. Licensure (Vacc & Loesch, 2000, p. 304)

The first activity reflects the training that occurs for professional helpers, while the second and third activities represent the credentialing process that occurs for practitioners.

Training

Professional helpers are trained in programs that are based on specific competencies and standards. By and large, professional helpers trained at the undergraduate level are found in human services programs and social work programs, and these programs are based on national standards developed by the Council in Human Service Education and the Council on Social Work Education. Many social work students also go on to obtain their master's degree in social work; often, this advanced degree is required in some states for licensure as a social worker. Professional counselors are trained in master's degree programs designed to meet professional criteria established by the Council for Accreditation of Counseling and Related Education Programs. Accreditation refers to the process in which a private association grants public recognition to a program that meets established guidelines based on evaluative data (Sweeney, 1995).

Most training programs begin with a series of courses that introduce the helping professions, settings, client populations, and professional ethics. Early in most programs, a counseling techniques laboratory or practice course introduces students to communication skills and entry-level counseling interventions and provides opportunities to try out these skills in an observable setting (either through a two-way mirror or a closed-circuit video). Such a course includes content that is presented in this text. Also, usually in conjunction with or concurrent with this prepracticum, students receive training in content referred to as counseling theories. Counseling theories represent various models and approaches to conceptualizing and helping clients. The helping and counseling strategies that we describe in Chapter 9 are representative of various counseling theories or approaches, and many of these theories are described in greater detail in our other text, *The Professional Counselor* (Hackney & Cormier, 2009). Typically, these courses are followed by a field-based practicum in which students work with real clients under the supervision of a skilled practitioner who serves as the student's supervisor. That supervision may include live observation, videotaped review, or audiotaped review. Whatever the medium, sessions are reviewed by the supervisor, and feedback is provided to the trainee for assessment and professional growth (see also Chapter 10).

Along with other coursework, most students take courses in group counseling (sometimes including a group practicum), educational and psychological testing, career counseling and development, research, human development, multicultural counseling, and substance abuse. Toward the end of the program, most trainees are required to complete an internship in a counseling setting related to their program. This may be in school counseling, agency counseling, college counseling, or another related setting. Programs in rehabilitation counseling, social work, human services, and marriage and family therapy differ in some of the didactic content, but the experiential portions are similar. These programs are also accredited by their respective accrediting organizations. Training programs and professional associations alike are also concerned with research, particularly practice research. This kind of research provides information about the efficacy of particular counseling approaches and interventions that—when supported by research—are called evidence-based interventions or best practices. The impetus for this kind of research, as Bradley, Sexton, and Smith (2005) noted, is that "on a daily basis, the practitioner is faced with the decision of how to take a counseling theory and implement it into counseling practice" (p. 491). Collecting data about client outcomes helps practitioners to "substantiate the treatment that is most effective or ineffective with a particular mental health disorder"(p. 491).

Credentialing

In addition to receiving a degree in counseling or a related field, most counselors and other help-giving professionals also seek to become a credentialed counselor following their training and degree. Credentialing has become an important issue in recent years because of health care reforms (i.e., managed care) in which the credentials of the counselor are important for obtaining third-party reimbursement. Sweeney (1995) defined credentialing as "a method of identifying individuals by occupational group" (p. 120). It involves either certification and/or licensing. Although certification and licensing are similar processes, they differ in several important ways. *Certification,* unlike licensure, is established through independent, nonlegislative organizations that help regulate the use of a particular title. Vacc and Loesch (2000) noted that "application of this title is more than self-anointment by those who refer to themselves as counselors" (p. 228). Counselors can be certified through the National Board of Certified Counselors (NBCC), rehabilitation counselors are certified through the Commission for Rehabilitation Counselor Certification (CRCC), and social workers are certified through the National Association of Social Workers (NASW). School counselors are also credentialed by the state in which they work (Myers, Sweeney & White, 2002). Human service professionals are in the process of becoming credentialed as a human services board-certified practitioner by the National Organization of Human Services (NOHS) and the Council for Standards in Human Service Education (CSHSE).

   Licensure is a legislatively established basis of credentialing that is considered even more desirable than certification because it regulates not only the title but also the practice of the profession. All states have passed legislation to license professional counselors. Social workers can also obtain social work licenses through state legislation, and some states have passed legislation to license marriage and family therapists. It is important to note that licensing laws, in particular, vary among different states, and "only by examining a specific law and the rules by which it is administered can one determine the full implications of the law in a given state" (Sweeney, 1995, p. 121).

   Myers, Sweeney, and White (2002) summarized a number of advantages to the credentialing process. First, it invokes a sense of pride that is important both for advocacy and job satisfaction. Second, credentialing increases a feeling of competence. Such competence not only helps professionals, but it should also be reassuring to the public or clients who see credentialed practitioners. Finally, credentialing promotes accountability within a profession by its members.

APPLICATION EXERCISE 1.3

Credentialing and Professional Identity

Continue with the interview you began in Application Exercise 1.2. Ask the helper you interviewed about his or her sense of professional identity. How was this person trained? What certification and/or license does this person have? What information did you gather about the code of ethics this person uses? With what professional organizations does this person affiliate? Present an oral summary of your findings to your class or write your finding in a written report.

Summary

This chapter has examined the meaning of helping in the context of human concerns and who the helpers are. Professional helpers are found in many settings and encounter a wide variety of human issues. Professional helpers can be distinguished from nonprofessional helpers by their identification with a professional organization, their use of an ethical code and standards of practice, and acknowledgment of an accrediting body that regulates their training, certification, and licensing of their practice. The effective helper brings to the setting certain personal qualities, without which the client would not likely enter into the alliance in which help occurs. These include character traits such as virtue and ethical decision-making, mindful awareness or neural integration, resilience and stamina, and cultural knowledge and sensitivity. The effective helper is committed to the sharing of resources, power, and privilege across diverse clients. Although the exact parameters of these skills may be defined by the helper's theoretical orientation, there is no denying that the effective helper has them and the ineffective helper does not. Increasingly, professional helpers are entering new employment settings and encountering more diverse groups of clients.

In the chapters that follow, we shall examine these skills and provide you with exercises and discussion questions to help in your integration of the material. Chapter 2 will look at the helping relationship and conditions that enable it to develop in positive directions to facilitate the client's progress. Chapters 3, 4, and 5 address the interpersonal skills of the helper in regard to attending to clients, recognizing communication patterns, and managing the counseling session. Chapters 6 and 7 focus on the cognitive and affective messages of clients and ways in which helpers can differentiate between and respond to these two types of messages. Chapters 8 and 9 address the helper's skills in conceptualizing issues and selecting and implementing strategies and interventions. Finally, Chapter 10 explores common challenges for helpers. It is important to note that all the skills and processes we describe in the following chapters are affected by both the social milieu and the cultural context of the practitioner and client.

Reflective Questions

1. In a small group of 3–5 class members, each of you should identify a preferred setting in which you would choose to be a professional helper. Discuss among yourselves why you chose the particular setting. Does it have to do with your personal qualities? Your perception of the demands of the setting? Your perception of the rewards of working in that setting?

2. Now choose a second-most-preferred setting (other than your first choice). Continue the discussion as directed in question 1. How did you find your reactions to be different in this second discussion? What might you learn from these differences? Did you perceive the other group members as having similar or different reactions to the second choice? What did you learn about them as a result? Share your reactions candidly.

3. Identify a person you have known who was, in your opinion, an exceptional helper. What qualities did this person possess that contributed to his or her helping nature? How do you think these qualities were acquired? Do you have any of these qualities?

4. In your opinion, what does it mean to help? To give help? To receive help? How are these processes related?

5. What has impacted your decision to become a helper? Consider the following sources of influence: your family of origin (the one in which you grew up), life experiences, role models, personal qualities, needs, motivations, pragmatic concerns, culture, and environment.

My Helping Lab

For each exercise, log on to MyHelpingLab at http://www.myhelpinglab.com and then click the Topics tab.

1. Click the Intro/Orientation to Counseling tab to locate the Counseling in Mental Health and Private Practice Video Lab. Then, click the Career Explorations tab. Your task is to review the interviews with the selected helping professionals. What did you learn about your future as a helping professional from watching these?

2. Click the Intro/Orientation to Counseling tab again. Then, click Multicultural Considerations Video Lab. Select the Cultural Considerations in Counseling Sessions video. Watch this video clip of the two helpers, and describe how you think the helpers' understanding of the clients' culture helped them work more effectively with this couple.

3. This time, click the Ethical, Legal, and Professional Issues in Counseling tab to locate the Professional Identity of Helpers tab. Choose the video lab for the following two selections: What is a Counselor? and Response to What is a Counselor. After watching these two clips, describe what you learned about roles and functions of professional helpers.

4. Click the Ethical, Legal, and Professional Issues in Counseling tab again to locate the Professional Practice in a Multicultural Society tab. Choose the Video Lab for the following two selections: A Cross-Cultural Miscommunication and Response to a Cross-Cultural Miscommunication. How would you assess the cultural competence of the helping professional you saw in this video clip?

Recommended Readings

Capuzzi, D. & Gross, P. (2008). *Introduction to the counseling profession, 5th edition.* Upper Saddle River, NJ: Pearson.

Clark, M. A. & Breman, J. C. (2009). School counselor inclusion: A collaborative model to provide academic and social-emotional support in the classroom setting. *Journal of Counseling and Development, 87,* 6–11.

Colbert, R., Vernon-Jones, R. & Pransky, K. (2006). The school change feedback process: Creating a new role for helpers in education reform. *Journal of Counseling and Development, 84,* 72–81.

Corey, M. S. & Corey, G. (2010). *Becoming a helper, 6th edition.* Belmont, CA: Brooks/Cole, Cengage.

Day-Vines, N. L., Wood, S. M., Grothaus, T., Craigen, L., Holman, A., Dotson-Blake, K. & Douglass, M. J. (2007). Broaching the subjects of race, ethnicity, and culture during the counseling process. *Journal of Counseling and Development, 85,* 401–409.

Dimmitt, C., Carey, J. & Hatch, T. (2007). *Evidence-based school counseling.* Thousand Oaks, CA: Corwin Press.

Gale, A. U. & Austin, B. D. (2003). Professionalism's challenges to professional helpers' collective identity. *Journal of Counseling and Development, 81,* 3–10.

Gibelman, M. & Furman, R. (2008). *Navigating human service organizations.* Chicago, IL: Lyceum Books.

Hepworth, D., Rooney, R., Rooney, D. G., Strom-Gottfried, K. & Larsen, J. (2010). *Direct social work practice, 8th edition.* Belmont, CA: Brooks/Cole, Cengage.

Osborn, C. (2004). Seven salutary suggestions for counselor stamina. *Journal of Counseling and Development, 82,* 319–328.

Ponton, R. F. & Duba, J. D. (2009). The ACA Code of Ethics: Articulating counseling's professional covenant. *Journal of Counseling and Development, 87,* 117–121.

Ratts, M. J., Toporek, R. L. & Lewis, J. A. (2010). (Eds.). *ACA advocacy competencies: A social justice framework for helpers.* Washington, DC: American Counseling Association.

Roysircar, G., Sandhu, D. S. & Bibbins, V. (2003). *Multicultural competencies: A guidebook of practices.* Washington, DC: American Counseling Association.

Sales, A. (2007). *Rehabilitation counseling: An empowerment perspective.* Washington DC: American Counseling Association.

Siegel, D. (2007). The mindful brain. New York: W. W. Norton.

Smith, E. (2006). The strength-based counseling model. *The Counseling Psychologist, 34,* 13–79.

Sue, D. W. (2010). *Microaggressions in everyday life: Race, gender and sexual orientation.* Hoboken, NJ: John Wiley & Sons.

Welfel, E. (2010). *Ethics in counseling and psychotherapy, 4th edition.* Belmont, CA: Brooks/Cole, Cengage.

West, J. D., Osborn, C. J. & Bubenzer, D. L. (2003). *Leaders and legacies: Contributions to the profession of counseling.* New York: Brunner-Routledge.

Wicks, R. J. (2007). *The resilient clinician.* New York: Oxford University Press.

Woodside, M. & McClam, T. (2009). *An introduction to human services, 6th edition.* Belmont, CA: Brooks/Cole, Cengage.

The Helping Relationship

C. Rogers. *Empathy Positive Regard Congruency*

Much of what is accomplished in counseling depends on the quality of the relationship between the helper and the client. The helping relationship is a different kind of relationship than one that occurs between close friends, family members, or even between nonprofessionals. It is a relationship characterized by security, safety, privacy, and healing. The roots of this particular kind of helping relationship lie in a theoretical approach to counseling called the person-centered approach. The *person-centered approach* derives principally from the work of one individual: Carl Rogers. Rogers emerged on the scene at a time when two psychological approaches—psychoanalysis and behaviorism—were dominant. Through his influence, the focus began to shift to the relationship between therapist and client, as opposed to the existing emphasis on the client's intrapsychic experience or patterns of behavior. In one of his early writings, Rogers (1957) defined what he believed to be the "necessary and sufficient conditions" for positive personality change to occur, including accurate empathy, unconditional positive regard, and congruence. These concepts have evolved over the years, and today, they are generally acknowledged by most theoretical approaches as *core conditions* in the therapeutic process. Exploration by a task force on empirically supported relationship variables has re-emphasized the contributions of these core conditions and the helping relationship to effective therapy processes and outcomes (Norcross, 2001). In other words, the therapeutic relationship makes specific contributions to the outcomes of counseling regardless of the theoretical approach, treatment type, or intervention strategies the practitioner uses. Norcross (2002) has observed that all communication skills as well as therapeutic strategies and interventions (such as the ones we describe in later chapters) are "relational acts" (p. 98).

THE IMPORTANCE OF THE RELATIONSHIP TO CLIENTS

The quality of the therapeutic relationship has the potential to be helpful and healing or hurtful and even damaging to clients. Many—if not most—clients who come to see us have missed out on the caring communication and healthy attachment to a caregiver in early life that is necessary for good health (physical and mental) and well-being. Instead of having experiences and expressions of oneself received and validated, clients may have had their experiences and expressions of self denied or judged. As a result, they develop narratives (or stories) and conclusions about themselves that are either too rigid or too chaotic, with not enough brain integration for them to regulate themselves effectively, particularly their emotions (Siegel, 1999). The therapeutic relationship has the potential to help repair some of these denied and judged experiences through collaborative communication and emotional processing of the dyadic experience between helper and client (Fosha, 2005). As a result, clients who feel cut off from themselves and their experiences have an opportunity to regain wholeness. Moreover, clients will be able to regain important connections with themselves and with other people; the relationship with the helper is the first step in this process.

Perhaps you can see from this why we discussed the importance of neural integration and mindful awareness as a positive quality for counselors in Chapter 1. If the helper brings a lot of leftover issues and unresolved personal "baggage" into the counseling session, it will be "in the room" with the client and will impede the quality of communication and the process of change. When helpers' unresolved issues get projected onto clients, we call this *countertransference*. And when clients' unresolved issues get projected onto helpers, we call this *transference*. Both helpers and clients can regulate unfinished business by learning to become aware of themselves and mindful of their feelings and emotions—what they are experiencing at any given moment in time. Indeed, some theoretical orientations view this as a primary goal of counseling and therapy (Fosha, 2002). This involves being aware of our own feelings as helpers and also being attuned to the feelings and experiences of our clients through the core or facilitative conditions previously mentioned. In the following sections of this chapter, we describe these core conditions in depth.

ACCURATE EMPATHY

There are numerous definitions of empathy in the counseling literature. The definition that we like is the following: the ability to understand the client's experience and feel with or emotionally resonate to the client's experience as if it were your own but without losing the "as if" quality (Rogers, 1957; Bozarth, 1997). Clark (2007) noted that empathy is a complex process and is often used in different ways and for different purposes in the helping relationship. When used effectively, empathy increases clients' sense of safety, their feelings of being understood, and their satisfaction with the helping process. Effective use of this core condition also decreases premature termination and promotes client exploration (Bohart, Elliott, Greenberg & Watson, 2002).

Empathic understanding involves two primary steps:

1. "Empathic rapport": Accurately sensing the client's world and being able to see things the way he or she does
2. "Communicative attunement": Verbally sharing your understanding with the client (Bohart & Greenberg, 1997a, pp. 13–14)

How do you know when the client feels you have understood? Client responses such as "Yes, that's it" or "That's exactly right" indicate some sort of recognition by the client of the level of your understanding. When your clients say something like that after one of your responses, you are assured that they feel you are following and understanding what is occurring.

Learning to understand is not an easy process. It involves skillful listening, so you can hear not only the obvious but also the subtle shadings of which the client is perhaps not yet aware.

Empathy also involves having good internal boundaries for yourself. An internal boundary helps to separate personal thoughts, feelings, and behavior from the thoughts, feelings, and behaviors of others (Mellody, 1989, p. 11). Rogers (1957) asserted that empathy is being sensitive to a client's experiencing a feeling. This is sometimes called resonant empathy (Buie, 1981). You can feel with the client without taking on the client's feelings and actually feeling them yourself. This is an area that occasionally poses problems, especially for beginning counselors. In your eagerness to be helpful, you may find yourself becoming so involved with the client that you get disconnected from yourself and what you are feeling. Instead, you take on the client's feelings and perhaps even find yourself obsessing about the client long after the session is over. Such immersion is not helpful because you lose your capacity to be objective about the client's experience. As a result, you may avoid seeing, hearing, or saying important things in the session. If you feel this is happening to you, you can talk it over with a supervisor. You also can get reconnected to yourself during a session by taking a minute to focus internally and privately on what you are feeling and by taking some deep breaths.

Understanding clients' perspectives alone is not sufficient. You also must verbally express to clients your sense of understanding about them. This kind of communication is, in effect, a kind of mirror—feeding back clients' feelings to them, without agreeing or disagreeing, reassuring or denying. For a client to know that the practitioner is empathic, it must be expressed or made visible to the client (Clark, 2007). For example, suppose your client, Precious, tells you that she is having a hard time in school since losing her pet as a result of being moved into a shelter after her dad lost his job. In making empathy visible to Precious, the helper might say something like the following: "Precious, I imagine you are pretty upset now about losing your pet and your home too."

Accurate empathy involves not only mirroring your clients' feelings but also some parts of the immediate process. For example, if clients continually ask many questions rather than discuss the issues that brought them to counseling, it would be appropriate to reflect on the obvious with statements such as:

- "You have a lot of questions to ask right now."
- "You seem to want a lot of information about this."
- "You are asking a lot of questions. I wonder if you are uncertain about what to expect."

Learning to develop accurate empathy with your client and with other people takes time and practice. This is in part because empathy is not only an understanding of the client's feelings but also an understanding of the client's experiences. As Bohart and colleagues (2002) observed, "truly empathic therapists do not parrot clients' words back or reflect only the content of those words"; instead, they also reflect back the moment-to-moment experiences, meanings, and implications of the words (p. 19). Effectively used, empathy helps clients to "symbolize, organize, and make sense" of their experiences (Bohart & Greenberg, 1997a, p. 15). In the above example, the helper goes beyond simply mirroring the feelings of the client Precious and also reflects empathically on her experiences, as in the following example: "Precious, it sounds like you are going through a lot of changes right now in your life and everything feels turned upside down at this time."

Several caveats about the effective use of empathy are worth noting. First, the effects of empathy are most useful when the other two core conditions of positive regard and congruence are also present. Second, empathy is not the same as sympathy. Empathy is about communicating your understanding of the client and her or his experience. Sympathy is about feeling sorry for or sad about the client. Finally, not all clients will perceive empathic understanding as useful; some may experience empathy as intrusive, directive, or foreign to them (Bohart et al., 2002, p. 102).

The Brain Connection and Empathy

In 1996, in Italy, a team of neuroscientists discovered neurons that fire in our brains called "mirror" neurons. These are neurons that are specifically tailored to mirror the emotions and bodily responses of another person and are located in various cortical regions of the brain, such as the frontal and parietal lobes. These mirror neurons link perception and motor action and interact with an area of the brain called the insula that makes a neural circuit in which behavioral imitation, emotional or felt resonance, and attunement of intentional states occur (Siegel, 2006). As a result, when you perceive the expressions of another person, the brain is able to create within the body an internal state that is thought to "resonate" with that of the other person. The implications of the mirror neuron system in the brain and the resulting potential for empathic attunement with our clients are profound. Siegel asserted that being empathic with clients extends beyond helping them feel better (p. 13). This empathic mirroring helps clients feel "felt" and ultimately leads to brain changes in clients through the establishment of new neural firing patterns and increased neural integration. For further information about this, see also the UCLA Center for Culture, Brain, and Development at http://www.cbd.ucla.edu.

Empathy and Mindfulness

In Chapter 1, we discussed the importance of mindful awareness as an integral quality of helpers. We now know that mindful awareness or mindfulness is not only useful for helpers but is also an important link to empathy. When we as helpers are mindful, we are more attuned to our own internal states by using our "sixth sense." In turn, being attuned to our own internal states helps us be attuned to the internal states of others, such as (but not limited to) our clients. In other words, mindfulness and empathy overlap to such a degree that being mindful augments our capacity to be empathic (Siegel, 2007). Stated another way, when we become frenetic or frazzled and lose our connection to ourselves, we are more likely to lose the relational connection and understanding with our clients too.

Cultural and Relational Empathy

Empathy also involves understanding the client's gender and cultural backgrounds. There is increasing evidence that men and women talk in different ways (Tannen, 1990) and that cultural/historical backgrounds affect the meaning the client conveys as well as the meaning the therapist interprets. O'Hara (1997) observed that "there is good evidence that people are not all in the world in the same way and that the way people experience themselves and their phenomenal world has differed historically across time and still differs from context to context" (p. 301). Chung and Bemak (2002) noted that in North America, the concept of empathy is derived largely from Western Eurocentric values. They believe there is a need for culturally sensitive empathy. Cultural empathy is inclusive, and reaches for understanding both among and between diverse groups. When used in the helping process, cultural empathy helps practitioners understand not just the individual sitting in front of them but also something about the client's worldview and context in which the client lives (Pedersen, Crethar & Carlson, 2008). A major way in which a helper's cultural empathy may be blocked is by one's state of *privilege*. Recall from Chapter 1 that privilege is an unearned advantage, such as being White, being able bodied, being heterosexual, or having economic resources. Because such privileges are unearned, it is easy to take them for granted and to underestimate the impact that lack of privilege has on others. For example, consider the kind of cultural empathy that would be conveyed if helpers could really understand the discrimination, oppression, and losses experienced by clients who may be of another race, ethnic origin, or religion or by clients who may be experiencing loss of health status or income.

Cultural empathy is also impacted by the mirror neurons we talked about earlier. The Italian researchers who discovered the mirror neuron system are also exploring the role of mirror neurons in communicating information about emotions and social life across cultures. The brain is undoubtedly behind our capacity to create and maintain cultural and relational empathy. Cultural empathy includes consideration of context and society in which both the counselor and the client live. When context is ignored and attempts to understand are made solely from an individualistic frame of reference, "blaming the victim" can result (O'Hara, 1997, p. 311). As an example of this, consider how the understanding of unwed teenage pregnancy is often confined to the individual teenage girl who presents with the pregnancy. Absent from this empathic quotient is the understanding of larger system issues about why the girl became pregnant in the first place (O'Hara, 1997). Ignoring social context overlooks the relational world in which clients live—the dyads, families, racial/ethnic/religious groups, social classes, occupational groups, and genders to which clients belong. As O'Hara noted, effective counseling is more than just a venture of two people—it is a "multilevel, relational situation" (p. 311). Theorists have coined the term *relational empathy* to describe this process (Jordan, 1997). Relational empathy involves empathy for oneself, other people, and the counseling relationship. In empathic interactions with the therapist, the client develops self-empathy as well as an increase in empathic attunement to others. This leads to "enhanced relational capacity and to an increase in self-esteem" (p. 345). For therapists to work effectively with clients from cultures different from their own, they must be able to step back from usual ways of knowing and be open to different ways of seeing things (Jenkins, 1997).

Chung and Bemak (2002) offered three specific ways counselors can foster cultural and relational empathy:

1. Have a genuine interest in learning more about the client's cultural affiliations
2. Have a genuine appreciation for cultural differences between the counselor and the client
3. Incorporate culturally appropriate help-seeking behaviors and treatment outcomes and expectations into the helping process as needed (p. 157)

Shame and the Empathy Bond

Another factor that is increasingly recognized as having a substantial impact on the helping relationship is shame. *Shame* is viewed as a central component or main regulator of a person's affective life. Normal shame is about values and limits; it is recognized, spoken about, and acknowledged. The shame that is considered problematic and a primary contributor to aggression, addictions, obsessions, narcissism, and depression is hidden shame—shame that is unacknowledged, repressed, or defended against that seems to result in either an attack on others or an incredible self-loathing (Karen, 1992).

According to Lewis (1971), shame is inescapable in the counselor-client relationship and has major implications for the empathic bonding of the counselor to the client. Karen (1992) quoted Lewis as follows: "However good your reasons for going into treatment, so long as you are an adult speaking to another adult to whom you are telling the most intimate things, there is an undercurrent of shame in every session" (p. 50). Lewis (1971) asserted that not only do counselors overlook shame in clients and bypass dealing with it, but they inadvertently add to a client's "shame tank" through judgmental interpretations. Value judgments about the client's culture can also contribute

APPLICATION EXERCISE 2.1

Accurate Empathy and Cultural Empathy

A. Hearing and Verbalizing Client Concerns

Using triads with one person as speaker, a second as respondent, and the third as observer, complete the following tasks. Then, rotate the roles until each person has had an opportunity to react in all three ways.

1. The speaker should begin by sharing a concern or issue with the listener.
2. The respondent should
   a. listen to the speaker and
   b. verbalize to the speaker what he or she heard.
3. The observer should note the extent to which the others accomplished their tasks and whether any understanding or misunderstanding occurred.

   Following a brief (five-minute) interaction, respond verbally to the following questions:

   SPEAKER: "Do you think the respondent heard what you had to say? Did you think he or she understood you? Did the listener seem to understand your culture? Discuss this with the respondent."

   RESPONDENT: "Did you let the speaker know you understood or attempted to understand? How did you do this? What blocks within you interfered with doing so? Did you struggle with the person's cultural affiliations?"

   OBSERVER: "Discuss what you saw taking place between the speaker and the respondent."

   Now reverse roles, and complete the same process.

B. Understanding Client Concerns

This exercise should be completed with a group of three to ten people sitting in a circle.

1. Each participant is given a piece of paper and a pencil.
2. Each participant should complete—in writing and anonymously—the following sentence: My primary concern about becoming a helper is

   _____

   _____

3. Papers are folded and placed in the center of the circle.
4. Each participant draws a paper. (If one person receives his or her own, all should draw again.)
5. Each participant reads aloud the concern listed and then talks for several minutes about what it would be like to have this concern. Other participants can then add to this.

   This process continues until each participant has read and discussed a concern. When discussing the concern, attempt to reflect only your understanding of the world of the person with this concern. Do not attempt to give a solution or advice.

   After the exercise, members should give each other feedback about the level of empathic understanding that was displayed during the discussion. Feedback should be specific so participants can use it for behavior change.

(continued)

C. Cultural and Relational Empathy

Consider your capacity to relate to clients who are both similar to and different from yourself along cultural dimensions. Explore and discuss the following four areas listed below:

1. What are your family's beliefs and feelings about the group(s) that comprise your culture of origin? What parts of the group(s) do they embrace or reject? How has this influenced your feelings about your cultural identity?
2. What aspects of your culture of origin do you have the most comfort "owning"? The most difficulty "owning"?
3. What groups will you have the easiest time understanding and relating to? The most difficult?
4. What privileges do you have as a function of being you? And of how and where you grew up and how and where you live now? Consider such dimensions as race, ethnic origin, gender, socioeconomic status, health status, age, sexual orientation, and so on. How might such a privilege(s) impede your understanding of a client and the client's context?

to a sense of shame. Lewis stated that when this happens, the client becomes enraged at the counselor, but because he or she cannot accept feeling angry toward someone who is a "helper," it is turned inward and becomes depression and self-denigration. Lewis cautions counselors to be alert to client states of shame so they can help clients work through and discharge the feeling. In this way, clients can move ahead. Otherwise, they are likely to continue to move in and out of shame attacks or shame spirals, both within and outside of the counseling sessions.

A major precursor to shame appears to be the lack of parental empathy. According to Miller (1985), a child's sense of self-esteem comes largely from the parents' capacity to tune in empathetically with the child—to mirror and reflect the child as she or he develops. As Karen (1992) pointed out, in therapy, "the same phenomenon requires a special sensitivity on the part of the therapist. The patient is hypersensitive about acceptance and abandonment and uncertain of whether he can trust the therapist with his wound—a wound that, he no doubt senses, the therapy session has great potential to exacerbate. The therapist must win over the hiding, shameful side of the personality and gradually help it to heal" (p. 65). The counselor does this by creating an empathic bond with the client—that is, an emotional connection—a genuine feeling for the client. Although empathy can be conveyed by certain techniques (such as the verbal expressions we noted earlier), there is ultimately no substitute for the counselor's ability to genuinely care for and feel with the client. Empathy appears to be the critical variable in the healing of pathological shame (Jordan, 1997).

Shame can also be culture-bound. Hardy and Laszloffy (1995) pointed out that every cultural group has pride and shame issues—that is, "aspects of a culture that are sanctioned as distinctively negative or positive" (p. 229). These are important issues to identify about a client's cultural group because they help to define appropriate and inappropriate behavior within a cultural context.

POSITIVE REGARD

In his early writings, Carl Rogers (1957) described positive regard as unconditional. More recent writers have relabeled positive regard as nonpossessive warmth. The effectiveness of positive regard appears to lie "in its ability to facilitate a long-term working relationship" (Farber & Lane, 2002, p. 185). Positive regard is associated with clients' perceptions of improvement on issues, and it sets the stage for the use of various helping strategies and interventions (such as those we describe in later chapters). Lack of positive regard often produces and contributes to ruptures in the helping relationship (Farber & Lane, 2002, p. 192).

Positive regard or nonpossessive warmth seems to be conveyed by helpers to clients through the dimensions of friendliness, helpfulness, and trustworthiness (Williams & Bargh, 2008). Neurobiological research has found an area of the brain (the insular cortex) that is related to the processing of interpersonal warmth information; this area of the brain appears to be linked to early attachment in infancy with the warm, physical contact with caregivers (Williams & Bargh, 2008).

Positive regard—or nonpossessive warmth—is often misconstrued as agreement or lack of disagreement with the client. Instead, it is an attitude of valuing the client. To show positive regard is to express appreciation of the client as a unique and worthwhile person. It is also to be noncritical—to provide an "overall sense of protection, support, or acceptance, no matter what is divulged" (Karasu, 1992, p. 36). In this context, it is important for counselors to not only feel positively about clients but to also convey these positive feelings to clients. As Farber and Lane (2002) noted, "This does not have to translate to a stream of compliments nor to a gushing of positive sentiment that, in fact, may overwhelm or even terrify some clients; rather, it speaks to the need for therapists to communicate a caring, respectful, positive attitude that serves to affirm a client's basic sense of worth" (p. 192).

Consider the following scenario:

> Lettia, the counselor, tells her supervisor that she has seen her client, Pedro, for three sessions. She says she feels annoyed and frustrated with him because he comes in every session and "whines about his low grades," which she believes are bad because of his constant partying.

Can you find any regard in Lettia's attitude toward Pedro? Instead of experiencing Pedro as a unique person of value and worth, Lettia feels "put off" and frustrated by her client. It is hard to work effectively with clients if you do not like, respect, and value them for who they are. In this situation, Lettia's lack of regard may not only be for this individual client but may also extend to aspects of his culture. Sometimes, issues in positive regard are exacerbated in cross-cultural counseling, making progress and change even more difficult.

Contrast this with the way Lettia speaks about her other client, Maria. Maria is a young woman who has a chronic health condition that limits her functioning in several ways. While Maria's progress in counseling is also slow, Lettia notes how much she looks forward to each session with Maria and how supportive she feels toward her. As you can see, regard for clients is closely related to empathy and also to the other core relationship condition we consider next: congruence or genuineness.

CONGRUENCE/GENUINENESS

Neither empathy nor positive regard can be conveyed in helping relationships unless the helper is seen by the client as genuine. Genuineness is also referred to by Rogers as *congruence,* a condition reflecting honesty, transparency, and openness to the client. Congruence implies that therapists are real in their interactions with clients. As Corey (2009) noted, this means helpers are "without a false front, their inner experience and outer expression of that experience match, and they can openly express feelings, thoughts, reactions, and attitudes that are present in the relationship with the

APPLICATION EXERCISE 2.2

Positive Regard

A. Overcoming Barriers to Positive Regard

Think about expressing to the client those limitations that may be blocking your sense of liking for the client and those strengths that increase your appreciation for the client. The following steps may assist you in expressing this:

1. Picture the other person in your mind. Begin a dialogue in which you express what it is that is interfering with your sense of positive regard. Now reverse the roles. Become the other person. What does the person say in response? Then, what do you say?
2. Complete this process again. This time, express the strengths you see in the other person—what you appreciate about that person. Again, reverse the roles. Become the other person. What does he or she say in response? Then, what do you say?

This exercise can be used with any client toward whom you have difficulty experiencing positive regard.

B. Expressing Positive Regard

Take a few minutes to think about a person with whom you currently have a relationship and for whom you experience positive regard. What kinds of things do you do to express your feelings of positive regard for this person? Jot them down.

_____

_____

_____

_____

There is no set answer to the preceding exercise because each person has a different style of communicating good feelings for another person. The first step, though, is positive regard—to feel comfortable enough to express warm feelings to someone else. Being free enough to spontaneously share feelings of regard for another human being is a process that can be learned.

Think again for a moment about several of your existing relationships with a few people close to you—perhaps your partner, parent, child, neighbor, or friend. Then, respond in writing to the following questions:

1. What is your level of expression of positive regard to these people?
2. How often do you say things like "I like you"; "It's nice to be with you"; "You're good for me"; "I enjoy you"; and so forth?
3. What is your feeling when you do?
4. What is the effect on the other person?
5. If your expression of such statements is infrequent, what might be holding you back?

Either now or later, seek out someone you like and then try to express these kinds of feelings to that person. Then, think again about the previous questions. Share your reactions with your partner. In doing this, you will probably note that warmth and positive regard are expressed both nonverbally and verbally.

client" (p. 174). Through being genuine and congruent, helpers model for clients not only the experience of being real but also the process of claiming one's truths and speaking about them. When this happens, there is usually more vitality and a greater "connection" in the helping relationship. As Jordan (1997) noted, "We all know the deadened, bored, or anxious feelings that occur in interactions in which people cannot risk being in their truth. . . . Inauthenticity takes us out of real mutuality" (p. 350). Take a moment to think about the fact that most clients come into the helping process in a state of incongruence, often either not knowing who they are or not feeling as if they can truly be who they are. In this respect, the congruence of the helper is even more important. It helps clients become more congruent, making it easier for them to own their feelings and express them without excessive fears (Klein, Kolden, Michels & Chisholm-Stockard, 2002, p. 196).

The beginning helper may find this condition easier to apply in theory than in practice. Questions inevitably rise when genuineness and congruence are examined. Some examples are the following: What if I really don't like my client? Should I let that be known? Wouldn't it destroy the relationship? Congruence means that the helper is honest but in helpful rather than destructive ways. Expressing your feelings should not take precedence over understanding the client's feelings. The helping relationship does not have all the mutuality present in many other relationships, such as friend to friend, partner to partner, and so forth. Corey (2009) cautioned that congruence does not mean that the helper impulsively shares all thoughts and feelings with clients in a nonselective way. A general guideline is to share your feelings when they are persistent and if they block your acceptance of the client. At times though, it may be better to just acknowledge these kinds of thoughts and feelings to yourself or to your supervisor, "as the cost of too much expressed internal reaction outweighs the benefit" (Sommers-Flanagan & Sommers-Flanagan, 2003, p. 104). In other words, an important part of congruence means developing a sense of awareness about all that you are and what the impact of this may mean for your clients. For example, Roberto became aware through supervision that the sessions with one particular client, Jessica, seemed to drag on and move more slowly than with his other clients. Roberto was not sure why, but after disclosing this to his supervisor, he realized it was because Jessica talked a lot in the sessions about things that seemed trivial to Roberto compared to what his other clients discussed. As Roberto was able to own and be congruent with these feelings with his supervisor, he noticed these feelings growing less intense. He also found a way to ask Jessica in the following session about her goals for counseling and about her own experience of the sessions so far. Interestingly enough, Jessica disclosed that she wished Roberto could take a more active role in the sessions so they could move along more quickly.

Steps in Congruence: Awareness and Discernment

Because congruence can be a more complicated process, consider the following two steps in the development of congruence in the helping relationship. The first step involves self-awareness or acknowledgement. The second step involves discernment or good clinical judgment.

Ask yourself what it means to be genuine. Can you tell when you are being yourself or when you are presenting an image that is different from the way you actually feel? In order to communicate congruence to the client, you must first learn to get in touch with yourself and your own truth—to become aware of who you are as an individual and what kinds of thoughts and feelings you have. This involves learning to discriminate among your various feelings and allowing them to come into your awareness without denial or distortion. A good question to ask yourself is, "What am I experiencing now?" Congruence also involves paying attention to what goes on in your body during a counseling session. Our bodies provide cues to us about what we experience and also what clients experience during sessions. Furthermore, body cues can "leak" out to clients, particularly if we are unaware of them. For example, clients may feel the effects of our prior late night through our lack of energy, sleepiness, and shallow breathing or they may sense our uptightness through our rushed speech and constricted breath.

Once you develop acknowledgement and awareness of all that you are and what you are experiencing and feeling, a second step in congruence involves discernment or good clinical judgment about expressiveness of your feelings to clients. Sommers-Flanagan and Sommers-Flanagan (2003, p. 105) suggest the following guidelines to develop such discernment:

- Examine your motives: Is your expression solely for the client's benefit?
- Consider if what you want to say or do is really therapeutic: How do you anticipate your client will react?

Once you decide that you are in a situation in which expression would benefit the client—and the client would be helped by such expression—consider the use of both self-disclosure and feedback statements, which we describe in the next section.

SELF-DISCLOSURE.   Expression of your thoughts, ideas, and feelings follows after your awareness of them. This process might also be called self-expression or self-disclosure. Hill and Knox (2002) defined *self-disclosure* as statements that reveal something about you (p. 255). Self-expression and disclosure are important ways of letting the client know that you are a person and not just a role; however, self-disclosure should be used appropriately and not indiscriminately in the counseling sessions. Hepworth and colleagues (2010) cautioned against self-disclosure of hostility in particular. It is important not to interpret self-disclosure to mean that you should talk about yourself; the primary focus of the interview is on the client. However, it is occasionally appropriate and helpful for you to reveal or disclose a particular feeling you may have about the counseling session or about the client. The clue to appropriateness is often determined by the question, "Whose needs am I meeting when I disclose this idea or feeling—the client's or mine?" Clearly, the former is more appropriate. As Zur et al. (2009) state, "Appropriate, ethical, and clinically driven self-disclosures are intentionally employed with the client's welfare in mind and with a clinical rationale" (p. 24).

There are several different kinds of self-disclosure:

- The helper's own issues
- Facts about the helper's role
- The helper's reactions to the client (feedback)
- The helper's reactions to the helping relationship

Usually, disclosure in the latter two areas is more productive. Many times, helpers are tempted to share their problems and concerns when encountering a client with similar problems. In a few instances, this may be done as a reassurance to clients that their concerns are not catastrophic. But in most other instances, a role reversal occurs—the helper is gaining something by this sharing with the client. Some research indicates that the helper who discloses at a moderate level may be perceived by the client more positively than the practitioner who discloses at a high or low level (Edwards & Murdock, 1994). Thus, too much or too little self-disclosure may limit the client's confidence in you as an effective helper. Furthermore, self-disclosure that occurs too frequently may blur the boundaries between helper and client and can be a precursor to problematic multiple or nonprofessional relationships with clients. (We discuss the slippery slope of this in Chapter 10.) On the other hand, lack of self-disclosure can turn clients away. Self-disclosure is an important way to build trust with adolescent clients, with clients who have substance abuse

APPLICATION EXERCISE 2.3

Dyadic Encounter: Congruence

To assist you in becoming aware of your own thoughts and feelings, select a partner and spend a few minutes with this dyadic encounter experience (Banikiotes, Kubinski & Pursell, 1981). It is designed to facilitate getting to know yourself and another person on a fairly close level. All you need to do is respond to the open-ended questions as honestly and directly as possible. Both of you should respond to one question at a time. The discussion statements can be completed at whatever level of self-disclosure you wish; there is no forced disclosure!

My name is . . .

The reason I'm here is . . .

One of the most important skills in getting to know another person is listening. In order to check on your ability to understand what your partner is communicating, the two of you should go through the following steps one at a time.

Decide which one of you is to speak first in this unit. The first speaker is to complete the following item in two or three sentences:

When I think about the future, I see myself . . .

The second speaker repeats in his or her own words what the first speaker has just said. The first speaker must be satisfied that he or she has been heard accurately.

The second speaker then completes the item in two or three sentences. The first speaker paraphrases what the second speaker just said, to the satisfaction of the second speaker.

Share what you may have learned about yourself as a listener with your partner. To check your listening accuracy, the two of you may find yourselves later saying to each other, "Do you mean that . . .?" or "You're saying that . . . " Do not respond to any sentence you do not want to.

When I am new in a group, I . . .

When I am feeling anxious in a new situation, I usually . . .

You're saying that . . . (Listening check)

Right now, I'm feeling . . .

The thing that turns me off the most is . . .

When I am alone, I usually . . .

I feel angry about . . .

Do you mean that . . . ? (Listening check)

Checkup

Have a short discussion about this experience so far. Keep eye contact as much as you can, and try to cover the following points:

How well are you listening?

How open and honest have you been?

How eager are you to continue this interchange?

Do you feel that you are getting to know each other?

(continued)

Then continue with the following:

I love …

I feel jealous about …

Right now, I'm feeling …

I am afraid of …

The thing I like best about you is …

You are …

Right now, I am responding most to …

issues, and in multicultural counseling situations (Egan, 2010; Sue & Sue, 2008). In other words, the decision about self-disclosure often varies with the *context* of the helping situation, including the setting, the type of client, and the theoretical orientation of the helper (Zur et al., 2009).

Often, clients may ask questions about the helper: Are you married? Why did you become a counselor? Are you in school? These are common questions clients ask in seeking information about the helper. In this case, it is usually best to give a direct, brief answer and then return the interview focus to the client. However, if this is a common occurrence with a particular client, there are other ways of responding. Continual client questioning of this sort often indicates that the client is anxious and is attempting to get off the "hot seat" by turning the focus onto you. There are better ways to handle this than spending the interview disclosing facts about yourself. Alternative ways of responding include:

1. Reflect on the client's feelings of anxiety: "You seem anxious about talking about yourself now."
2. Reflect on the process: "You seem to be asking a lot of questions now."
3. Make a statement about what you see happening: "I think you feel as if you're on the 'hot seat' and that asking me questions is a good way for you to get off it."

SHARING AND FEEDBACK STATEMENTS. Some helpers are able to acknowledge their feelings and determine when these can be best expressed in the interview but are not sure how to express these kinds of thoughts and feelings to the client. Self-disclosure or expressions of congruence are often characterized by sharing and feedback statements—statements that convey to the client your sense of what is going on and your feelings about it. These kinds of statements are illustrated by the following examples:

"I am glad you shared that with me."

"If that happened to me, I think I'd feel pretty angry."

"I don't feel that we're getting anywhere right now."

Other examples of sharing responses are:

CLIENT: It's hard for me to say so, but I really do get a lot out of these sessions.

HELPER: That makes me feel good to hear you say that.

or

HELPER: I'm glad to know you feel that way.

APPLICATION EXERCISE 2.4

Self-Disclosure

Think about yourself in the following instances:

1. You have a client who describes herself as shy and retiring. During the third interview, she says: "I'd like to be like you—you seem so outgoing and comfortable with people. Why don't you just tell me how you got that way?" Do you then consider it appropriate to share some of your experiences with her? Do you think your response to this might vary depending on the client's cultural affiliations? If so, how?

2. You have had one particular client for about seven individual sessions. After the first session, the client has been at least several minutes late for each session and waits until almost the end of the interview to bring up something important to discuss. You feel that he is infringing on your time. This is preventing you from giving your full attention and understanding to the client. You have acknowledged to yourself that this is bothering you. Is it appropriate to go ahead and express this to him? If so, what would you say?

Take a few minutes to think about yourself as the practitioner in these two examples. Now write in the following space what you would do in each example concerning self-disclosure.

_____

_____

_____

There is no right or wrong answer to these two examples; each counseling interaction is somewhat different. Ultimately, you, as the helper, will have to make a decision for yourself in each instance, taking into consideration the client and the context. In the first instance, rather than sharing facts about yourself, there may be more productive ways of helping the client reach her goals. For example, she might be more involved if you suggest role reversal. You become the client; have her be the outgoing and comfortable counselor she sees. In the second instance, the client, by being late, is not fulfilling his share of the responsibility or he is indirectly communicating something about his feelings that needs to be discussed.

Note that in the helper's sharing statements, the communication is direct; it focuses on the helper's feelings and on the client. It is a better statement than a generalized comment, such as "I hope most clients would feel the same way." A sharing and feedback statement should avoid the trap of "counseling lingo or language." To begin a sharing and/or feedback statement with "I hear you saying . . ."; "It seems that you feel . . ."; or "I feel that you feel . . ." gets wordy, repetitive, and even phony. Say exactly what you mean.

POSITIVE FEEDBACK STATEMENTS: ENCOURAGEMENT AND STRENGTHS PERSPECTIVE.

Positive feedback statements are also related to the quality of congruence. Like self-disclosure, these kinds of statements help clients see their helper as a real human being. Johnson (2009) has pointed out that both self-disclosure and feedback statements can reveal things to clients they do

APPLICATION EXERCISE 2.5

Expressing Helper Feelings

Sharing and feedback communicate to the client that you have heard or seen something going on and that you have certain thoughts or feelings about it that you want to communicate. Sometimes, you will want to say not only what you feel about a specific instance or experience but also how you feel about the client. This will be more effective if your feelings are expressed as immediate ones—that is, expressed in the present rather than in the past or future. This is the meaning of keeping the process of relationship in the here and now, using what is going on from moment to moment in each session to build the relationship. It is represented by the type of statement that communicates, "Right now, I'm feeling . . ." or "Right now, we are . . .."

To experience this here-and-now kind of communication, try to get in touch with yourself this instant. What are you feeling this very moment as you are reading and thinking about this page, this paragraph, this sentence? Write down four or five adjectives that express your present feelings. Tune in to your nonverbal cues too (body position, rate of breathing, tension spots, etc.).

APPLICATION EXERCISE 2.6

Using Sharing Statements

With a partner, engage in some sharing-type statements that are direct, specific, and immediate. Can you tune in to your feelings as you engage in this kind of communication? What does it do for you, and what effect does it have on the other person? Jot down some of these reactions here. List the sharing statements you have made to your partner.

not know about themselves. Like self-disclosure, feedback statements should never be made against the client (Claiborn, Goodyear & Horner, 2002, p. 229).

In a review of related research about feedback, Claiborn, Goodyear, and Horner (2002) concluded that positive feedback is more acceptable than negative feedback and that this is especially true early in the helping relationship. Hepworth and colleagues (2010) noted that positive feedback statements can focus on client strengths and effective coping and can empower clients. According to the authors, tapes of sessions between workers and clients reveal a dearth of responses that underscore client strengths, successes, assets, coping behaviors, and areas of growth.

We spoke of strengths counseling in Chapter 1. Human strengths are important because they are protective against illness, both physical and emotional (Vailant, 2000). Also, clients may be more likely to change when helpers focus on strengths rather than deficits (Smith, 2006). This is probably because focusing on strengths builds hope and fosters resilience—in other words, focusing on strengths with clients has "healing effects" (p. 36). One way to focus on client strengths is the intentional use of encouragement—that is, "feedback that emphasizes individuals' efforts or improvement" (p. 41). Positive feedback statements or compliments are a key component of the encouragement process with clients (De Jong & Berg, 2008).

Positive feedback statements are useful when you have warm and supportive feelings for clients that are truly genuine. Consider the following examples offered by Hepworth and colleagues (2010, p. 117):

> HELPER TO INDIVIDUAL CLIENT: I'm pleased you have what I consider [an] exceptional ability to 'self-observe' your own behavior and to analyze the part you play in relationships. I think this strength will serve you well in solving the problems you've identified.
>
> HELPER TO CLIENT WHO IS A MEMBER OF A COUNSELING GROUP: I've been touched several times in the group when I've noticed that, despite your grief over the loss of your husband, you've reached out to other members who needed support.

In making positive feedback statements, there are some guidelines to consider that are fundamental to effective feedback processes. Such statements express a feeling of acknowledgment and ownership by the helper, as in "When something happens, I feel thus and so" or "When I see you, I think. . . ." Note that these statements use the personal pronoun or "I" messages. They avoid judgment and evaluation. Most of all, they do not accuse or blame, as in the following statement: "You are a real problem to work with because you are always late." In other words, they preserve the dignity and self-respect of the other person involved in the relationship. Furthermore, an effective feedback statement does not contain advice; it is not a "parenting" or scolding statement. It should also concern a behavior or attitude the other person has the capacity to change or modify. For example, it would not be helpful to use the following kind of feedback statement: "I just don't like the way you look. Why don't you do something about your complexion?" Focus your feedback statements on behavior rather than personality traits, and be specific rather than general.

Feedback is usually more effective when it is solicited. Thus, feedback statements that relate to clients' goals or to aspects of the counseling relationship may be better received by clients because of their involvement in this process. In any case, though, you can determine the effects of your feedback by the clients' reactions. If your clients are defensive, give detailed explanations or justifications or make strong denials, this is a clue that perhaps you have touched on an issue too soon. At this point in the relationship, clients need an indication of your support and acceptance. It is also important to give clients a chance to explore their feelings about and reactions to these feedback statements.

A CLIMATE OF SAFETY

The primary reason why the conditions of a therapeutic relationship are so important is to help clients feel safe. When clients feel safe, they feel trusting and free to be open. When clients do not feel safe, they often feel self-protective, guarded, and subdued. It is the helper's

APPLICATION EXERCISE 2.7

Focusing on Strengths: Positive Feedback Statements

A. Characteristics of Feedback

With a partner, try some feedback-type statements similar to the examples described in the preceding section. Be sure your responses include a description of your partner's behavior as well as your reactions to it. For example, you might say something like "I appreciate (your feeling) your taking the time to talk with me (partner's behavior)."

List the feedback statements you make to your partner. What are the effects on you? On the other person? On the relationship?

B. Positive Feedback Statements and Focusing on Strengths

In a small group, construct a positive feedback statement that focuses on a positive ingredient or strength that each member brings to the group. This may refer to a specific behavior you have seen each person demonstrate in the group or it may refer to something you appreciate about that person. Share your statements verbally in the group. Make sure there is time for the group member to respond to your positive feedback statements.

_____

_____

_____

_____

responsibility to offer the kind of climate in which clients feel the sense of safety they need in order to ask for and accept help. If a client has come from a particular kind of family or relationship in which there was a lot of stress—such as abuse or incest—then the helper's effort to provide a safe environment will need to be even more intentional and more intensive. Clients—particularly those who have had their trust broken in the past—will often test the helper. They will likely not believe that the therapist's initial efforts to be understanding, sincere, accepting, and warm are really true. They may want to find out if they really mean something—if they really are valued as the helper says they are. This reason may account for all kinds of client feelings and behaviors that are projected or reflected in or outside a session, including acting out, calling the practitioner on the phone, being late to a session, becoming angry, and so on. It is as if clients long for a warm, caring empathic helper but, due to their history, fear this, and in their fear, they resist, attack, or retreat (Karasu, 1992, p. 21). According to Teyber (2006), there is nothing that "casual" about these testing behaviors by clients, as they are the client's attempts to assess safety or danger in the helping relationship (p. 287). Establishing a climate of safety means that helpers provide a more effective response to clients than they have received or expect to receive from others; clients feel safer when the helper does not respond in a familiar yet problematic way that they have come to expect (Teyber, 2006, p. 159, 287).

A climate of safety is a basic prerequisite to progress in counseling and, as Teyber (2006) observes, such progress can often be seen immediately, as in the following examples:

- The client expresses more confidence in oneself or in the helper.
- The client reports feeling better as symptoms or difficult feelings subside.
- The client is able to bring up new content in the session.
- The client becomes more congruent, forthright, and honest. (p. 288)

Efforts to provide a safe, therapeutic environment for clients need to be ongoing and persistent. This is also especially true in working with clients who do not have privileges and power from the mainstream culture and who have experienced discrimination and oppression.

Summary

Although the helping relationship has some marked differences from other interpersonal relationships, it does serve as a model that the client can use to improve the quality of relationships outside the counseling room. From the view of your clients, the helping relationship is described as a special place outside the usual context of family, friends, and work where they can express themselves freely to a respectful and supportive person (Lilliengren & Werbart, 2005).

Clearly, the helping relationship cannot succeed without the presence of accurate empathy or understanding of the client's world. When you assume that you understand but you do not, you and your client detour from a constructive and helpful course and risk the dangers of false conclusions and failure. In a similar manner, if you do not value your client or if you do not consider the client's problems and concerns to be real, you are denying the most reliable information about your client's perceptions. Lacking this information, you cannot help your client develop in more constructive directions. Finally—and underlying both accurate empathy and positive regard—the degree to which you can be honestly and consistently yourself, knowing yourself, and sharing yourself with your client in congruent ways will establish the ultimate parameters of the helping relationship.

A recent study of clients in counseling described the critical incidents that, from the client's perspective, helped to forge a strong helping relationship (Bedi, Davis & Williams, 2005). These were described by clients as specific things the helper said or did. They included the following:

- Active listening: The counselor remembered what I said.
- Self-disclosure: The counselor recalled an experience similar to my own.
- Encouragement: The counselor focused on what I was doing well.
- Validation of feelings: The counselor understood my fears and my frustration over situations.

Bedi and colleagues (2005) concluded several things about the helping relationship from the client's perspective. First, clients see the strength of the helping relationship as related to things the helper does rather than things the client does. Second, as helpers, we may overlook behaviors and comments that seem simple or benign to us but have tremendous impact on clients for establishing a positive therapeutic relationship.

Although the behaviors presented in this chapter can be learned and incorporated into your style and repertoire, there is a dimension yet to be acknowledged. The integral human element of the helping relationship cannot exist by mechanical manipulation of certain behaviors at given moments. Your relationship with each client contains its own uniqueness and spontaneity that cannot—without the loss of both genuineness and sincerity—be systematically controlled prior to its occurrence. However, your spontaneity will increase rather than decrease once you have become comfortable with a variety of counseling techniques. While you are learning counseling responses, this ease may not be quite as apparent because you will need to overlearn them. However, once the responses suggested in this book have become second nature to you, your spontaneity as a helper will begin to emerge. You will be on your way to becoming the helper you hope to be.

Reflective Questions

1. How do you approach a new relationship? What conditions do you require to be met before you open yourself to a closer relationship?
2. What were the "unwritten rules" in your family and in your culture about interactions with non-family members? How might these rules affect the kind of relationship you are able to offer clients?
3. If you were a client, what conditions would you look for in your helper?
4. Under what conditions do you feel safe? Open and able to disclose? Trusting? Does this vary with persons of different ages, gender, values, and ethnic origins?
5. How have your own childhood experiences influenced your relationships with others as an adult? In exploring this for yourself, can you see potential connections between the childhood experiences of your clients and the way they may relate to you and to others?

My Helping Lab

For each exercise, log on to MyHelpingLab at http://www.myhelpinglab.com and then click the Topics tab.

1. Choose the Video Lab, and watch the following selection: Empathy as a Foundation for Engagement. Watch this segment and then comment on how the two practitioners conveyed empathic understanding to this client as her grief unfolds.
2. Click the Process, Skills, and Techniques tab again. This time, locate the Cognitive and Behavioral Interventions tab, choose the Video Lab, and then watch the Example of Counselor Self-Disclosure selection. What did you think about this clinician's use of self-disclosure in this clip? How was it used? Did it seem to elicit something positive in the session?
3. Click the Theories tab. Then, click the Person-centered tab. Choose the Video Lab, and watch all the segments under this series. There are five segments in which a helper works with a young girl (youth) and six segments in which a helper works with a woman (individual). Comment on what you saw in all these segments about the relative effectiveness of the helper's uses of the facilitative conditions of empathy, positive regard, and genuineness. Did you notice any differences between the sessions with the child and the sessions with the individual adult? Did you feel a climate of safety was established in both sessions? If so, how? In your eyes and ears, how would you describe the helping relationship in these two sessions?

Recommended Readings

Brammer, L. M. & MacDonald, G. (2003). *The helping relationship, 8th edition*. Boston: Allyn & Bacon.

Breggin, P., Breggin, G. & Bemak, F. (Eds.). (2002). *Dimensions of empathic therapy*. New York: Springer.

Chi-Ying Chung, R. & Bemak, F. (2002). The relationship of culture and empathy in cross-cultural counseling. *Journal of Counseling and Development, 80*, 154–159.

Clark, A. J. (2007). *Empathy in counseling and psychotherapy.* NY: Erlbaum.

Hepworth, D. H., Rooney, R. H., Rooney, G. D., Strom-Gottfried, K. & Larsen, J. A. (2010). *Direct social work practice, 8th edition.* Belmont, CA: Brooks/Cole, Cengage.

Johnson, D. W. (2009). *Reaching out: Interpersonal effectiveness and self-actualization, 10th edition.* Upper Saddle River, NJ: Pearson Education.

Norcross, J. C. (Ed.). (2002). *Psychotherapy relationships that work.* New York: Oxford University Press.

Pedersen, P., Crethar, H. & Carlson, J. (2008). *Inclusive cultural empathy.* Washington, DC: American Psychological Association.

Zur, O., Williams, M., Lehavot, K. & Knapp, S. (2009). Therapist self-disclosure and transparency in the Internet age. *Professional Psychology, 40,* 22–30.

Attending to Clients

We have identified several conditions that affect the development of the helping relationship. Those conditions—accurate empathy, positive regard, and genuineness or congruence—are called *core conditions* because they are central to the therapeutic process. Although these core conditions are necessary, the helper must also bring other skills and knowledge to the therapeutic process. Certainly, the first of these skills is the ability to *listen* actively and attentively to the client. This objective is not as simple as it might appear. It involves more than an attentive ear. Have you ever talked to someone who was fiddling with a pencil, staring around the room, or seemed otherwise distracted as he or she listened to you? If you have—and who has not?—you will recall how this felt. The listener may have heard all that you said, but you probably interpreted his or her behavior as a lack of interest, concentration, or attention. That being the case, you probably found it difficult to continue the conversation. Clients exhibit the same sensitivity to whether the helper is paying attention to what they say. Attending skills are used by the helper to assure, support, and/or reinforce the client. These skills are very important for the client who is feeling vulnerable, uncertain, or insecure. One precondition for the existence of attending behaviors is an awareness of the client's communication. This awareness must then be communicated through your undistracted attentiveness to the client. Attentiveness is one way of saying, "I am following both your message and your metacommunication; I am invested and involved in your story." Ivey et al. (2007, p. 91) summarize decades of research on helper attentiveness in the following two statements:

    1. Clients respond better and more positively, verbalize at greater length, and indicate a stronger willingness to return to see helpers who are attentive.

    2. Experienced and seasoned helpers typically do better with attending skills, while inexperienced or beginning helpers have room to grow on dimensions of attentiveness.

    In the following section, we describe the primary dimensions of helper attentiveness.

COMMUNICATION OF ATTENTIVENESS

Attentiveness is communicated primarily through four dimensions: facial expressions, eye contact, bodily positions and movement, and verbal responses (Cormier, Nurius & Osborn, 2009). You may have noted that the first three of these channels are all nonverbal. On the surface, attending to clients appears relatively simple. However, it is easier said than done. Egan (2010) listed a number of obstacles to the attending process:

1. Being judgmental
2. Having biases
3. Pigeonholing clients
4. Attending to facts
5. Sympathizing
6. Interrupting

These are all ways in which we disrupt our attentiveness to and with clients.

Another issue in the communication of attentiveness involves the various meanings that people attach to different gestures or words because such meanings have been learned. Some of the meanings are fairly standardized; others have distinct regional or cultural variances. For example, do you prefer to have people look at you when you talk to them? Most European Americans do, but some Native Americans do not, and studies suggest that some inner-city African-American youths do not. It is important to remember that some cultural groups have sanctions on direct visual contact during some types of interpersonal interactions. When you are telling someone what you think, what would be your reaction if that person began to frown? If the frown was not consistent with your feelings, you probably would begin to question the inconsistency between your message and the listener's response. If you feel strongly about a topic and the other person does not seem to care about it, are you likely to continue telling the person about your feelings? No—because most of us want to know that our feelings are falling on concerned ears.

For these and other reasons, your behavior can contribute to your client's feelings of security. The increased sense of security that occurs as clients are talking about themselves can become a self-reinforcing phenomenon. Most of you have probably had the experience of entering a new activity and feeling nervous and unsure of yourselves. But as you stayed with the activity and nothing bad (perhaps even some good things) happened, before long, your self-confidence began to grow. So it is with the helping process. As the client begins to experience your acceptance, your understanding, and your commitment, the feelings of vulnerability, uncertainty, caution, or lack of trust begin to dissipate. In the following sections of the chapter, we describe nonverbal and verbal ways to increase your attentiveness with clients by using the four dimensions we mentioned above—facial expressions, eye contact, bodily movement and positioning, and verbal responses. We also explore the contextual variables surrounding these dimensions because as we indicated earlier, the meanings of certain gestures or words are learned and vary by region and culture.

Facial Expressions

Knapp and Hall (2006) have observed that the face is the primary means by which people communicate information about their emotional states. Facial expressions convey basic emotions such as anger, disgust, fear, sadness, and happiness. Unlike most other aspects of nonverbal attending behavior, facial expressions do not seem to vary much among cultures. These basic emotions seem to be represented by the same facial expressions across cultures, although individual cultural norms may influence how much and how often such emotions are expressed (Mesquita & Frijda, 1992). For example, anger is often conveyed cross-culturally through the eyes and by changes in the area of the mouth and jaw. However, men and women both within and between cultures may express anger in different ways and at different times. For example, some persons may reject the idea of releasing anger because they have learned it is "unchristian" or "unlady-like" (Kelley, 1979, p. 24). Your facial expressions communicate messages to the client that are as meaningful as those you receive from the client's facial expressions. As Egan (2010) notes, "an averted face is often a sign of the averted heart" (p. 131).

A primary—although often not intentional—way that helpers use their facial expressions is to reinforce client behavior. For example, Almedar, your client, reveals that he was invited to join an honorary society at his school. Because Almedar's prior success at school has been limited, in hearing this, your own face "lights up." This in and of itself encourages Almedar to share more of this part of his story with you. Another aspect of facial expressions and attentiveness has to do with *mirroring*. It is important for your facial expressions to reflect those of the client: If the client expresses pleasure, you look happy; if the client conveys sadness, you show concern. The same mirror neurons in the brain that we discussed in the previous chapter that help to create resonant empathy are also related to the mirroring of facial expressions between helpers and clients.

ANIMATION.   Animation in facial expression gives clients the feeling that you are alert and responding to ongoing communication. An absence of facial expressions (a deadpan look) will suggest a lack of interest, awareness, or presence to clients. You can surely remember talking with someone who is "vacant" in lack of facial responsiveness. And you can surely remember the effect this had on you, and we doubt it was pleasant. The most noticeable expression is the smile. The appropriate use of smiles can have a powerful effect on clients, particularly when used in conjunction with occasional head nods. However, continuous smiling has a negative effect, just as do frequent frowns, which can communicate disapproval. On the other hand, occasional frowns communicate your failure to follow or understand a particular point and are therefore often useful.

Eye Contact

What is the effect of eye contact in the helper-client relationship? Research into interpersonal interaction indicates that eye contact has more than one effect and that these effects do vary across cultures. It may signal a need for affiliation, involvement, or inclusion; it may reflect the quality of an existing relationship; or it may enhance the communication of a complex message. Eye contact can also produce anxiety in the other person. A gaze lasting longer than about ten seconds can signal aggressiveness rather than acceptance. An averted gaze may hide shame over expressing something seen as culturally taboo.

In some cultures, client eye contact is appropriate when listening. In other cultures, an individual may look away as a sign of respect or may demonstrate more eye contact when talking and less eye contact while listening. Effective eye contact—eye contact that reinforces clients and makes their communication easier—lies somewhere between the fixed gaze and "shifty eyes" or frequent breaks of eye contact. Look at clients when they are talking. Occasionally, permit your eyes to drift to an object away—*but not far away*—from the client. Then, return your eyes to the client. Let yourself be natural. At the same time, avoid making stereotypical judgments about the client's eye contact or lack thereof. As Knapp and Hall (2006) comment, the meanings and effects of eye contact vary both within and across cultural groups. For some clients, less eye contact is typical of their culture and should not be construed to mean anything else. In other words, eye contact varies from client to client and

APPLICATION EXERCISE 3.1

Facial Expressions

A. Facial Attentiveness

With a partner, designate one of you as the speaker and the other as the listener. While the speaker shares one of his or her concerns, the listener's tasks are the following:

1. Do not respond with *any* facial expression or animation whatsoever while the speaker is talking; maintain complete facial passivity.
2. After two or three minutes, respond with a facial reaction that is opposite to the feelings and concerns being expressed by the speaker. For example, if the speaker is talking seriously, smile and look happy.
3. After another three minutes or so, respond with facial animation and expression that mirror the kind and intensity of feelings being expressed by the speaker.

Discuss the different results produced by these three approaches. Reverse roles and repeat the exercise. What can you conclude about facial attentiveness as a result of this exercise? What have you learned about yourself and your facial gestures? What do you want to change about your facial gestures, and how do you intend to bring about this change? If possible, repeat this activity with a person from a distinctly different culture than your own. Do your conclusions change in any way?

B. Recognizing Facial Cues

Find two people with whom to work. Designate one of you as the speaker for round 1, the second as the listener, and the third as the observer. Roles are rotated for round 2 and round 3. For each round, the listener feeds each of the four incomplete sentences to the speaker. The speaker repeats the sentence and adds the first completion that comes to his or her mind. The observer watches for changes and cues in the speaker's facial expressions as he or she works with all the incomplete sentences in the round. For this to be most effective, when you are in the role of the speaker, take your time, breathe deeply, and say whatever comes into your mind without thinking about it or censoring it. The observer shares the observations with the speaker after the round is over. When you are in the role of the speaker, only disclose what feels comfortable to you.

1. Anger
   a. When I get angry . . .
   b. I get angry when . . .
   c. I feel disgusted that . . .
   d. One thing that makes me mad is . . .
2. Sadness
   a. When I get sad . . .
   b. I get sad when . . .
   c. I feel "blue" that . . .
   d. One thing that makes me sad is . . .
3. Fear
   a. When I get afraid . . .
   b. I feel afraid that . . .
   c. I get afraid when . . .
   d. One thing that makes me afraid is . . .

APPLICATION EXERCISE 3.2

Eye Contact

Perhaps you can better grasp the effects of eye contact by participating in the following dyadic exercise. With a partner, determine who will be the talker and who will be the listener. While the talker speaks, the listener should listen but avoid eye contact with the speaker. Then, discuss the following questions: What are the effects on the speaker? How well did the speaker feel that he or she was able to communicate? Try the exercise again, but this time, maintain eye contact with the speaker as described in the previous section. What effect does this have? Reverse roles, and repeat the exercise. Discuss how the effects may vary depending on the gender and culture of the participants.

within and between cultural groups, and eye contact patterns may involve changes in duration as well as frequency (Knapp and Hall, 2006). Some clients may favor more direct eye contact because their cultural identifications emphasize visual contact during interactions, while other clients identify with cultures that sanction a lot of eye contact during some kinds of interpersonal interactions. Other clients may avoid eye contact because of their clinical disorder. For example, some clients with autism, depression, or social anxiety may not be able to bear the intensity of a gaze between themselves and the helper. Another variable that impacts eye contact during the helping process is distance or space between the helper and client. As physical space is increased, eye contact often increases too; as physical space is decreased, eye contact also often decreases.

Body Positions and Use of Space

Body positions serve important functions in a helping session. Body positions and movement are involved in regulating the space or distance between the helper and a client, greeting of a client, terminating a session, and taking turns (that is, the exchange of speaker and listener roles within a conversation) (Cormier, Nurius & Osborn, 2009). Body movement and comfort with physical space (closeness or distance) vary among cultures and with gender. Generally, among Euro-Americans, counselors and clients sit face to face. Even an intervening object such as a desk is often considered a distraction—a barrier to attentiveness. Yet, as Ivey, D'Andrea, Ivey, and Simek-Morgan (2007, p. 93) noted, in some Eskimo and Inuit cultural groups, persons sit side by side when discussing a personal issue. European–Americans usually prefer several feet of distance between chairs; however, those from contact cultures may be more comfortable with closer distances (Watson, 1970). Many Latino/a clients prefer closer distances between helper and client and also client and helper dyads of the same race (Knapp and Hall, 2006). Yet, individual differences among clients may be as important in use of space and distance as cultural patterns. For example, the effects of space also vary with a client's expression of feelings. A client who has just expressed a lot of anger often requires more personal space than someone who is feeling sad or experiencing a lot of pain. In short, the concept of space has no universals.

Gender also dictates what is considered appropriate space. Some females may be more comfortable with a closer distance to the helper, especially if the helper is female. However, many female clients may feel intruded upon if a male helper positions himself too close for comfort. Clients with a history of severe physical and/or sexual abuse may require greater space, particularly at the beginning stage of the helping process. To be respectful of all clients, it is important to allow *them* to choose the appropriate amount of distance from the helper in the counseling interactions.

One important aspect of body communication involves the amount of tension conveyed by the body. Astute helpers will note the degree of tension or relaxation in a client's body. A body that is blocking or holding back a feeling may be tense, with shallow, fast breathing. A relaxed body posture indicates comfort, both with the counseling setting and with the topic being discussed. Selective body tension communicates action. It may reflect a "working" moment for you—involvement with the client, movement toward a goal, or preparation for something new.

Shifts in body position, such as leaning forward or backward, often signify an "important segment of the encounter" (Knapp and Hall, 2006, p. 152). Body tension that is continuous will probably communicate discomfort with the client, the topic, or yourself. To be comfortable with yourself, it is important to begin from a base of relaxation because this is what will be mirrored to the client. Exercise 3.3 may help you achieve a desired state of relaxation.

Visible Behavior

Together, facial expressions, eye contact, and body messages constitute the helper's visible behavior. The impact of visible behavior on communication is considerable, as the following exercise will prove.

APPLICATION EXERCISE 3.3

Relaxing

Muscle Relaxation

While sitting down, raise your hand and arms three to four inches above the armrests of the chair and then let them drop. Feel the tension flow out of your arms. Repeat this, and try to increase the relaxation. Let your back and buttocks be in contact with as much of the chair as possible. Feel the chair pressing against your body. Tense the muscles in your legs and then release the tension. Feel the surge of warmth in your muscles as your legs relax. Repeat this tensing and releasing of leg muscles several times, each time achieving a little more relaxation. Now take three or four deep breaths slowly. After each breath, slowly release the air from your lungs. Do you feel more relaxed than when you started?

Do this exercise again—this time without any interruptions between different body exercises. This is a good exercise to do just before seeing a client. It is one of the ways by which you can prepare yourself for the session. As you do the exercise more often, you will find it easier and quicker to achieve a surprisingly comfortable state of relaxation.

APPLICATION EXERCISE 3.4

The Impact of Visible Behavior

Egan (2010) has described an exercise that illustrates the importance of what you see in another person when you communicate. This exercise will give you an opportunity to measure the effect of your facial and body gestures on the person receiving your message. Select as your partner a person you have wanted to involve in a conversation. Sit down facing each other. Each of you close your eyes—and keep them closed throughout the conversation. Talk to each other for about five minutes. Then, open your eyes, complete the conversation, and discuss the differences between visual and nonvisual communication. What compensations did you have to make while talking without sight? How successful do you believe you were in your communication attempts? What, in particular, were you missing in terms of visual feedback from your partner?

VERBAL BEHAVIOR AND SELECTIVE ATTENTION

The things you say will have an immediate impact on your clients. Many studies have shown that the helper's responses can mold and shape the direction of the client's responses. In other words, whatever topic you respond to with a verbal acknowledgment, the client will probably continue to talk about it. Topics that you do not respond to often get cut off or interrupted. This process is called *selective attention*. Egan (2010) has aptly noted that if helpers think everything that their clients say is key, then nothing is key. One of the implications of this is that, as helpers, we are constantly sorting out all the various messages and "story lines" we get from clients. What is important? What is more relevant? Less relevant? Are there patterns of messages or story lines we do not want to respond to with attentiveness, such as with the client who is always talking about how everyone else is the problem?

Ivey, Gluckstern, and Ivey (1993) have suggested that what the helper chooses to focus on says more about the helper than the client. These authors also stated that it is important to notice what topics the helper selectively attends to so the clients are not inadvertently or unconsciously steered away from topics they need to discuss just because they are uncomfortable for the helper. If you become aware of this happening, it is useful to consult your supervisor (see also Chapter 10). Several points should be considered in terms of your verbal impact. Fit your comments or questions into the context of the topic at hand. Do not interrupt clients or quickly change topics. Stay with the topics that clients introduce, and help them develop and pursue them. This implies more than a technique; it is a highly conscious awareness of what is going on between you and your client. It is called *verbal following*.

Egan (2010) proposed some useful questions that may help you listen and attend to clients, especially with the skill of verbal following:

- What are the main ideas reflected by the client's message?
- What are the most important experiences described in the client's messages?
- What themes are apparent in the client's messages?
- What is the client's worldview?
- What is most important to the client?
- What does the client need you to understand?

APPLICATION EXERCISE 3.5

Verbal Following

A. Roleplay of Verbal Following

In the roles of helper and client, choose a partner and sit in pairs. Concentrate on using the verbal reinforcing behaviors discussed in this chapter. In your responses, react only to what the client has just said; do not add a new idea. Let your thinking be as close as possible to that of the client.

Prevent your facial gestures, body gestures, and verbal responses from distracting the client. After five minutes, stop the exercise and then discuss the following with your client: What was your client most aware of in your behavior? How well did your client think you understood his or her communication? What, if any, behavior got in your client's way? Now reverse roles, and repeat the exercise. What effect did your own gender and culture have on this activity? What about the client's gender and culture?

B. Verbal Following and Shifts in Focus

Shown here are some client statements followed by helper responses. Describe each helper response: Do you feel that it is a response to the client's statement? If not, describe the nature of the inappropriate response, such as shift of topic, focus on others, or focus on past.

CLIENT A: I think I just have to go away for a while. The pressure is really building up.
HELPER: What would Bob say to that?

The helper did/did not (circle one) respond to the client's statement. If the helper did not respond to the client's statement, the nature of the inappropriate response was _____.

CLIENT B: She doesn't really care anymore, and I've got to learn to accept that.
HELPER: You are fairly sure that she doesn't care.

The helper did/did not (circle one) respond to the client's statement. If the helper did not respond to the client's statement, the nature of the inappropriate response was _____.

CLIENT C: Grades are the biggest problem I have in school. I can't get poor grades and bring shame to my family.
HELPER: What did you do last year?

The helper did/did not (circle one) respond to the client's statement. If the helper did not respond to the client's statement, the nature of the inappropriate response was _____.

CLIENT D: The job I have isn't fun, but I'm afraid that if I quit, I might not get another job.
HELPER: Jobs are really getting hard to find.

The helper did/did not (circle one) respond to the client's statement. If the helper did not respond to the client's statement, the nature of the inappropriate response was ._____.

These exchanges illustrate some of the common pitfalls that await the helper. In the exchange with client A, the response was probably inappropriate. The helper seems to have

(continued)

jumped topics by bringing up Bob. In addition, the helper ignored the client's reference to the pressure and its effect on him. The response given to client B could be quite appropriate, although it is not the only possible appropriate response. The helper is responding directly to what the client said. The inappropriateness of the response to client C is more obvious. The helper really did not respond to any of the key ideas in the client's statement. Instead, for some reason, the helper decided to collect information about the client. Moreover, the helper also ignored the social and cultural implications of the client's situation. Finally, the response to client D is also inappropriate. The client is talking about feelings ("isn't fun"; "afraid"). The helper's response has nothing to do with the client. Instead, the helper shifted the focus to a social commentary on the current economic scene.

Of course, the helper does not distract clients by asking these questions directly. Rather, these questions are part of the helper's process in listening and attending to clients, and they reflect the helper's interest in the client's world (Egan, 2010).

Vocal Characteristics and Minimal Verbal Followers

The use of a well-modulated, calm, but energetic vocal tone and pitch will reassure clients of your own comfort with their problems. The use of intermittent one-word phrases (*minimal verbal followers*) serves much the same purpose as head nods and eye contact. These are verbal signs that you are listening and following what the client is saying. The more common minimal verbal stimuli are "mm-hmm," "mmm," "ah," and so forth. There is one hazard that should be mentioned: Overuse of these vocal stimuli can produce a parrot-like effect that has negative results. Later chapters will describe how you can use minimal verbal stimuli and other types of reinforcing behaviors to assist clients in developing their thinking.

LISTENING FOR CONTEXT

Egan (2010) observed that clients are more than the sum of their verbal and nonverbal messages. Listening in its deepest sense means listening to the ways in which clients are influenced by the contexts in which they live, move, and have their being. Egan added that key elements of this context become part of the client's story, whether they are mentioned directly or not. Many of the elements of context were discussed in Chapter 1. They have to do with such things as the client's religion or faith heritage, race, ethnicity, gender, sexual orientation, social and economic class, occupation, geography, age, and so on. Often, these elements of context form a central part of the client's identity, and not to attend to them is to render the client invisible. For example, for some clients, being Jewish may be a core aspect of their identity and being in the world, whereas for others, the core aspect may be race, sexual orientation, money, social class, or health status. Listening for context not only involves attending to and acknowledging these elements of context surrounding clients but it also involves attending to and clarifying the meaning that clients give to these contextual elements. A case example might illustrate this process.

APPLICATION EXERCISE 3.6

Culturally Appropriate Behavior for Helper Attentiveness

Now that you are aware of behavioral descriptions of inappropriate social behaviors and attending behaviors in the counseling setting, can you deduce some appropriate behaviors? Be specific as to nonverbal components (face, eyes, tone of voice, rate of speech, etc.), body language components (head, arms, body position, etc.), and verbal components (choice of words, types of responses, etc.). List them on a sheet of paper.

For the second part of this activity, go back over the list you just created. Consider instances in which your list of helper attentiveness behaviors may not be culturally appropriate for some clients. Think about examples, and discuss them with a partner or in a small group.

Sondra is a lesbian who "came out" many years ago—so many years ago that at this point in time, being a lesbian was an important but not the only important part of her identity. Sondra stated in your counseling session that she at times felt annoyed because people were always responding to her sexual orientation as a rather singular factor; that is what they paid attention to. Sondra believed there were many other interesting aspects to her life and her identity, and she felt annoyed when other people were not interested in learning more about these. On the other hand, your client Angela was upset when you did not mention in the session the fact that she was African American. She felt you overlooked something that was critical to how she saw herself and that you were not attentive to this important part of her identity. She wondered aloud how well the two of you would be able to work together in counseling because you had "missed" communicating your awareness and attentiveness about this important part of her narrative/story.

Summary

One of the major goals in counseling is to listen attentively and to communicate this attentiveness through the use of eye contact, intermittent head nods, a variety of facial expressions, relaxed posture, modulated voice, minimal verbal followers, and verbal responses that follow the client's topics. As we have seen in this chapter, many of these components of attentiveness vary depending on the gender and culture of both helper and client.

Because helpers cannot attend to everything, attentiveness is selective, and in counseling sessions, helpers make moment-by-moment decisions about what is most important. In addition to listening to verbal and nonverbal messages, helpers also need to pay attention to the context surrounding client stories and lives. Ivey, Gluckstern, and Ivey (1993) concluded, "Listening to another person and giving them your full attention is one of the greatest gifts you can give" (p. 5).

Reflective Questions

1. How much do you rely on reactions (gestures or verbal responses) from the other person when you are trying to communicate an important message?
2. What is your typical response when you feel that you are failing in your attempt to communicate with another person—that is, when you get a lack of response from them?
3. What goals or objectives have you set for yourself in terms of improving your ability to be a good listener? What do you plan to do to achieve these goals?
4. What are some additional examples for social behaviors that you would find distracting if you were involved in a sensitive discussion of your private life?
5. Recall an incident in which you were sharing a significant moment with another person and that person displayed some distracting behavior. What was the effect of that person's behavior on you? What did you decide was the reason for that person's behavior?
6. What do you notice about nonverbal behavior among persons from varying cultures?
7. What effect does your own culture have on the way you seem to attend and respond to clients?

My Helping Lab

For each exercise, log on to MyHelpingLab at http://www.myhelpinglab.com and then click the Topics tab.

1. Click the Process, Skills, and Techniques tab to locate the Establishing the Therapeutic Relationship tab. Choose the Video Lab for the following two selections: Encouraging Clients to "Listen to their Center" and Examples of Active Listening in Session. Review these two clips and then comment on these questions:
2.
   1. In the first clip, the client talked a great deal in the session. How did the practitioner use attending skills to listen to her?
   2. In the second clip, what nonverbal and verbal attending skills did the practitioner use, and what effects did these seem to have on this particular client?
   3. In these two clips, the helper and client differed on several cultural dimensions, including race, gender, and age. Did you think the helper's attending skills were impacted by these differences? If so, how?
3. Click the Theories tab to locate the Existential-Humanistic Theory tab. Under the Video Lab for this tab, click the following selection: Relating Non-Verbals to Congruency. After watching this interaction, respond to these questions:
   1. What did you notice about the practitioner's use of attending explicitly to the client's facial expressions? How did this advance the session?
   2. What did you notice about the practitioner's own facial expressions in this clip?
   3. Were there any cultural issues underlying the client's presenting concern about fear of making a mistake that in your opinion were not addressed by the practitioner in this clip? If so, what were they, and how would you have attended to this aspect of the client's story?

Recommended Readings

Cormier, S., Nurius, P. S. & Osborn, C.J. (2009). *Interviewing strategies for helpers, 6th edition.* Belmont, CA: Brooks/Cole, Cengage.

Egan, G. (2010). *The skilled helper, 9th edition.* Belmont, CA: Brooks/Cole, Cengage.

Ivey, A., D'Andrea, M., Ivey, M. B. & Simek-Morgan, L. (2007). *Theories of counseling and psychotherapy: A multicultural perspective, 6th edition.* Upper Saddle River, NJ: Pearson.

Ivey, A., Gluckstern, N. & Ivey, M. B. (1993). *Basic attending skills.* North Amherst, MA: Microtraining Associates.

Knapp, M. L. & Hall, J. (2006). *Nonverbal communication in human interaction.* Belmont, CA: Brooks/Cole, Thomson.

Lindahl, K. (2003). *Practicing the sacred art of listening.* Woodstock, VT: Skylights Path Publishing.

Communication Patterns in the Helping Process

As the helper-client relationship develops, communication patterns emerge. Issues related to the locus of control and responsibility in the session, choice of topics, timing, and other therapeutic logistics are undefined at the outset of the helping process. In the first few sessions, these issues are resolved—either openly or tacitly—and become apparent through understanding the communication patterns that evolve.

There are many ways to think about patterning in the helping process. Some patterning takes the form of ritual, whereas other patterning is responsive. That is, some of the behaviors become ritualized as a function of routine; for example, the client always chooses the chair facing the window or the helper always begins by asking, "What is on your mind today?" And so forth. Other patterns are negotiations between the practitioner and client, the intent of which may be to settle such matters as "Are we really going to work today?" or "I want you to take charge because I'm feeling overwhelmed." Frequent topic shifts made by the client in early helping sessions may be an expression of client anxiety and of a need to control something about the process. If the helper is unaware of these shifts in communication and also of the client's underlying affect, progress may be impeded. However, as you will see later in this chapter, communication styles and patterns are greatly influenced by cultural variables such as ethnicity, race, gender, and disability, and particular communication patterns do not always have the same meaning across clients.

RITUALIZED PATTERNS OF COMMUNICATION

Ritualized patterns may be either situation-specific or idiosyncratic to the individuals involved. For example, we have already mentioned examples of situation-specific patterning with the client who always chooses a certain chair to sit in. This act of repeated choice may arise out of a very simple condition. It was the chair selected by the client at the initial session, and its continued selection in subsequent sessions offers familiar ground and reflects that the client feels no need to make a different choice. However, if the client arrives for the fifth session and, with no explanation, chooses a different chair, the act of choice may contain unspecified meaning. In other words, through the act of choosing, something is communicated, but what is communicated is unclear until the helper explores this with the client.

Ritualized Helper Patterns

The same situation may apply to the helper. Most experienced helpers develop a style of interaction with their clients. Although their style takes individuals into account, it is nonetheless patterned and, as such, is a kind of trademark of that particular practitioner's work. For example, one clinician may use the first several minutes of the session as relationship time and may communicate this to clients. A different clinician may view the first few minutes as history-taking time. However, should a client arrive in a distraught state, that pattern may be suspended and therapeutic work may begin immediately.

Ritualized Client Patterns

Clients also become involved in ritualized patterns of communication. Often, these patterns evolve out of assumptions about what the helper wants or expects from the client. For example, a client may assume that the helper expects to hear an account of the week's worries. The fact that this happened in the second session led the client to think such an account is expected, so he or she continues the practice in subsequent sessions. Thus, although the activity may have little to do with the ensuing process, it remains a part of the pattern. Often, such patterns are useful to clients because they provide stability and predictability. Occasionally, however, the purpose or intention behind the pattern outlives its usefulness, and the helper needs to gently challenge the pattern.

INTERACTIVE COMMUNICATION PATTERNS: RACE, ETHNICITY, GENDER, AND DISABILITY

Most patterning—and certainly the most significant patterning that occurs in helping sessions—is interactive in nature. It has been suggested by Hackney and Cormier (2009) that most clients approach counseling with two conflicting motivations: (1) "I know I need help" and (2) "I wish I weren't here." Given this dual set of motivations, the client may be expected to convey conflicting and even contradictory communications at times. Similarly, helpers must resolve the potential conflict that was mentioned in Chapter 2 regarding unconditional positive regard and congruence. As you recall, these can be occasions when the helper's feelings about the client may be pulled in two different directions. We mention these conflicting tendencies because they can confuse the communication process. It is essential that the helper remains aware of such conflicts in communication patterns. In addition to these contradictory communications, interactive communication patterns are also influenced by cultural variables such as race, ethnicity, gender, and disability.

Communication and Race and Ethnicity

Sue and Sue (2008) have noted that different racial/ethnic groups differ in their communication styles. They suggested:

> Whether our conversation proceeds with fits or starts, whether we interrupt one another continually or proceed smoothly, the topics we prefer to discuss or avoid, the

depth of our involvement, the forms of interaction (ritual, repartee, argumentative, persuasive, etc.) and the channel we use to communicate (verbal-nonverbal vs. non-verbal-verbal) are all aspects of communication style. Some refer to these factors as the *social rhythms* that underlie all our speech and actions. Communication styles are strongly correlated with race, culture, and ethnicity. (p. 161)

For example, "in traditional Japanese culture, children have been taught not to speak until addressed. Patterns of communication tend to be vertical, flowing from those of higher prestige and status to those of lower prestige and status. Likewise, there are many cultural groups in which restraint of strong feelings is highly valued. It is equated with wisdom and maturity" (Sue, 1992, p. 12).

Sue and Sue (2008) have provided other examples of different communication patterns, such as the following: "Many Black clients may use a communication style that is often 'high-key, animated, heated, interpersonal, and confrontational' and often "Blacks tend to act as *advocates* of a position" (p. 173). In contrast, White, middle-class communication styles are usually characterized more as "detached, objective, impersonal, and nonchallenging," and Whites often act as a "*spokesperson*" rather than an advocate (Sue & Sue, 2008, p. 173). Unfortunately, a culturally uninformed helper may view varying patterns of client communication in pejorative ways. For example, an Asian client practicing restraint of strong feelings may be viewed by a culturally uninformed practitioner as being "repressed, inhibited, or avoiding feelings" (p. 159).

Pedersen and Ivey (1993, p. 14) have identified four possible communication barriers in the cross-cultural helping process: verbal and nonverbal language problems, interference from preconceptions and stereotyping, erroneous evaluation, and stress. For example, clients who are bilingual or trilingual or who do not speak standard English or who have a pronounced accent or limited command of standard English may be misunderstood by helpers. Other language barriers may exist with clients from different geographic locations. For example, a client from Russia may not understand certain English phrases and idioms or a Jewish client may use Yiddish phrases to describe certain things to the practitioner. Sue and Sue (2008) concluded that the lack of bilingual therapists and the requirement that the culturally different client communicate in English may limit the person's ability to progress in counseling (p. 136). As you can imagine, from the client's point of view, having a helper who does not understand the way you talk and express yourself can seriously dampen your desire to return for future sessions.

Generally speaking, clients belonging to different cultural groups will be more receptive to communication patterns that are similar to their own and that are respectful of their values. For example, American Indians, Asian Americans, Black Americans, and Hispanic Americans tend to prefer more active and directive forms of helping rather than more passive, nondirective communication (Sue & Sue, 2008, p. 177). A communication mismatch can occur between cross-cultural helping dyads if the helper focuses on more passive-attending skills (such as those described in Chapter 3) and the client prefers a more active communication approach. As Sue and Sue (2008) conclude, "when the counseling style of the counselor does not match the communication style of his or her culturally diverse clients, many difficulties may arise: premature termination of the session, inability to establish rapport, or cultural oppression of the client" (p. 178). Some beginning helpers have difficulty understanding how differences in communication styles in culturally diverse helping dyads may result in these conditions. To that question, Sue and Sue (2008) reply that the helping process represents a "special type of temporary culture" (p. 178). Misunderstandings and breakdowns in the communication process in cross-cultural counseling dyads are more likely to occur if helpers assume that certain rules and patterns of speaking are universal and possess the same meaning.

Implications for Practice

Many helpers develop their communication style from the perspective, standards, and worldview of their own ethnicity and race. As a result, there may be limits on how much practitioners can adapt or change their communication styles to match those of their clients. At the same time, practitioners can stretch, grow, and cultivate nuances and variances within such styles to enhance communication with a wide range of clients.

Sue and Sue (2008, pp. 179-182) recommend a variety of ways to "grow your communication style," especially with clients who are culturally diverse:

1. Become aware of and seek feedback about your own communication style and how it tends to impact others, especially clients. Become aware of how your preferred communication style may work with some clients but not with others.

2. Expand your repertoire of helping styles and roles in order to shift your helping style to meet the cultural dimensions of your clients.

3. Become knowledgeable about how race, culture, and gender impact communication styles. This helps to avoid the notion that there is a preferred helping communication style that is effective with all clients.

4. Obtain additional training and education on a variety of theoretical approaches and orientations, particularly those that consider not only individual characteristics but also contextual and systemic factors. This helps the tendency to view client problems as residing primarily within the individual client.

5. Think holistically about clients, for example, recognizing that people are not just a product of their thinking or behavior, but are "feeling, thinking, behaving, cultural, spiritual, and political" beings.

Communication and Gender

Communication patterns are also influenced by gender. Gender has been linked to such communication variables as amount of talk time, swearing, interrupting, and use of silence (Gilbert & Scher, 1999). New research reported in various magazines and newspapers in the last several years has noted differences in brain-wave patterns between the genders, resulting in differences in how women and men think. Also, the structure of the brain is somewhat different between men and women. Differences in brain structure as well as differences in wiring within the brain between genders may provide some explanation for why women tend to be less aggressive than men—perhaps they are more easily able to filter out physiologically arousing feelings.

In a groundbreaking book on the effect of gender in couples therapy, Worden and Worden (1998) noted differences on issues of autonomy and connection as well as expression of anger and power, resulting in differences in communication in the counseling process. These kinds of learned gender roles and schemas are also evident in gay, lesbian, and bisexual men and women because they are also "not immune from the social-psychological construction of gender" (p. 19). Gender roles and schemata cannot help but spill over or infiltrate the helping process, so both ritualized and responsive patterns between same-gender and different-gender helper and client pairs are likely to vary somewhat.

A qualitative research study that assessed perceptions of male and female clients by female and male counselors found a great deal of consistency and similarity among the counselors' descriptions of clients of both genders (Vogel, Epting & Wester, 2003). However, two primary areas of difference emerged. Both female and male counselors tended to view female clients as emotionally vulnerable. At the same time, these counselors viewed the male clients as having difficulties in self-control. What is striking to us about these differences is that they seem to reflect more traditional gender role notions. As the authors explain, this may be because the clients in this study actually did have different presentations in the session or it may be because there was some unintentional gender bias impacting the counselors' perceptions of the clients (Vogel et al., 2003). In either case, they conclude that practitioners need to "increase the range of affective and behavioral responses that they consider healthy and appropriate for each of the sexes" to promote gender-fair counseling (p. 139).

In a comprehensive review of gender issues in the helping process, Enns (2000) observed that "power differentials" are reflected in communication patterns (p. 613). For example, use of language that conveys standards and expectations based on male norms communicates a subtle but biased power differential between the genders. Similarly, heterosexist biases are conveyed when noninclusive language is used to refer to intimate partnerships and parenting. Part of the use of gender-sensitive language means that helpers are sensitive to the ways in which all people—including those who hold unearned privilege—may feel disempowered by patriarchal norms and values. Brown (1994) noted that "while the wounds of patriarchy to women are more obvious, the stories of patriarchal power and control damage men as well" (p. 118). Furthermore, she concluded that even the separation of linked cultural oppression into the descriptive categories people use—such as gender, race, sexual orientation, religion, age, social class, health status, and so on—are themselves artifacts "of patriarchal structures that promote disconnections and silences" (p. 70).

Fixed gender roles not only result in differing communication patterns between women and men, but they may also produce gender-role stress and shame-proneness for both, impacting communication. As Efthim, Kenny, and Mahalik (2001) asserted, helpers need to be attentive to the links between gender, shame, guilt, and externalized communication patterns. They stated that "clients who seem rigidly committed to traditional gender role norms may be shame-prone, and so the counselor should exercise care when communication centers around feelings of not 'measuring up' as a woman or man" (p. 79). From their research, these authors also noted that "male clients who are stressed about being in contexts in which traditional male dominance is threatened or in which tender emotions are being expressed may rely on externalizing defenses.... . [That is,] they may speak in the language of threat and counterthreat, particularly regarding the danger of being perceived as 'feminine' or of being seen as failing to prove their masculinity. Female clients, on the other hand, may respond with either overt shame or externalization when coping with stress in domains where male power has a direct impact on them: concerns about body image, feeling vulnerable about victimization, and discomfort with situations calling for assertive behavior" (p. 436).

The overall goal of recognizing gender patterns in communication during helping sessions is to develop awareness of any gender-stereotyped patterns that could potentially harm the client. Pittman (1985) coined the term *gender broker* to describe the function of practitioners in helping clients examine socialization and communication styles, old and new. All the ethical codes of conduct in human services promote the idea of being respectful, informed, and nondiscriminatory in the theory and practice of gender communication.

Implications for Practice

Both women and men are impacted by traditional gender-role situations (Gilbert & Scher, 1999). Hoffman (2001) and Bartholomew (2003) have offered a number of suggestions for gender-sensitive communication:

1. Support clients' desires to break free from the oppression of traditional gender norms.
2. Communicate empathy for the plight of both genders.
3. Use gender inquiry questions to help understand messages clients have received about gender, such as, "Do you remember anything that happened when you were growing up that strengthened your sense of being a girl or boy?" or "What did you learn about how you should be acting as a girl or boy?" and "How do these messages affect you?"
4. Attend to ways in which other aspects of culture affect gender development in clients' lives. For example, how have dimensions such as religious affiliation, ethnicity, geography, age, and so on impacted the client's sense of being a woman or a man? Have these other dimensions restricted or expanded the client's sense of gender?

Communication with Clients with Disabilities

An increasing number of clients are persons with chronic health issues and conditions that have some disabling effects. Some of these clients have sensory disabilities involving sight or hearing; some have a condition limiting basic physical activities; others have a condition that impacts their learning, remembering, or concentration; and still others have a condition that impacts their ability to work at a job. While this is not a conclusive list of disabilities, perhaps it does give you a sense of the wide range of clients whom you may see. While some disabilities are more visible than others, the word itself refers to "the functional limitation a person experiences as a result of an impairment" (American Psychological Association, 1999, p. 2). While some disabilities are the result of progressive, chronic conditions, others are not, and in these instances, the client with a substantial disability may be healthier than the clinician (American Psychological Association, 1999, p. 2).

When clients with disabilities present to helpers, the potential impact on communication styles and patterns may often be either unknown or minimized by helpers. For example, through the American with Disabilities Act, many strides have been made in improving accessibility in buildings, increasing access to education, and opening up employment opportunities for persons with disabilities. However, much less attention has been given in general to communication and interaction with people with disabilities. A helper's sense of discomfort in working with someone with a disability—particularly a client with a visible disability—may consciously or unconsciously result in the helper's communication withdrawal, for fear of saying the wrong things. As a result, the client may feel more invisible or more stigmatized simply by the helper's absence of or limited communication. Issues in communication patterns between helpers and clients with disabilities may include awkward or biased use of language, shorter interactions and prematurely terminated helping sessions, greater interpersonal distance between helper and client during the session, and restricted or stiff oral communication. Helpers also may shut down their communication patterns by unasked questions, by wondering how helpful they should be, or by internal reactions about their own real or potential disability status. For example, as Daughtry, Gibson, and Abels (2009) have observed, many helping professionals have disability-related biases and anxieties that result in considerable interpersonal distance in the interaction. In addition, some clients with disabilities may have conditions such as hearing and visual impairments that require assistive communication devices, and these devices may somewhat alter the communication flow between client and helper. In the following section, we make recommendations for communicating with clients with disabilities. Some of these recommendations come from our own experience, and others are recommended by Daughtry et al. (2009, p. 204).

Implications for Practice

1. Be aware of and sensitive to language. *Language* has the possibility of healing or hurting. Use affirmative phrases, such as the "client with a disability" rather than "my disabled client," and avoid using the word "handicapped" to refer to any client! Similarly, a helper can refer to his or her client as a person with a psychiatric disability rather than a crazy person or a client who uses a wheelchair rather than a client confined to a wheelchair or a client who has a hearing or visual impairment rather than a client who is deaf, dumb, suffers a hearing loss, or is blind. This is language that considers the person first rather than the disability, avoids sensationalizing the disability, and avoids verbs that suggest images of passivity (American Psychological Association, 1999). Similarly, it is important to avoid using descriptors that refer to clients with disabilities in ways that evoke pity, such as "afflicted by," "the victim of," "struck by," "crippled with," and so on. These sensitivities help because it is through language usage "that we can conjure up images of people actively engaged in life, and we can avoid stereotypical phrases that suggest helplessness or tragedy" (American Psychological Association, 1999, p. 1).

2. Use supportive, nonverbal communication. For example, it is appropriate when meeting a client with a disability to offer to shake hands, using either the right or left hand. Also, when working with a client using crutches or using a wheelchair, place yourself at eye level with the person. Do not pat a client in a wheelchair on the head or shoulders. Avoid shouting at a person with a hearing impairment. Look directly at the client and speak clearly, slowly, and expressively, especially if this is a client who is reading lips.

3. Develop a communication style that is direct and respectful rather than avoidant or condescending. Address clients with disabilities in the same way you would other clients. For example, do not talk with clients with disabilities as though they are childlike or ill. Address clients with disabilities by their first names only if this is a practice you use with all your clients. If some clients have difficulty in speaking or understanding, listen carefully, do not rush the communication in the session, and do not pretend to understand when you do not. Instead, rephrase what you do understand, and give the client time to respond. Avoid finishing or completing sentences for the client. At the same time, if you do not understand a particular client because they use a communication aid or have difficulty with speech, do not automatically assume they cannot understand you! If the client with a disability has a communication issue, he or she will probably let you know and indicate a preferred method of communicating. You can facilitate the communication process by *asking the client what she or he needs from you as a communicator and then adapt your communication style accordingly!*

APPLICATION EXERCISE 4.1

Communication Patterns

A. Race And Ethnicity

In a small group, discuss ways in which communication patterns may vary among clients from differing ethnic groups and of different races. Relate your observations to the helping process. Discuss what your preferred communication style in the helping process seems to be. How might this help or hurt you in working with a client whose ethnic group and race differs from your own?

B. Gender

Observe the way men and women talk, even in ordinary, noncounseling conversations. What similarities and differences do you note? How do you think these similarities and differences will affect the helping situation?

C. Clients With Disabilities

With a partner, discuss experiences (or lack of) you have had in working with clients with disabilities. What do you notice about the communication patterns? If you have not yet had much experience in this area, what do you anticipate as you think about working with clients with disabilities both in terms of your own internal reactions and your oral and nonverbal communications?

SILENCE

For most beginning helpers, silence can be frightening. It seems to bring the total focus of attention on them, revealing their most glaring weaknesses as helpers—at least this is how many helpers describe their experiences with silence. As a result, their tendency is to say something—anything—to prevent silence. Typically, a question is asked. Often, it is a bad question—one that can be answered by a minimal response from the client. The answer to the question is relatively unimportant because the question was not well-thought-out by the helper. The helper may not even be listening to the answer. Such a state of affairs suggests that it is the helper's responsibility to keep the client talking, that talking is the only evidence that the client is working, and that silence is probably nontherapeutic or a waste of time. None of these assumptions are valid. In fact, a recent study of the effects of silence during actual counseling interviews found that significantly higher amounts of silence were linked to greater rapport, whereas lower amounts of silence were associated with less rapport (Sharpley, Munro & Elly, 2005). As Karasu (1992) has noted, the importance of silence is frequently overlooked, as "therapists tend to underestimate the power of listening and overestimate the power of speaking" (pp. 81–82).

Because clients react to silence in this way, you can use silence as a counseling technique and as a way of responding to clients. Silence has another meaning that is important to acknowledge. After a period of hard work in the session or after a moment of significant insight, the client often needs time to absorb the experience—to fit it into his or her existing system. This results in an integration silence—one in which the client is fully experiencing the therapeutic moment. You may not encounter this in your first helping sessions, but you will as you gain experience.

Types of Silence

Silence can be a therapeutic moment as well as a self-conscious moment. But what makes one silence different from another? What are the dimensions of silence in a counseling session? Silence can be broadly categorized as helper-induced or client-induced. Helper-induced silence occurs when the focus of the interview is on the helper. In other words, if the helper-rather than the client—is feeling responsible for the moment and responds with silence, that is a helper-induced silence. Conversely, if the client has been talking, assuming responsibility, and then stops, that is a client-induced silence.

HELPER-INDUCED SILENCE.   Helper-induced silence can be examined in two contexts: the helper's intentions and the consequences of the silence. Helper intentions can vary widely. The underparticipatory helper gives very little verbally. It is a style of behavior that may reflect the helper's interpersonal interactions with people in general. It does not reflect therapeutic intention. Rather, it may indicate a generalized tendency to hide, to withhold, and to protect oneself from other people. It arises out of fear.

A second form of silence is that which occurs unsystematically. It is like being at a loss for words. Its intention is probably to give the helper time to absorb and comprehend all that is going on at the moment. Again, it is not intended by the helper to be a therapeutic moment, although the effect is often therapeutic. Many times, a helper will fail to respond to the moment for personal reasons, and the effect is to encourage the client to continue more deeply into the topic or the feeling. When this happens, the helper is more apt to feel lucky rather than competent.

The third form of helper-induced silence is that which the helper has deliberately presented. It may be that the helper has been very active and has decided to reduce that activity, thus transferring more responsibility to the client. Or it may be that the helper senses a momentum on the client's part that will lead to insight, commitment, or new relevant issues. In this case, the helper chooses not to respond in order to not interfere with or impede the client's psychological momentum.

CLIENT-INDUCED SILENCE.   Client-induced silence also has varied intentions and consequences. As noted with helper-induced silence, client silence is affected by the issue of responsibility and what to do with it. If the client is feeling irresponsible or underresponsible, the intention behind the silence may be antitherapeutic or antigrowth. For example, suppose Betty has developed a life pattern of avoiding some personal issues. When these issues arise, her natural response is to deny or ignore them by deflecting attention from her. In the counseling setting, she may be aware that these personal issues are the source of her difficulties. Yet, her natural reaction continues to be avoidance, deflection, or resistance. In this example, Betty's silence would reflect an attempt to transfer momentary responsibility over to the helper and away from herself. If she is successful, the consequence would be yet another time when important issues are avoided and underresponsibility is rewarded.

Another reason that clients lapse into silence is to try to catch up on the progress of the moment. Counseling sessions sometimes move very quickly, covering a lot of ground and incorporating and relating many issues to one another. There is a need to stop, catch one's breath, observe the progress, or comprehend the implications. This is a very therapeutic type of silence. It allows clients to fit the new growth or insight that has occurred into their existing system. In effect, the client alters the existing system to include what has just been learned. There are also times when client-induced silence results from a client opening some new door to his or her awareness. For example, Robert—who, with his wife Carolyn, had been in counseling for several weeks— lapsed into a silence during a discussion of "families of origin" (a technique used to identify styles, expectations, and rules of interpersonal living). After a silence of a minute or more, he stated to the therapist and his wife, "I've been living with Carolyn for six years and thinking that I was overcoming the life I had with my parents. Now I can see that I have been more a reflection of my parents' home than I realized. I wonder what I really do believe in and want from my own family."

Silence also has different meanings from one culture to another. Sue and Sue (2008) stated that there are "complex rules" regarding the cultural appropriateness of the use of silence:

> U.S. Americans frequently feel uncomfortable with a pause or silent stretch in the conversation, feeling obligated to fill it in with more talk. Silence is not always a sign for the listener to take up the conversation. While it may be viewed negatively by many, other cultures interpret the use of silence differently. The British and Arabs use silence for privacy, while the Russians, French and Spanish read it as agreement among the parties. In Asian culture, silence is traditionally a sign of respect for elders. Furthermore, silence by many Chinese and Japanese is not a floor-yielding signal inviting others to pick up the conversation. Rather, it may indicate a desire to continue speaking after making a particular point. Oftentimes silence is a sign of politeness and respect rather than a lack of desire to continue speaking. (p. 166)

Patterns of silence may also vary with gender. A woman may wait for a pause in the conversation to make a point; a man may interrupt a conversation to offer a fact. When expressing feelings, a woman may do so with great verbal facility; a man may pause frequently or present his feelings more hesitantly. Silence and pauses can also vary with clients with certain disabilities. For example, with clients using assisted communication devices, rhythms and pauses of communication may change. Or consider the client who is on Social Security disability due to severe and incapacitating depression. With this client, perhaps there are more silent periods during the session than periods of conversation, especially in initial sessions.

How do you know what kind of silence is occurring? The intention of a client-induced silence must always be inferred. By watching the client closely and by being sensitive to the themes, issues, and feelings being expressed, you will be gathering clues to what is happening. Is the client relaxed? Are the client's eyes fixed on something without being focused? This may mean the client is thinking about or pondering something, examining a new idea, or ruminating around in his or her mind. Or is the client tense, appearing nervous, looking from one object to another, and avoiding eye contact? If so, this may mean that he or she is avoiding some topic or idea. Again, we remind you to be careful about assigning universal meanings to client pauses and silent periods, as these meanings do vary with individuals.

THERAPEUTIC SILENCE.   Skilled helpers often use silence as their best technique for specific situations. This does not suggest that they are inactive. There is always nonverbal behavior that adds meaning to the silence, thereby communicating a therapeutic message to the client. The messages that the helper may seek to communicate include: "I want us to move a bit more slowly"; "I want you to think more about what you just said"; "I don't accept the message you just presented"; or "I care very much about you and your feelings in this moment." Silence can also be soothing to clients. There are other therapeutic messages that can be communicated through silence, but these tend to be the most common.

Pacing the Helping Session

Helping sessions can be compared to a musical score. They have variations in theme, timing, activity, and inactivity. As you acquire self-comfort and skills, you will become aware that different times in an interview have very different qualities. The helper is a conductor of sorts for this therapeutic score. There are times when the client is hyperactive, babbling, or overreacting, and the desired objective is to slow down the pace of the session. You can always verbally call attention to the client's activity; oftentimes, silence achieves the same objective. You may not respond with total silence. Occasional verbal responses let the client know that you are still a participant. But you may want to monitor your reactions and not respond to all that stimulates you.

The use of silence to *pace* the session is especially important in initial interviews when the conditions of trust and safety are being built. Especially in these sessions, it is important to let the client determine the pace. As Hutchins and Cole-Vaught (1997) noted, "The helping interview may be one of the few opportunities clients have to express their thoughts and feelings without being rushed or pressed to perform. This luxury of unhurried time allows more complete expression than is typical in most interactions" (p. 104). In using silence to pace a session, it is important to explain the purpose of silence to clients, especially those in beginning sessions, so they are not scared away (Sommers-Flanagan & Sommers-Flanagan, 2003, p. 63).

Silent Focusing

One of the ways in which silence is most useful is to focus attention on the moment. It is like stopping to listen to an echo. Throughout the book, we will be suggesting ways in which you can help clients hear themselves. Silence is the first of these ways. Sometimes, clients make totally irrational statements. By not responding to the statement, you allow the clients' messages to remain present—to continue to be heard even by the clients themselves. Other times, clients may make a statement of such relevance that you want to give them time to absorb the impact of that relevance. This would be the case when a client has just acknowledged a significant insight and needs time to fit this insight into an existing system of meanings.

Responding to Defenses

Occasionally, clients come to the interview filled with emotions that belong to other people or situations, yet they spill them out on you or the helping process. Or you may make a statement to which the client responds defensively. These situations often reflect a lack of client awareness, although they are moments when the potential for awareness is great. The temptation for you may be to give the client insight into the situation. Often, it is more meaningful to allow clients to give themselves that insight. This can be done by using silence as your response.

Silent Caring

Silent caring occurs in those moments when no words are an adequate response to the feelings that are present. It may be a moment of quiet weeping for the client or it may be a moment of heavy melancholy. Whatever the feeling may be, it is one of those moments when experiencing the feeling fully is more important than making it go away. You can communicate your compassion and involvement very clearly with caring silence.

Guidelines for Using Silence

After all is said and done, there are specific therapeutic guidelines to follow in using silence effectively with clients. Sommers-Flanagan and Sommers-Flanagan (2003) and Sharpley et al. (2005) have summarized these:

- When a client pauses after making a statement or after hearing your paraphrase, let a few seconds pass rather than immediately jumping in with further verbal interaction. Given the opportunity, clients can move naturally into very significant material without your guidance or urging. Give them a chance to associate to new material.
- As you are sitting silently and waiting for your client to resume speaking, tell yourself that this is the client's time to express himself or herself, not your time to prove you can be useful. If you assume the role of an "expert" interviewer, you will probably feel greater responsibility (i.e., as if you need to say the right thing or ask the right question).
- Try not to get into a rut regarding your use of silence. When silence comes, sometimes wait for the client to speak next and other times break the silence yourself.
- Avoid using silence if you believe your client is confused, experiencing an acute emotional crisis, or psychotic. Excessive silence—and the anxiety it provokes—tend to exacerbate these conditions. Silence is also not useful in some culturally diverse helping situations; for example, if a gay client says to a straight helper, "I don't feel safe here at school" and if this report is met with silence, this kind of silence may make the client feel less safe and more invisible.
- If you feel uncomfortable during silent periods, relax. Use your attending skills to look expectantly toward clients. This will help them understand that it is their turn to talk.
- If clients appear uncomfortable with silence, you may give them instructions to free associate (i.e., tell them "just say whatever comes to mind"). Or you may want to use an empathic reflection (say something like "it's hard to decide what to say next").
- Remember that silence is at times the most therapeutic response available.
- Remember to observe your body and face while communicating silence. This is important because there is a big difference between communicating a cold and a warm silence. (Sommers-Flanagan & Sommers-Flanagan, 2003, pp. 63–64)
- Give clients the opportunity to stop or terminate the silence that you initiate. This contributes to greater rapport and gives clients the chance to decide when to speak again rather than having this decided for them by you (Sharpley et al., 2005).

APPLICATION EXERCISE 4.2

Being Comfortable with Silence

Some people often have to learn to be silent. Perhaps you find silence to be intense and uncomfortable. If so, this exercise will help you become more comfortable with silence. Team up with two other people. One person will be the talker, one will be the listener, and the third person can be the timekeeper. Invite the talker to talk about anything he or she wishes. You will listen and respond. But before you respond, allow a pause to occur. Begin with five-second pauses. Gradually increase the duration of pauses until you are allowing fifteen seconds to pass before responding. The timekeeper should sit in a position from which he or she can signal the number of seconds to you without distracting the talker. After a ten-minute discussion, rotate roles and repeat the exercise until all three of you have had a turn as listener.

As a variation on this exercise, consider your contacts with people you encounter every day. Become conscious of your interaction patterns. Do you interject your reactions as soon as the other person has completed a communication? Do you interrupt the other person, thus preventing the slightest possibility of a silence? During the next few days, monitor your response behavior. When someone speaks to you, pause and think about the message for a few seconds and then give your response. Record any feedback you receive from your friends or acquaintances regarding your communication behavior.

Summary

The practice of helping involves a sense of both personal authenticity and professional skills. Both authenticity and skills are maintained by patterns of behavior that emerge as the helper matures and grows in experience. Similarly, clients evolve patterns of behavior that reflect their personal qualities, their problems, and their culture. We have noted in this chapter how these patterns affect and are affected by the helper's communication patterns and styles.

Helpers must be careful to avoid imposing their communication styles and values on clients and must be sensitive to communication styles from culturally diverse clients, as race and ethnicity play a large role in communication patterns. Gender expression of language also affects the helping process. Again, it is crucial for helpers to be sensitive to the ways in which gender roles are expressed through language and to be aware of the difficulties that patriarchal gender norms have created for both women and men. As the helper's comfort level with the helping setting improves, these patterns may be examined for their effect on the session. Helpers must also be sensitive to language usage and verbal and nonverbal communication patterns in their interactions with clients with disabilities.

More subtle—and perhaps of greater concern—are the helper communication patterns that become ritualized. Ritualized patterns exist for expediency's sake. They are the behavioral shorthand that allows more efficient functioning. The problem is that efficient functioning may not be effective functioning, particularly in the helping relationship. Another communication pattern impacted by culture, gender, and disability status involves the use of silence. Again, silence can be used therapeutically or accidentally. When accidental, any positive effects may be from luck rather than intention. The intentional use of silence can contribute greatly to the helping relationship and the establishment of rapport between helper and client.

Reflective Questions

1. What types of messages can be communicated with a silence? How many of these messages might occur in a helping session? How can you tell one message from another?

2. What do you think your own tolerance/comfort level is with silence? Are you more comfortable with silence that is initiated by you or the client? What about silences that are terminated by you or the client?

3. Provide examples that illustrate how the meaning and use of silence may be affected by working with clients with disabilities, by race, and by gender.

4. Discuss some examples in which you have observed communication patterns being influenced by culture, such as race and ethnicity.

5. Describe your reactions to the idea that gender affects communication.

6. Discuss ways to enhance your communication and interactions with clients with disabilities.
7. How do you think the communication styles and patterns discussed in this chapter relate to you?

8. What do you think of the notion of ritualized communication patterns for both helper and client?

My Helping Lab

For the following exercise, log on to MyHelpingLab at http://www.myhelpinglab.com and then click the Topics tab.

1. Click the Theories tab to locate the Existential-Humanistic Theory tab. Choose the video lab for the Using Silence in Session selection. After reviewing this clip, consider the following questions:

1. How comfortable would you be initiating a helping session in the same way that the practitioner did on the tape?
2. If you would start the session differently, how would your approach be different?
3. What did you think the function of the silence was that you viewed in this helping interaction?

Recommended Readings

Bartholomew, C. G. (2003). *Gender-sensitive therapy: Principles and practices*. Prospect Heights, IL: Waveland Press.

American Psychological Association (1999). Enhancing your interactions with people with disabilities. Washington, DC: Author.

Daughtry, D., Gibson, J & Abels, A. (2009). Mentoring students and professionals with disabilities. *Professional Psychology, 40*, 201–205.

Hoffman, R. M. (2001). The measurement of masculinity and femininity: Historical perspective and implications for counseling. *Journal of Counseling and Development, 79*, 472–485.

Nutt, R. & Brooks, G. (2008). Psychology of gender. In S. D. Brown & R. W. Lent (Eds.). *Handbook of counseling psychology* (176–193). New York: John Wiley & Sons.

Sharpley, C. F., Munro, D. M. & Elly, M. J. (2005). Silence and rapport during initial interviews. *Counseling Psychology Quarterly, 18*, 149–159.

Sommers-Flanagan, J. & Sommers-Flanagan, R. (2003). Clinical interviewing. New York: John Wiley & Sons.

Sue, D. W. & Sue, D. (2008). *Counseling the culturally diverse*. New York: John Wiley & Sons.

Vogel, D. L., Epting, F. & Wester, S. R. (2003). Counselors' perceptions of female and male clients. *Journal of Counseling and Development, 81*, 131–140.

CHAPTER 5

Managing the Helping Session

We have discussed the qualities of a therapeutic relationship and how effective helpers attend to and understand the client, but we have not yet discussed the structure within which all this occurs. Experienced helpers enter each session with a sense of who they are, what they wish to do and to be in the session, and how they will represent themselves to the client. This is true in the first session as well as in the twelfth session. As we mentioned in the previous chapter, experienced helpers develop a personal style that they carry into the relationship. That style provides the structure for how to begin the process, how to develop it, and how to end it.

In this chapter, we will consider some awkward and sensitive times in the helping relationship that require structure. Many helpers and clients have difficulty with beginnings and endings, whether they be the beginning or ending of a helping interview or the beginning or ending of a helping relationship. As you read this chapter, you will find suggestions and thoughts that may help you make smoother transitions into and out of these moments. There are two types of beginnings that will be examined: beginning the first interview you have with a client and beginning subsequent interviews. Similarly, we examine the two types of termination: termination of a session and termination of the helping relationship. In addition, we explore the ethical issues surrounding these two key transitional times in helping sessions and also some ideas for managing in-between helping sessions.

THE FIRST INTERVIEW

Your first interview with a client will have a special set of dynamics operating. It is the beginning of a potentially significant relationship. As such, there are hopes and expectations, fears and reservations, acute awareness of some conditions, and an amazing lack of awareness of other conditions—all of which have a bearing on the session. With so many emotional issues operating, you might be wondering how you can possibly have a successful first interview. Helpers deal with this issue in one of two ways. Some practitioners choose to work with the relationship dynamics that are operating. Others choose to make the first session an *intake interview* and collect needed information about the client. Whichever choice you make, you must still attend to the other issue later. If you focus on interpersonal dynamics in the first session, in the second or third interview, you will want to collect information. If you use the first session as an intake session, you will soon afterward need to acknowledge relationship dynamics. If you wish to focus on relationship dynamics, then the content of Chapter 2 is particularly relevant. Specifically, you will want to achieve an accurate sense of the client's world and communicate that understanding back to your client. Learning to understand means putting aside your own agenda long enough to allow the client's world to enter your awareness. It means not worrying about yourself—Am I doing the right thing? Am I looking nervous?—and trying to avoid "analysis paralysis" (C. Helbok, personal communication, Nov. 20, 2002). Until you have had the experience of several beginning sessions, this will be a difficult task. Of course, you will have an underlying set of objectives in this session:

- To reduce your client's initial anxieties to a level that permits him or her to begin talking
- To refrain from excessive talking because that takes time away from your client
- To listen carefully to what your client is saying and attempt to reconstruct in your mind the world that he or she is describing
- To be aware that your client's choice of topics gives insight into his or her priorities for the moment

CULTURAL VARIABLES AND THE FIRST INTERVIEW

Whether you choose to focus primarily on establishing a relationship or on gathering information in an initial counseling session often depends somewhat on your setting as well as the client's cultural affiliation. Some settings specify that the initial session be an intake interview; this initial history-gathering session may even be conducted by an intake worker rather than the counselor assigned to work with the client. The client's culture also influences your focus in an initial interview. Sue and Sue (2008) observed that some culturally diverse clients may approach the helper initially with caution, not feeling safe to self-disclose until and unless the helper self-discloses first. This trepidation may be reinforced with white counselors whose sole focus in the initial session is individualistic rather than contextualistic—that is, viewing the client's problems as residing within the individual rather than society or the context and environment in which the client resides. Moreover, some research reported by Sue and Sue (2008) has found that many Asian-American and African-American clients prefer a more structured and logical approach (e.g., an intake information session) to an affective and reflective one. In any initial session, regardless of approach, helpers need to exert caution and move slowly, as asking very personal questions in an initial session may be perceived as lacking respect (Sue & Sue, 2008). It is important to be flexible enough in your helping style to adapt your style in an initial session to meet the cultural diversity of your clients.

STRUCTURING OF INITIAL MOMENTS

In opening an interview, there are some logistics that require your attention. An initial guideline is to be on time. This communicates respect. The beginning point can be as simple as a smile and greeting from you, along with a simple introduction and a motion to show the client where to sit. For example:

> "Hello. I'm Bill Janutolo. Please have a seat here or in that chair if you wish. I realize this is our first meeting together, and I'm interested in getting to know you and something about what brings you here today."

In initial moments with clients, the helper sets the tone. Initially, you want to welcome the client and begin the interview in a warm and friendly fashion. Then, you proceed to give the first interview some structure (D. Fosha, personal communication, Jan. 13, 2006). There are questions that must be resolved. How long will the interview be? (Often, the length of the interview depends on the age of the client, with shorter interviews for children and elderly clients.) How do you want your client to address you? What should your client expect the sessions to be like? What are your client's rights? What will be your role? Answers to these and other questions provide the structure for the relationship.

Structuring has been defined as the way the clinician defines the nature, limits, roles, and goals within the helping relationship (Brammer, Abrego & Shostrom, 1993). It includes comments about time limits, number of sessions, confidentiality, possibilities and expectations as well as supervision, observation, and/or tape-recording procedures. Describing the helping process and providing structure reduces the unknowns and thus reduces the anxiety of clients. It also permits clients the opportunity to check out their expectations. Structuring conveys to clients the message that they are not going through the counseling process alone (D. Fosha, personal communication, Jan. 13, 2006). Kottler (1991) summarized the ingredients of effective structuring in initial sessions as follows:

- Providing a general overview and preview of the helping process
- Assessing the client's expectations and promoting positive ones
- Describing the helper's expectations
- Orienting the client to a new language and new behaviors
- Helping the client to increase tolerance for frustration and discomfort
- Obtaining client commitment (pp. 141–144)

Not only does structuring provide a sense of safety for clients, but it also fulfills the helper's ethical obligation to inform clients about the nature of the helping process at the outset (American Counseling Association, 2005; National Association of Social Workers, 1999). There are also aspects of structuring to consider in working with diverse clients. For example, with children, structuring is more limited, and much of it occurs with the adult who is giving consent for the minor to be seen by a helper. With culturally diverse clients, structuring needs to occur in a way that generates "a mutually satisfying set of procedures that honor the cultures inherent to the therapy, the therapist, and the client" (Helms & Cook, 1999, p. 169). One of the most important aspects of providing structure to clients has to do with giving information about the helping process—known as informed consent—and clarifying concerns about confidentiality.

Informed Consent

Simply put, informed consent has to do with providing information to clients about the potential helping process and the benefits and risks of being a client and securing the client's agreement about the process. While writing this section, Sherry and one of her friends recently attended training in an energy healing modality. Well into the training, we learned that there was a special diet we should have followed several days prior to the training as well as during the training, including no chocolate. While we were told of this information, Sherry was melting her daily piece of antioxidant dark chocolate in her mouth! We were also notified near the end of the training that we might experience some unusual sensations for a few weeks after the training! Needless to say, had we been informed about this kind of information prior to the training, we may have made different decisions. Because the trainer did not provide informed consent either before or at the very beginning of the training day, we did not have the option of deciding to forego the training. (Note: This training was for personal development only and was not a continuing education–approved event).

In the helping professions, we are required by our ethical codes to disclose to clients some information about the benefits, risks, and alternatives to treatment procedures. As Corey, Corey, and Callanan (2010) observe, "professionals have a responsibility to their clients to make reasonable disclosure of all significant facts, the nature of the procedure, and some of the more probable consequences and difficulties" (p. 161). Informed consent is also a legal issue. It is not just a matter of providing information to clients about the helping process (also called *notice*) but also of negotiating an agreement with the client based on such information and facts. Clients must have the capacity to make an informed decision, the comprehension to understand the information supporting their decision, and the competence to make an informed consent decision without being pressured or coerced.

Corey et al. (2010) recommend some of the primary issues that helpers need to address to assist in obtaining consent with clients at the beginning of a helping relationship. As we will see later in this chapter, these issues not only impact the beginning of the helping process, but they also potentially structure and give notice about the termination of the helping process. The particular issues recommend by Corey et al. (2010, pp. 161–162) include the following:

- What are the goals of the therapeutic endeavor?
- What services will the helper provide, and what are the qualifications of the helper to provide these services?
- What is expected of the client, and what is the client's role in the process?
- What are the benefits and risks of engaging in counseling for the client?
- What are the financial arrangements?
- What might the approximate duration or length of the helping sessions be?
- What are the limitations of confidentiality, and in what situations does the helping professional have mandatory reporting requirements?

We discuss this last question in the following section.

Confidentiality

According to Welfel (2010), "confidentiality refers to an ethical duty to keep client identity and disclosures secret" (p. 116). You will want to emphasize the issue of confidentiality to new clients. Does it mean you will talk to no one? What are the implications if you are being observed by a supervisor or if you are tape-recording the session? Will you keep a written record? If so, what are the client's guarantees that the record will be kept confidential? What about e-mail communication? Or faxes?

According to ethical guidelines for helping professions, the helper is generally obligated to treat the client's communication in a confidential manner; that is, the helper agrees not to share information given by the client with other persons. However, there are some exceptions to this general policy, such as when the client requests release of information, when the court orders information, when the client is involved in litigation, and when the client's condition indicates harm to self or others. The current ethical codes of most helping professional organizations are written in such a way to allow mental health professionals to disclose confidential information (with certain restrictions) when they believe the client is of immediate danger to others, based on some kind of a risk assessment procedure that assesses the client's capacity for and history of violent behavior. This exception to confidentiality stems from a court case in 1974, which has evolved over the years such that in some (but not all) states, the helper has a *duty to warn* and/or a *duty to protect* the one in danger or at risk from the client's threatened actions. These actions often include notifying or warning the intended victim and protecting the victim by securing protection from loved ones or police, by increasing the frequency of the sessions with the client, or by hospitalizing the client. In the case of self-danger, the "legal and ethical responsibility to protect the client from harm is unequivocal" (Welfel, 2010, p. 132). Some states also have legal statutes that require helpers to report instances of child and elder abuse or to testify under subpoena. Because these statutes vary from state to state, it is important to know the guidelines for your particular state, to consult with supervisors and colleagues about clients at risk, and to document in writing all actions and decisions.

With respect to clients and initial interviews, the important point is to discuss with clients both the protection and the limits of confidentiality as a part of the structuring process. Here is how one helper begins a session with structuring:

> "Juanita, we have about an hour together. I'm not sure what brings you here, but I'm ready to answer any questions you have and also to listen to whatever you tell me. You can talk about whatever you wish—this is your time. And whatever you do talk about is kept between you and me. We call this confidentiality. It means that I keep what you say to me to myself. This is very important to me and to you. However, I do need to let you know there are some exceptions to this that I need to share with you up front so that you're aware of what they are. If you tell me about abusing a child or an elderly person, I'm mandated to report this, as these are both against the law in this state. And the other exceptions would be if I was ordered by a court of law to provide information or if you were involved in litigation and also if you requested that I share information. Finally, if you gave me information that led me to conclude there was serious risk of harm to yourself or someone else, there would also be some limits to the complete confidentiality of this material. Do you have any questions about what this might mean before we get started? I want to be really sure that you understand what this may mean before we get started here today, so let's take some time to talk about this, as your safety and privacy are important to me as well as to you."

If you are working under supervision, also add that you will be consulting with your supervisor who is also obligated to honor the confidentiality of the client's communication except in the instances you just noted to the client.

TIMING OF CONFIDENTIALITY.   Most ethical codes for helping professions require that confidentiality and its limitations be discussed as early as possible—usually at the beginning of the helping process during the initial interview. This early timing is important for several reasons. First, it is intended to give clients enough upfront information to help them become informed about and consent to the conditions under which counseling occurs. Many clients are unaware that confidentiality is not always absolute. Second, should a disclosure by the counselor become necessary during the course of subsequent sessions, lack of information about it is not only unethical but also contributes to a client's sense of betrayal.

PRIVACY REQUIREMENTS. A federal government rule called the Health Insurance Portability and Accountability Act (HIPAA) also affects helpers and confidentiality. The act gives regulations for electronic as well as traditional paper health care–related charts. Part of the HIPAA regulations is designed to protect client privacy by delineating the steps that providers have to take to secure client information. Perhaps the most controversial aspect of HIPAA has to do with the medical privacy regulations stipulating that for the "first time in the 227-year history of America, the federal government has granted itself the right to review everyone's medical record" (Freeny, 2003, p. 42). Medical record information includes psychiatric diagnosis, symptoms, treatment plans, appointment times, and summaries of sessions. As Freeny (p. 44) points out, these items are now handled under HIPAA as routine medical information about which "covered entities" may receive information without explicit client consent. Fortunately, practitioners' notes are considered psychotherapy notes under HIPAA regulations and do require a specific client authorization for release. Under HIPAA, all health care (including mental health) professionals are required to provide clients with an NPP (Notice of Privacy Practices) that tells clients what information can be released under HIPAA without explicit consent and what clients can do if they believe their personal health information was disclosed in unauthorized ways. (However, this notice does not substitute for an informed consent discussion as we described earlier). For additional information on HIPAA, we recommend the website for the U.S. Department of Health and Human Services at http://www.hhs.gov/hipaafaq. Because issues around confidentiality and privacy are complex, it is wise to consult with your supervisor, a colleague, or a trusted attorney when questions about these issues arise. We also discuss some of the ethical challenges around these issues in Chapter 10.

Encouraging the Client to Talk

After providing this initial structure, you and your client are ready to begin work. The obvious beginning is to get your client to talk, to indicate his or her reason for entering counseling, and perhaps to indicate in some form what he or she hopes to achieve as a result of counseling (the client's first statement of goals). Your beginning will be an invitation to the client to talk. The nature of this invitation is important. A good invitation is one that encourages but does not specify what the client should talk about. This is called an unstructured invitation or an open-ended lead.

UNSTRUCTURED INVITATIONS. The unstructured invitation has two purposes: It gives the client an opportunity to talk, and it prevents the helper from identifying the topic the client should discuss. An unstructured invitation is a statement in which the helper encourages clients to begin talking about whatever is of concern to them, such as:

- "Please feel free to go ahead and begin."
- "Where would you like to begin today?"
- "You can talk about whatever you'd like."
- "Perhaps there's something particular you want to discuss."
- "What brings you to counseling?"
- "What brings you to see me now?"

By contrast, a structured invitation—one that specifies a topic—gives clients little room to reflect on the motives, goals, or needs that brought them to counseling. An example of a less desirable structured invitation to talk might be: "Tell me about what careers you're considering." The client is obviously tied down to a discussion of careers by this invitation, thus delaying or even negating a more relevant issue. (Note: If careers are what the client wants to discuss, an unstructured invitation allows this topic to emerge as well as a structured invitation would.) Other responses that solicit information include open, closed, and clarifying questions.

OPEN-ENDED QUESTIONS.   Open-ended questions require more than a minimal or one-word response by the client. This type of question is introduced with either *what*, *where*, *when*, or *how*. You will find that it is very difficult to ask questions that clearly place the focus on your client. Fairly often, it happens that helpers ask questions that allow the client to respond with either a "Yes" or a "No." The result is that the client assumes no responsibility for the content of the interview. The purpose of the open-ended question is to prevent this from happening. The following questions are examples of open-ended questions:

- "What are you thinking when you're silent?"
- "How do you plan to find employment?"
- "When do you feel anxious?"

CLOSED QUESTIONS.   When your objective is to get the client to talk about anything, closed questions are not good responses. However, when you want the client to give a specific piece of information, a closed question can be the best response available, such as:

- "How old were you when your parents died?"
- "How many brothers and sisters do you have?"
- "What medication are you taking now?"
- "Have you ever received counseling or therapy?"

CLARIFYING QUESTIONS.   Requests for clarification can be used for soliciting information as well as for encouraging the client to elaborate on his or her feelings. It is important to keep in mind that such requests can be overused or underused. When overused, they can become distractors that repeatedly interrupt the client's train of thought. However, when they are underused, the helper may have difficulty understanding what the client is saying. Sometimes, the practitioner is reluctant to seek clarification because it might impede or distract the client from the topic. If you are simply unable to follow the client's train of thought, it is more important to seek clarification than it is to allow the client to proceed. Here are some examples:

- "Could you go over that again for me?"
- "Could you explain that relationship to me again?"
- "What did you mean a while ago when you said your parents were pretty indifferent?"

The Application Exercise 5.1 will help you develop the skills involved in initiating the interview.

CLIENT REACTIONS TO INITIAL INTERVIEWS

Client reactions to initial interviews often depend on whether they have had any prior experience with counseling and, if so, whether that experience was a positive or negative one. Clients who have had positive experiences with the helping process are not as likely to have the same fears and reservations as clients who have had negative or mixed experiences or who have never seen a helper before. Most clients approach initial helping sessions with some mixture of both dread and hope (D. Fosha, personal communication, Jan. 13, 2006). And all clients need to feel a sense of safety or

APPLICATION EXERCISE 5.1

Initiating an Interview

This is a class exercise that requires a videotape system. Have class members select partners. Each pair is to decide who is to be the helper and who is to be the client. The exercise is to last for five minutes. The helper is to work toward achieving the following goals:

• Set the client at ease (body relaxed, voice without tension).
• Help the client to start talking about anything (use unstructured invitation).
• Get the client to identify a current concern (acknowledge that the client came to counseling for a reason; ask about the reason).

Following each exercise, reverse roles and then repeat the procedure. Then, when all pairs have had the opportunity to do the exercise, replay the tape and discuss the encounters by using the following format:

• Ask the helper for his or her reaction to the tape.
• Describe those behaviors that were helpful in the exercise.

they are unlikely to return for more sessions. It is the helper's task to provide safety and security and to recognize and address any client fears and reservations. From the get-go, helpers want to create a new kind of environment for clients. A general principle to remember in initial sessions is that the safer a client feels, the wider the range of self-exploration that ensues (D. Fosha, personal communication, Jan. 13, 2006). Sommers-Flanagan and Sommers-Flanagan (2003) noted that common client fears at the beginning of the helping process include the following sorts of questions:

• Is this professional competent?
• More importantly, can this person help me?
• Will this person understand me and my problems?
• Am I going crazy?
• Can I trust this person to be honest with me?
• Will this interviewer share or reject my values (or religious views)?
• Will I be pressured to say things I don't want to say?
• Will this interviewer think I'm a bad person? (p. 142)

In addition, Sue and Sue (2008) have added that for some culturally diverse clients, their fears and trepidation are initially centered on concerns such as the following:

• Before I open up to you (self-disclose), I want to know where you're coming from.
• How open and honest are you about your own racism, and will it interfere with our relationship?
• How well will you, the helper, be able to understand my cultural status and affiliations?

These kinds of client concerns are likely to appear in initial interviews, regardless of whether you approach the initial interview as a time to establish the relationship or as a time to gather pertinent information, as in an intake interview, which we describe in the following section.

INTAKE INTERVIEW CONTENT

We have described the intake as an information-gathering interview, but we have not indicated what that information should be. This section presents a suggested outline of topics to cover and the rationale for their importance. Morrison (2008) has written a helpful guide for the first interview. An assumption behind the intake interview is that the client is coming to counseling for more than one interview and intends to address problems or concerns that involve other people, other settings, and the future as well as the present. Most helpers try to limit intake interviews to an hour or perhaps ninety minutes or probably no more than forty-five minutes for younger clients. In order to do this, you must assume responsibility and control over the interview. The following is a suggested outline. Variations in this outline will occur depending on the setting and on certain client variables, such as age, gender, race, class, ethnicity, sexual orientation, and health/ability and disability status.

I. Identifying Data

A. Client's name, address, and telephone number at which client can be reached. This information is important in the event the helper needs to contact the client between sessions. The client's address also gives some hint about the conditions under which the client lives (large apartment complex, student dormitory, private home, etc.).

B. Age, gender, ethnic origin, race, partnered status, occupational status, and educational status as well as languages, citizenship, and immigration status. Again, this is information that can be important. It lets you know if the client is still legally a minor, and it provides a basis for understanding information that will come out in later sessions.

II. Presenting Issues—Both Primary and Secondary

It is best when these are presented in exactly the way the client reported them. If the issue has behavioral components, these should also be recorded. The following questions can help reveal this type of information:

A. How much does the concern interfere with the client's everyday functioning?

B. How does the concern manifest itself? What are the thoughts, feelings, and so on, that are associated with it? What observable behavior is associated with it?

C. How often does the concern arise? How long has the concern existed?

D. Can the client identify a pattern of events surrounding the concern? When does it occur? With whom? What happens before and after its occurrence?

E. What caused the client to decide to enter counseling at this time?

III. Client's Current Life Setting

How does the client spend a typical day or week? What social, spiritual, and religious activities, recreational activities, and so on, are present? What is the nature of the client's vocational and/or educational situation? What is the client's living environment like? What are the client's most important current relationships? What sorts of financial stressors is the client experiencing?

IV. Family History

A. Recognize the plurality in contemporary practice of the definition of families. Be careful not to assume that the client's family is like your own. For example, leave room for the possibility that the client may have a family of choice by adoption to describe rather than a biological family. Once the client has identified something about his or her family, you can assess for family history by using the following as examples:

B. Names, ages, and order of brothers and sisters and relationship between the client and siblings if siblings are present, either biological or adopted.

C. Is there any history of emotional disturbance and/or substance abuse in the family?

D. Description of family stability, such as number of family moves, significant losses, and so on. This information provides insights in later sessions when issues related to client stability and/or relationships emerge.

E. If the client is a minor and the biological or legal custodial parents are divorced, obtain a notarized copy of the custody agreement, as this will impact informed consent for counseling. (You cannot counsel a minor unless all custodial parents give consent.)

V. Personal History

A. Medical history: Has the client had any unusual or relevant illness or injury from prenatal period to present, including hospitalizations, surgeries, or substance use?

B. Educational history: What is the client's academic progress through grade school, high school, and post–high school? This includes extracurricular interests and relationships with peers.

C. Military service record: Has the client served on active duty? Has the client or members of the client's family been deployed? Has the client experienced war, terrorism, or natural disaster service of any kind? Note setting and duration.

D. Vocational history: Where has the client worked, at what types of jobs, for what duration, and what were the relationships with fellow workers? Has the client suffered any employment termination or job losses?

E. Spiritual and religious history: What is the client's prior and current faith heritage, religious values and beliefs, and current spiritual practices?

F. Legal history: Has the client had any run-ins with the law, such as speeding tickets, accidents, time in prison, bankruptcy, divorce and custody issues, fights, weapons, or violence?

G. Substance use history: What is the client's past and current use of substances? Note the client's drug(s) of choice, including prescription medicines, frequency, the amount of substance use daily and weekly, and any particular consequences of substance use the client has experienced.

H. Sexual relationship history: Be careful not to assume the client's sexual orientation in exploring sexual history. Use with discretion questions such as the following: Where did the client receive sexual information? What was the client's dating history? Any engagements and/or marriages and/or partnerships, legal or nonlegal? Other serious emotional involvements prior to the present? Reasons that previous relationships terminated? How and in what way and with what effects? Are there any children?

I. Counseling experience: Wĭhat experience has the client had with counseling, and what were the client's reactions? Who referred the client?

J. Traumatic experiences: Has the client encountered neglect or physical, emotional, or sexual abuse? Medical traumas or accidents? Natural disasters? Oppression? Discrimination?

VI. Description of the Client During the Interview

In this section, you can overview some of your primary observations and impressions about the client, being very careful, however, not to impose your own cultural biases, norms, and value judgments. Examples of things that could be included here are the client's physical appearance, including height and weight, dress, posture, gestures, facial expressions, voice quality, and tensions; how the client seemed to relate to you in the session; the client's readiness of response, motivation, warmth, and distance; and so on. Do there appear to be any perceptual or sensory functions that intrude on the interaction? (Document with your observations.) What are the stream of thought, regularity, and rate of talking? Are the client's remarks logical? Connected to one another? What is the client's first language? Second language? What information have you gathered about the client's race, ethnicity, and general cultural affiliations? How might this information impact your impressions and observations?

VII. Summary and Recommendations

Here, you will want to acknowledge any connections that appear to exist between the client's statement of a problem and other information collected in this session. What is your understanding of the problem? What are the anticipated outcomes of counseling for this person? What type of counseling do you think would best fit this client? If you are to be this client's clinician, which of your characteristics might be particularly helpful? Which might be particularly unhelpful? How realistic are the client's goals for counseling? How long do you think counseling might continue? Is there anything in the client's history that seems like a red flag to you?

In writing up the intake interview, there are a few cautions to be made. First, avoid psychological jargon. It is not as understandable as you might think. Second, be as concise as possible and avoid elaborate inferences. Remember, an inference is a guess—sometimes an educated guess. An inference can also be wrong. Try to prevent your own biases from entering the report. Only include information that is directly relevant to the client and the counseling services to be offered. Remember that it is your responsibility to take steps to safeguard client privacy and confidentiality of communication. Make sure that the word *confidential* is stamped on the report itself—on each page if it is more than one page in length. Do not leave drafts of the reports around on your desk or in your mailbox or opened up on your computer screen.

Using Intake Interview Information

Following the intake interview but before the second session, you will want to review the write-up of the intake interview. Helpers develop different approaches to using this information. Some practitioners look primarily for patterns of behavior. For example, one helper noted that her client had a pattern of incompletion in life: He received a general discharge from the Army prior to completing his enlistment, dropped out of college twice, and had a long history of broken relationships. This observation provided food for thought. What happens to this person as he becomes involved in a commitment? What has he come to think about himself as a result of this history? How does he anticipate future commitments? Another practitioner uses the intake information to look for signals that suggest how this client might enter the helping relationship. Is there anything to indicate how the client might relate to females? Is there something in his life at present that common sense would suggest is a potential area for counseling attention? For example, is the client in the midst of a divorce? Is the client at a critical developmental stage? The main caution is to avoid reading too much into the intake information. It is far too early for you to begin making interpretations about your client.

Many practitioners supplement the intake interview information with some additional sort of structured assessment that may include diagnostic questions about the client's presenting concern, such as depression, anxiety, or substance abuse, or also may include the use of formalized, written questionnaires and instruments, such as inventories that measure depression or anxiety that yield yet additional information about potential diagnoses and client concerns and strengths. Often, such instruments can be administered at the end of the intake interview or near the beginning of the follow-up interview. These can be introduced to the client simply by indicating that you would like the client to complete a form or two to assist you in determining more about the client's presenting concerns and formulating a plan for treatment. Once such forms are used, it is important to score them promptly, use the information they provide efficiently, and provide feedback to the client about what the instrument yielded.

HANDLING SUBSEQUENT INTERVIEWS

Handling subsequent interviews involves several dimensions and tasks, including re-establishing rapport, eliciting essential information, and focusing in depth (Hepworth et al., 2010). Once you have established a relationship or rapport with your client, subsequent interviews will require that you reinstate the relationship that has developed. Reinstating the relationship usually amounts to acknowledging the client's absence since the last interview. This includes being sensitive to how your client's world may have changed since your last contact and your reactions in seeing the client again. This can be done with a few short statements, such as "Hello, Marvel. It's nice to see you again." This might be followed by some observation about the client's appearance: "You look a little hassled today" or "You're looking more energetic today." Or you might begin by asking, "How are you feeling today?" These types of questions focus on the client's current or immediate condition and reduce the likelihood that the client will spend the major part of the session recounting how the week has gone. If your client needs a bit of small talk to get started, it probably means that he or she needs time to make the transition into the role of help-seeker or help-taker. The important point is that you probably will not need to go to the same lengths in establishing rapport as was necessary when counseling was first initiated. However, keep in mind that some degree of relationship-building occurs in each and every session.

In addition to rapport-building, subsequent interviews are also characterized by information-gathering and focusing in depth. As Sommers-Flanagan and Sommers-Flanagan (2003) observe, "as an interviewer, you must obtain certain information to formulate the case and make recommendations. Your ears are tuned to pick up information, and you use nondirective and directive responses to encourage your client to elaborate more fully in some areas than others" (pp. 151–152). The question becomes, "What does the helper do with information that's gathered during the helping interviews?" Basically, the helper uses such information to make clinical judgments and inferences; such judgments and inferences are the basis upon which the clinician assesses the client's personal style and level of functioning, determinations about who is the actual client and how much therapy may be needed, decisions about the client's diagnosis—including diagnostic formulations and areas of strengths—and ideas about the most appropriate or efficacious approach to take with a particular client.

Another way in which helpers make use of clinical information is to help clients focus in depth in subsequent interviews. For example, some clients—out of fear or lack of trust—may withhold important parts of their story in initial interviews and may not reveal issues that bear significant weight until they feel very safe with the helper. Sometimes, clients presenting issues will shift significantly in subsequent situations, often due to internal processing or to external situations or both. For example, Eduardo was working with Sammy, who was exploring issues related to his partner when Sammy's mother passed away suddenly and unexpectedly. At this point, the focus of the sessions shifted somewhat away from the initial concern to the more immediate situation at hand and Sammy's resulting grief and sadness. At a later point, additional sessions shifted back to Sammy's ongoing concerns with his partner.

There are several ways that practitioners can help clients focus in depth, as suggested by Hepworth et al. (2010). One way is for the helper to explore and assess the cognitions of the clients, as thought patterns, beliefs, and attitudes are also "powerful determinants of behavior" (Hepworth et al., 2010, p. 49). For example, focusing in depth on cognitive patterns may reveal dogmatic or rigid thinking, misinterpretations, and nonproductive beliefs. Hepworth et al. (2010, p. 49) recommend the following kinds of questions to focus in depth on cognitions:

- How did you come to that conclusion?
- What meaning do you make of?
- How do you explain what happened?
- What are your views (or beliefs) about that?

We suggest additional strategies to focus in depth on cognitive processes in Chapter 6.

Another way is for the helper to assess and tune into the client's affective or emotional functioning, as emotional or affective patterns can impact the client's behavior in many contexts and can also provide clues about the client's interpersonal functioning. For example, the helper may use questions to focus in depth on affective functioning, such as the following ones recommended by Brooks-Harris (2008, p. 199):

- What feelings related to this concern have you been experiencing?
- Do you ever feel sad, afraid, angry, or ashamed in this situation?
- Do these feelings help you resolve things or do they make things worse?
- Are there other emotions you might be feeling at a deeper level?
- Are there feelings you express in order to get a reaction from someone?
- Which emotions are you likely to express, and which do you tend to hide?
- Are there times when your feelings seem too intense for the current situation?
- Do you ever feel like your emotions are restricted or muffled or you can't express what you're really feeling?

We suggest additional ideas in Chapter 7.

TERMINATING THE INTERVIEW

The beginning practitioner is often unsure about when to terminate the interview and may feel ready to conclude either before or after the client is ready. A general guideline is to limit the interview to a certain amount of time, such as forty-five or fifty minutes. Rarely does the helping interview need to exceed an hour in length, as both client and helper have a saturation point. With children, sessions may only be twenty to forty minutes in duration, and some part of this time may be spent in play therapy.

There is also a minimal amount of time required for counseling to take place. Interviews that continue for no more than ten or fifteen minutes make it very difficult for the helper to know enough about the client's concern to react appropriately. Indeed, helpers sometimes require five to ten minutes just to reorient themselves and to change their frame of reference from their preceding attention-involving activity to the present activity of counseling.

Acceptance of time limits is especially important when the client has a series of interviews. Research has shown that clients, like everyone else, tend to postpone talking about their concerns as long as possible. Without time limits, the presumed one-hour interview may extend well beyond an hour as a result of this postponing tendency. It is the one instance in which the client can easily manipulate the helper.

Sommers-Flanagan and Sommers-Flanagan (2003) have identified two factors basic to the closing process of the interview:

1. Both the client and the helper need to be aware that the interview is "winding down."
2. Terminating a session involves what has already occurred, so no additional information should be sought or discussed during the last few minutes. (p. 157)

If the client introduces a new topic near the end of a session, the practitioner can suggest discussing it at the outset of the next session. The rare exception to this would be when the client presents a truly urgent and immediate concern. Sommers-Flanagan and Sommers-Flanagan (2003) have summarized the main tasks necessary for terminating an interview effectively:

1. Leave enough time for closing the session so that you and the client do not feel rushed.
2. Reassure clients by validating their expressions of concerns and any self-disclosure that has occurred in the interview.
3. Instill hope about the helping process and try to solidify a follow-up appointment or any referral you make.
4. Empower the client by giving [him or her] an opportunity to ask questions or make comments as the session wraps up. (pp. 157–159)

Some ways to accomplish these tasks are discussed next.

Other Termination Strategies

Often, a brief and to-the-point statement by the helper will suffice for closing the interview:

- "It looks as if our time is up for today."
- "Well, I think it's time to stop for today."

This type of statement may be preceded by a pause or by a concluding kind of remark made by the client. Another effective way is to use *summarization*. Summarization provides continuity to the interview, is an active kind of helper response, and often helps the client to hear what he or she has been saying. It is essentially a series of statements in which the helper ties together the main points of the interview. It should be brief, to the point, and without interpretation. An example of a helper's use of summarization at the end of an interview is the following:

> "Essentially, you've indicated that your main concern is with your family—and we've discussed how you might handle your strivings for independence without their interpreting this as rejection."

Another possible termination strategy is to ask the client to summarize or to state how he or she understood what has been going on in the interview, as in the following example:

> "As we're ending the session today, I'm wondering what you're taking with you; if you could summarize this, I think it would be helpful to both of us."

Mutual feedback involving both the client and the helper is another possible tool for termination of an interview. If plans and decisions have been made, it is often useful for both individuals to clarify and verify the progress of the interview, as in the following example:

"I guess that's it for today; I'll also be thinking about the decision you're facing. As you understand it, what things do you want to do before our next session?"

Mutual exploration involves the client and helper assessing the experience of the helping session or sessions together. Whether the process has gone well or poorly, mutual exploration provides an opportunity to process what the experience has been like, as in the following example:

"Now that we're about out of time for today, can you share with me what it's been like for you?"

Boundary Issues in Terminating an Interview

It is up to the helper to set boundaries for terminating a session, but some clients for various reasons—such as anxiety, dependence, or reactivity—challenge these limits. For example, a client may abruptly end a session and say "That's it for me today" before the allotted time has occurred. Other clients may wait until you initiate termination and then say something provocative, such as, "Well, actually the real reason I came today is because I had to file for bankruptcy yesterday" or "I have something I must tell you before I leave today."

In both of these situations, it is the helper's responsibility to maintain time boundaries established at the beginning of the session—which, as we mentioned earlier, will vary with the age of the client and the setting in which you work. The rare exceptions to this would be with a client who is desperately anxious to leave early and with a client who brings up a recent traumatic event or a serious threat against oneself or someone else, such as, "Last night, I got in the car with a loaded gun and drove over to the house of the man who is having an affair with my wife."

As Sommers-Flanagan and Sommers-Flanagan (2003) have noted, beginning interviewers often feel guilty about maintaining time boundaries. But, according to the authors, disregarding these boundaries usually does not serve clients well in the long run (p. 162). "Reality is not always easy, and neither is closing an interview or therapy session, but by doing so in a kind, timely, professional manner, the message you give your client is: 'I play by the rules, and I believe you can, too. I will be here next week. I hold you in positive regard and am interested in helping you, but I can't work magic or change reality for you'" (p. 162).

TERMINATING THE HELPING RELATIONSHIP

The process of terminating a helping relationship can evoke various and even conflicting reactions for the helper. Some may think of it as a loss experience if the relationship has been highly meaningful or certainly as a "letting go" (Murdin, 2000). Others may consider termination to be an index of the helper's success or failure. From the client's point of view, termination may be a symbol of success or it may be a re-enactment of many former goodbyes in life. Whatever the interpretation, it is apparent that termination possesses an emotional dimension that can be intense. Often, it evokes an awareness of what the client means to us and vice versa. Through the process of termination, both helper and client are usually changed (Murdin, 2000, p. 211).

APPLICATION EXERCISE 5.2

Opening and Terminating the Interview

Use the following triadic exercise to review styles of opening and terminating the interview. With one class member as the speaker, another as the respondent, and a third as the observer, complete the following tasks by using the Observer Rating Charts (see Figures 5.1 and 5.2).

FIGURE 5.1   Observer Rating Chart: Opening the Interview

Counselor Response	Order
Unstructured invitation	
Open questions	
Closed questions	
Clarifying questions	

FIGURE 5.2   Observer Rating Chart: Terminating the Interview

Counselor Response	Order
Time limits	
Summarization of feelings	
Mutual feedback	
Structuring next session (time, date, etc.)	

Opening the Interview

SPEAKER:	Talk about yourself; share a concern with the listener.
LISTENER:	Respond to the speaker as if you were opening an interview. Try out the responses mentioned in the chapter: unstructured invitation and open, closed, and clarifying questions.
OBSERVER:	Observe the kinds of responses made by the listener. Keep a frequency count of the types of responses made. Share your report with the listener.
RECYCLING:	If, as the listener, you did not use at least two of the four response classes in your interaction with the speaker, complete the interaction again.
ROLE REVERSAL:	Reverse the roles and then follow the same process.

Record the order and frequency of responses used. If the counselor's first response was unstructured invitation, place a 1 in the space provided in the Observer Rating Charts. If the second counselor response was an open question, place a 2 in the appropriate space, and so forth.

Terminating the Interview

SPEAKER: Continue to explore the same topic you introduced in the preceding interaction.

LISTENER: Respond to the speaker as if you were terminating an interview. Try out at least one of the procedures mentioned in the section as approaches for termination of the interview (acknowledgment of time limits, summarization, or mutual feedback).

OBSERVER: Observe the procedure for termination used by the listener. Share your report with the listener.

RECYCLING: If, as the listener, you did not use any of the termination procedures or if, for some reason, termination did not occur with your speaker, complete the interaction agaain.

ROLE REVERSAL: Reverse the roles and then follow the same process.

Perhaps the most useful way to conceptualize termination is to think of it as a transition rather than an event (Hackney & Cormier, 2009). As the helping relationship develops and as the client is able to address and resolve the issues that necessitated counseling, the prospect of termination becomes a therapeutic stage in the process. More often than not, the helper becomes aware of the approaching termination first. Concerns related to the timing of termination, the preparation for termination, and the anticipation of therapeutic problems related to termination become dominant in the helper's mind.

When Should Termination Occur?

Some counseling theories provide guidelines for the timing of termination. These include such possibilities as letting the client determine the timing or having the clinician establish the date of termination at the outset of the helping process (Hackney & Cormier, 2009). Such issues will depend on your own theoretical orientation. However, there are some pragmatic factors that contribute to the question of timing. For example, the client may be under a managed health care plan that dictates a certain number of sessions per year, such as twenty. At the end of the specified number of sessions, several scenarios could occur. The helper may be able to negotiate with the client's plan for a few more sessions if the goals have not been reached. Alternatively, the helper and client may reach some kind of private payment agreement if termination does not seem clinically indicated. However, if the client is unable to pay and the insurance company does not authorize additional sessions, helping professionals "still have a fiduciary obligation to assist, stabilize, and/or refer" those clients who continue to need care (Younggren & Gottlieb, 2008, p. 501).

Hackney and Cormier (2009) have summarized some of these pragmatic considerations in termination as follows:

- When counseling has been predicated on a behavioral or another form of contract, progress toward the goals or conditions of the contract presents a clear picture of when counseling should end.
- When clients feel that their goals have been accomplished, they may initiate termination.

- When the relationship appears to not be helpful—either to helper or client—termination is appropriate.
- When contextual conditions change—for example, the client or helper moves to a new location—termination must occur.

Preparing Clients for Termination

Clients should be made aware throughout the helping process that there will come a time when counseling is no longer appropriate. This does not mean that they will have worked out all their issues nor will it mean that they have acquired all the tools and awareness necessary for a satisfying life. It does mean that they have grown to the point at which they have more to gain from being independent of the helping relationship than they would gain from continuing the relationship. Murdin (2000) noted that an important indicator of client readiness for termination is the client's ability and willingness to discuss reasons for wanting to terminate (p. 41). We believe that human beings are happier and more self-fulfilled when they are able to trust their own resources. Of course, healthy people rely on others, but they do so out of self-perceived choice rather than self-perceived necessity.

Occasionally, you will know in the first session with your client that the relationship will last a certain length of time. For example, if your client is seeking premarital counseling and the wedding is to take place in two months, the time constraints are apparent. People going to university counseling centers may know that vacations dictate the amount of time allowed for counseling. In such cases, it is appropriate to acknowledge throughout the relationship that these time constraints exist.

When the relationship is more open-ended and determined by the client's progress, the termination stage begins well before the final session. The client's presenting concerns, goals for counseling, and progress in counseling should be reviewed from time to time (Vasquez, 2005). Hackney and Cormier (2009) refer to this as termination by degree (p. 34). We believe that for any relationship that has existed more than three months, the topic should be raised three to four weeks prior to termination. This allows the client time to think about and discuss the ramifications of ending counseling with the helper. In addition, termination should also take into account both the nature of the client's issues and the nature of the helper's theoretical or treatment approach (Younggren & Gottlieb, 2008, p. 503). Clients with more severe issues usually require a longer termination period that provides more follow-up care than those with less severe issues. Also, terminating with a client after a long-term psychodynamic relationship is somewhat different than terminating with a client who was seen briefly with a cognitive-behavioral approach.

Cultural Variables and Termination

It is important to recognize that not all cultural groups share the same values and beliefs about the dimension of time, and this can also affect the termination process. For example, European Americans generally have a highly structured and future-oriented view of time, but some clients from other cultural groups have a much more casual view of time (Ivey et al., 2007). In cross-cultural helping situations, the time element of termination needs to also be discussed, negotiated, and understood from the client's perspective.

Also, many clients of color terminate the helping process at a much earlier time than other clients. Often, these clients are the decision-makers as to when to stop counseling, presumably because it is not relevant enough to them and their experiences, particularly their culturally linked experiences (Sue & Sue, 2008). Therefore, it is presumptuous to assume that in all situations, the "control" of the termination process is in the helper's hands.

Introducing Termination

Introducing termination can be done by saying something similar to this:

> "We've been dealing with a lot of issues, and I believe you've made a lot of progress. One of our goals all along has been to reach the point where counseling is no longer needed. I think we're reaching that point, and probably in about three or four weeks, we'll be stopping."

You can anticipate some of the reactions that your clients will have to this. They may feel good about their progress, nervous about the prospect of being on their own, or sad to see a significant relationship ending—to name but a few reactions. It is also important for the client to summarize both what has been achieved and what remains undone (Murdin, 2000, p. 150).

Occasionally, it is appropriate to terminate gradually. This can be done by spacing the time between interviews. If you have been seeing your client weekly, change the appointments to every other week or once a month. Or you may schedule a six-month check-in that gives your client the sense of an ongoing relationship—one that leaves the door open—should that be necessary. Even with these gradual transitions, you will still have as a major concern the transition of a significant relationship.

In all cases, it is important to emphasize the client's continued growth once counseling has ended. This includes summations of what the client has learned, discussions of other resources and support systems the client can make use of in her or his life, and the invitation for follow-up sessions as necessary. Kottler (1991) observed that "some people believe that therapy never ceases, that clients continue their dialogues with us (as they do with deceased parents) for the rest of their lives" (p. 173). Finally, it occasionally happens that the ending of a helping relationship has a character of finality. Perhaps you or your client is moving. Or you may be referring your client to another helping provider. In such instances, there may be a grieving process connected with termination. It is appropriate to view this grieving process as necessary and therapeutic in its own right. It is as important for the helper as for the client. Occasionally, a client may terminate simply by canceling the next appointment and there is no formal termination that occurs, yet the helper may still feel some grief. It is a symbolic or ceremonial conclusion—an acknowledgment that the relationship had importance and that reality dictates that it ends. In such cases, it is better not to hang on to it; that would only make the transition more difficult. If you are making a referral to another practitioner, you must give up your role as helper for both ethical and practical reasons.

Challenges to Termination

Murdin (2000) summarized a number of possible different challenges to the termination of counseling and psychotherapy. For example, she noted that clients sometimes leave suddenly and/or prematurely for fear of losing their own power. She observed that "the whole ending process involves questions about who has the power and whether or not it can be given up or shared" (p. 38). Studies have revealed that one-third of all clients do not return to counseling after only one or two sessions (Vasquez, 2005). These are likely to be clients who did not find counseling to be very useful for them. In other instances, clients just stop coming to see you because they feel ready to leave but are afraid to raise the issue of termination or do not see a way to "exit." Other clients may terminate the helping process prematurely because they have difficulty in regulating affective reactions, are emotionally unstable, and may be upset or irritated with the helper yet avoidant of communication about their feelings. In these situations, a note or phone call may be useful to collaborate with clients about various options: Do they want their file terminated?

Do they want to come in for a review session? Do they want to return to counseling—either with you or with someone different? (Vasquez, 2005, p. 21). A review of over thirty-five years of scientific literature on premature termination resulted in a number of other recommendations for preventing counseling "dropouts," including preparation, time-limited counseling, negotiation, case management, motivational interviewing and enhancement, strengthening the therapeutic relationship, and facilitating a safer environment for the expression of client feelings (Ogrodniczuk, Joyce & Piper, 2005).

At the other end of the continuum are clients who fight the termination process and have trouble saying goodbye for fear of losing the helper and his or her compassion (Murdin, 2000, p. 37). Even in instances where the termination point has been decided at the outset of the helping process—such as in time-limited counseling—challenges to the termination process can and do still occur. For instance, it is not uncommon for clients to have a crisis as the end of the contract approaches. Often, these clients may try to persuade the helper to work beyond the agreed-upon ending time. Murdin (2000) recommends that, in most cases, the helper should keep faith in the client and abide by the agreed-upon ending date (p. 151). She states that "in time-limited work, the therapist must be prepared to work for an ending right from the beginning and must not waver from the view that an ending is desirable" (p. 155). Murdin recommends that before agreeing to any changes in the termination date, helpers should search themselves and their own motivations for extending the time (p. 153). For any exception that may be made to the original contract, she also believes it is better to initiate a new contract than to extend the existing one (p. 153). Challenges to termination often occur because the attachment produces a fear of loss. The greatest difficulty in termination of counseling lies in "hidden anxieties" about this loss (p. 37). The fear of loss can result in such emotions as anger and jealousy (in addition to the sadness we mentioned earlier). Occasionally, clients' fear of loss may be so great they even pursue helpers by stalking them. Obviously, there is a great deal that helpers can do to promote a healthy attachment with clients and to avoid an unhealthy attachment, such as extreme dependence or adoration (Murdin, 2000).

Ethical Issues in Termination

In both the United States and the United Kingdom, numerous ethical complaints made by clients have to do with termination issues that clients felt were handled improperly (Murdin, 2000). Terminating the helping relationship does pose potential ethical and legal issues for helpers if not managed appropriately. Generally, it is important for helpers to avoid sudden endings. If a situation—such as a severe illness—requires a sudden termination, the helper still has continued responsibilities to the welfare of the client. "When incapacity or absence suddenly strike, psychotherapists must make sure that those being treated have access to emergency resources, and if the psychotherapist is unable to return to practice within a reasonable time, appropriate referrals must be arranged (Younggren & Gottlieb, 2008, p. 502). And the helper has certain ethical responsibilities in the referral process. These include protecting the client's privacy and confidentiality unless there is a written client release on file, providing the client with choices of several other professional helpers, and ensuring that these other helpers are regarded as competent and ethical professionals (Welfel, 2010). When a helper is incapacitated in a sudden and severe manner, other qualified helping professionals will need to fulfill these responsibilities.

It is also important to remember that clients who have not received any structuring about the termination process at the outset of the helping process may be more likely to feel abandoned and angry when the practitioner suggests termination is appropriate or when the practitioner becomes ill or moves away. Therefore, an important ethical issue in terminating the helping process effectively involves discussion of this issue as part of the informed consent process that we described earlier in this chapter. As Younggren and Gottlieb (2008) note, in reality, "effective termination begins during the initial psychotherapy session or another early session in which matters of informed consent are discussed . . . . Through this mechanism, practitioners explain the details of the treatment relationship and make contracts with patients regarding what the psychotherapist will and will not do. This is also the time for the practitioner to explain what he or she expects of the patient. It is through this clarification of the professional-patient relationship that much of the difficulty associated with the closure of psychotherapy can be avoided" (p. 502). A part of this discussion should very clearly include client financial obligations and insurance limitations. If a client is using health insurance and has a very restricted plan, it is important to explain this before counseling ensues to ensure that client expectations are reasonable and realistic and that the client still retains the potential choice to consent or not consent to treatment under these conditions.

APPLICATION EXERCISE 5.3

Working With Notice and Informed Consent

Because informed consent is such a critical and integral process in both beginning and ending sessions in the helping process, this activity gives you an opportunity to develop and refine your skills in providing informed consent. Recall that the activity of providing *notice* gives clients information about the helping process at the outset, while *informed consent* involves obtaining the client's agreement about the information you have provided.

In this activity, we suggest you divide into triads, with one person assuming the role of helper, one person assuming the role of a novice, inexperienced, new client, and the third person assuming the role of observer and feedback provider. As the helper, your task is to conduct a fifteen- to twenty-minute beginning helping interview in which you provide information to the client about the helping process. Make sure that you thoroughly cover issues of privacy, confidentiality, and limits to confidentiality as well as issues that may impact termination, such as insurance reimbursement limits, financial responsibilities, expectations of clients, and so on. Following the practice interview, the observer should provide feedback about the thoroughness of your informed consent process. Each of you can trade roles so that you are in each of the three roles one time. Sometimes, it is also useful to tape-record or videotape an informed consent session. We suggest you attempt to discuss the following issues in these practice sessions:

- The goals of helping
- The kinds of services you provide to clients
- Your qualifications
- What you expect from the client
- The potential benefits and risks of helping
- The financial arrangements and responsibilities
- Privacy, confidentiality, and the limits of confidentiality

Another potential ethical issue in termination involves continuity of care. Perhaps the client decides to terminate and return to see you at a later point. Or perhaps the client takes a break and later returns to your setting and sees another practitioner. In either case, a written summary of your progress with the client provides the basis for you or someone else to begin sessions with the client at a later date without having to start all over again. The structure of *discharge summaries* or *termination reports* varies among settings. However, generally speaking, most termination reports consist of the following kinds of information:

- Identifying information about the client (name, age, gender)
- Duration of counseling; dates and number of sessions with the client
- Summary of client's presenting issues and possible diagnostic codes for problems
- Type and method of counseling (treatment and intervention strategies)
- Summary of counseling and therapeutic progress
- Recommendations for future treatment (including referrals)

Obviously, the need for a more detailed summary is evident when the termination occurs prematurely and/or when the client objects to it. In these cases, "the record should include documentation that allows the reader to understand the rationale for ending therapy as well as the ethically appropriate and clinically indicated steps the practitioner took to do so in a reasonable manner" (Younggren & Gottlieb, 2008, p. 503).

Summary

Beginning interviews, subsequent interviews, and ending interviews all present different challenges for both helpers and clients. At the outset of the helping process, both individuals might experience some anxiety and uncertainty. It is important for practitioners to establish safety and trust from the beginning of the process, as many clients have both fears and reservations about the helping process. This is especially true for many culturally diverse clients and for clients who have had either no prior experience or negative experience with counseling. Structuring and disclosure can ease client fears and insecurities about the process. Both rapport and information gathering are important tasks in the initial stage of the helping process. One of the most important topics to address at the beginning of the helping process is confidentiality and its limits. Through the process of providing notice and informed consent, the helper provides information to the client about the helping process and secures client agreement based on such information and facts. This sort of process not only facilitates the beginning of counseling but also impacts subsequent helping sessions and even potential termination issues.

Termination—both of helping sessions and of the helping process—evokes its own set of challenges and emotions. It is important for helpers to terminate an interview as well as the helping process in a way that empowers clients. Clients who feel disempowered, such as some culturally diverse clients, might choose to terminate early or suddenly, often because counseling does not feel relevant to them or the helper does not understand their worldviews or aspects of oppression and discrimination are recreated for them in the helping process.

Both the termination of interviews and the termination of the helping process require the practitioner to manage a transition effectively. This transition becomes more difficult if either the helper or the client has any hidden anxieties about separation and/or loss. It is important for helpers to address feelings of loss, to prepare clients for termination over a period of time, and to help clients find ways to support their growth after counseling has ended.

Reflective Questions

1. Discuss what it might be like to be a client seeking help for the first time from an unknown practitioner. Now discuss this as it applies to a cross-cultural dyad.
2. Discuss the positive and negative perceptions that a client might have after going through an intake interview.
3. Discuss the transition the helper needs to make from a beginning interview or two to a subsequent session. What changes for the helper? For the client?
4. From a helper's perspective, what do you think are the most important elements in terminating a significant relationship? From the client's perspective?
5. What are the ethical issues in beginning or continuing to help a client who is also receiving counseling from another practitioner?

My Helping Lab

For each exercise, log on to MyHelpingLab at http://www.myhelpinglab.com and then click the Topics tab.

1. Click the Ethical, Legal, and Professional Issues in Counseling tab to locate the Confidentiality and Privileged Communication tab. Under this tab, choose the Video Lab for the following two selections: Misinformed Consent and Response to Misinformed Consent. Watch the Misinformed Consent clip first and then discuss what mistakes this beginning helper made in the notice and informed consent process with this client. Then, watch the second clip to determine if your responses are similar to the two experts in the Response to Misinformed Consent.
2. Click the Process, Skills, and Techniques tab to locate the Practical Issues: Ethical Dilemmas Video Lab. Then, choose the Two Different Methods for Ending a Session selection. In this selection, two different practitioners end a session with a client. Contrast the two different kinds of endings. What did you like and dislike about each kind of session termination?

Recommended Readings

Hackney, H. & Cormier, L. S. (2009). *The professional counselor, 6th edition.* Upper Saddle River, NJ: Pearson.

Morrison, J. (2008). *The first interview, 3rd edition.* New York: Guilford Press.

Murdin, L. (2000). *How much is enough: Endings in psychotherapy and counseling.* London: Routledge.

Ogrodniczuk, J. S., Joyce, A. S. & Piper, W. E. (2005). Strategies for reducing patient-initiated premature termination of psychotherapy. *Harvard Review of Psychiatry, 13,* 57–70.

Sommers-Flanagan, J. & Sommers-Flanagan, R. (2003). *Clinical interviewing, 3rd edition.* New York: John Wiley & Sons.

Sue, D. W. & Sue, D. (2008). *Counseling the culturally diverse, 5th edition.* New York: John Wiley & Sons.

Welfel, E. (2010). *Ethics in counseling and psychotherapy, 4th edition.* Belmont, CA: Brooks/Cole, Cengage.

Younggren, J. N. & Gottlieb, M. C. (2008). Termination and abandonment: History, risk, and risk management. *Professional Psychology, 39,* 498–504.

CHAPTER

6

Responding to Cognitive Content

In the last chapter, we talked about opening and closing an interview. As the interview ensues, the helper responds to the client in many ways—both verbally and nonverbally. Because your responses will have an impact on clients and the topics they discuss, it is necessary to be aware of the effect your responses will have. One very important effect deals with the changing pattern of the client's verbal behavior. As verbal interaction and communication begin, topics arise; some topics are developed, some are modified, and some are diverted into new topics. As an active participant in the helping process, you must be sure that your responses will influence the direction of topic development in such ways as choosing from among the topics that are to be discussed and the length of time allotted to the topics. Responding to client content suggests alternatives and conscious choices that you will have to make in the interview. Then, when one choice has been made, the effect of that choice will become the basis for further alternatives. The following example will illustrate the types of choices you, the helper, will be making. Suppose your client says, "I've known what this operation would do to my plans for a long time."

Your choices for responding are several:

- Paraphrase the client's remark: "You have known about the impact of this operation for quite a while now."
- Ask a question directly related to the client's statement: "What will it do?"
- Say "mm-hmm."
- Reflect the client's feelings about the operation: "You feel very certain about the consequences of the operation."
- Respond with silence and simply wait to see what the client does or says next.

Obviously, these five responses will produce different responses from clients. The client in this example may proceed to talk about the operation, about plans, or about how she anticipates events. In any case, your response would shape or mold the topic development and, as a result, influence the future matters the client discusses.

Because your responses greatly influence the nature of topic development, you will be faced with the decision of which kind of content to respond to and, thus, emphasize. Very often, the client's particular response contains both a cognitive message and an affect message. Cognitive messages usually deal with people, places, and things, whereas affect messages primarily reflect feelings and emotions. Typically, in early interviews, the affect message is disguised. The disguises may be thin but nonetheless necessary to the clients. It is their way of protecting themselves until they can determine the kinds of things to which you are willing to listen. Once you are able to hear the affect message (and this comes with practice), you will have to make some decisions. It is important that you respond to that portion of the client's communication that you think is most significantly related to the client's concerns.

The process of choosing between client cognitive and affective topics is called *differentiation*. Whether you choose to respond to the cognitive portion or the affect portion depends largely on what is happening in the interaction at that moment and on what the client needs. In other words, choosing to respond to the cognitive content serves one objective, whereas choosing to respond to the affect content serves another objective. This process of differentiation not only involves the client's comfort level but also the helper's comfort level (or lack thereof!). Some helpers are too uncomfortable with feelings or emotions to focus on affect even when the client is leading them in that direction, while others seem to focus always and exclusively on affect and feelings while ignoring important and relevant insight and cognitive understanding. It is helpful during work with your supervisor or faculty advisor to determine if your own tendency is to respond more naturally to either cognitive or affective content. Whatever your natural inclination is, you can work to broaden your range of responses, thus enhancing the potential of the helping process.

Some theoretical approaches to counseling (e.g., the phenomenological) favor an almost exclusive emphasis on affect, whereas others (e.g., rational-emotive, cognitive-behavioral, reality therapy) suggest that the primary emphasis should be on the cognitive process. Of course, there are many variables influencing this sort of emphasis. In working with one client who intellectualizes frequently, the helper may focus primarily on affect in an effort to get the client to recognize and accept his or her feelings. However, the same helper—with another client who intellectualizes—may choose to emphasize cognitive elements if the counseling time is too limited for the client to feel comfortable with emotions. There are certainly times when emphasis on the affective takes precedence over the cognitive and vice versa. Generally, though, during the interview process, it is important to respond to *both* affective and cognitive topics. This is because, for all clients, there are times when feelings govern thoughts and times when thoughts and their consequences govern or influence feelings. The important point is not which comes first but which type of intervention is likely to be the most effective for each particular client. In this chapter, we will work with content choices of a cognitive nature, as opposed to affective or feeling-type choices. (In Chapter 7, we will explore affective content and responses to it.) In other words, the emphasis now is on your recognition and demonstrated ability to identify and respond to client thoughts or ideas dealing with problems, situations, people, or things.

RECOGNIZING ALTERNATIVES

Each comment of the client presents alternatives to you in terms of content to which you may respond. How you respond to one alternative will shape the next remark of the client. Your task is to accurately identify the kinds of content presented by the client and the alternatives to which you, as the helper, can respond.

RESPONDING TO ALTERNATIVES

The process of selecting alternatives can best be illustrated by excerpts from actual interviews:

> CLIENT: I like this type of a setup where you can talk directly to people and talk with them. Uh, I don't like big crowds where I don't know anybody and they don't know me.
>
> HELPER: You'd rather not be in big crowds.

In this example, the client's response contained two basic communications: I like to talk directly to people, and I don't like big crowds in which individuals get lost. The helper chose to respond to the second communication in the client's response. Had the helper responded by saying "You prefer situations that permit you to get to know people," the topic of focus would have been on getting to know people and the necessary conditions for this. As it was, the response led to a topic focus on the ambiguity of not knowing people. This does not necessarily mean that one response was more appropriate than the other; it is used only to point out the available alternatives.

A study of counseling interview typescripts suggests that when the helper has alternative communications to which he or she may respond, the tendency is to respond to the final component of the response. Perhaps this is because of the immediacy of the final part of the response; but if so, that is a poor criterion. It is more logical that the helper respond to the part of the client's communication that has greatest bearing on the client's concern and is therefore most important.

The helper may also be tempted to respond to that portion of the client's communication that he or she finds most interesting. In this case, the interview tends to center on those topics that the helper may identify with or be dealing with personally. Again, the helper must ensure that the choice of alternative topics reflects a decision about the client's needs rather than the helper's. This is especially true in instances of cross-cultural counseling. If the helper chooses to respond to the portion of the client's communication that is most interesting to the helper, this may be a reflection of the helper's personal and cultural biases and cultural worldview and may not be relevant to the client's culture. In cross-cultural counseling, there are often barriers or stumbling blocks to intercultural communication (Pedersen & Ivey, 1993). They are not as likely to be barriers for those within the same culture because of shared meaning. Assuming similarities instead of differences in cross-cultural counseling is one such barrier. The helper cannot safely assume that what he or she chooses to attend to is what is of most importance to the client from a different culture.

VERBAL RESPONSES TO COGNITIVE CONTENT

There are several types of responses you can use to focus on and elicit specific content expressed in the client's communication. The responses presented here can be used specifically to respond to the cognitive content of the client's communication—that is, ideas that deal with problems, situations, people, and things. Although these are not the only possible ones, five verbal responses will be identified here for this purpose: silence, minimal verbal activity, paraphrase, questions, and summarization of content. Emphasis will be directed toward the latter three. The use of silence and minimal verbal activity has already been noted in previous chapters. Their use as verbal responses to cognitive content in client messages will be presented here briefly.

APPLICATION EXERCISE 6.1

Identifying Alternative Topics

To give you practice in identifying topic alternatives, carefully read the following client statements. Then, identify and list all the different topics in each client response.

1. "I don't know just exactly how it does work, but in connection with the Air Force or the Army, you can serve for a bunch of time and then they pay for college. But I would not want to join up and then get deployed."

   _____

   _____

   _____

2. "I realize that some people have a bad opinion of gays in the service but, uh, they shouldn't really. We can fight just as well as the next person."

   _____

   _____

   _____

Feedback

The correct answers to the exercises above are as follows:

1. **a.** I don't know just exactly how it does work.
   b. You can serve in the armed forces to get college paid for.
   c. I don't want to join up and get deployed.

2. **a.** I realize that some people have a bad opinion of gays in the service.
   b. They shouldn't really.
   c. We can fight just as well as someone not gay

Silence

Silence affects the course of topic development by indicating that the helper does not want to select or direct the topic at the given time it is used (see Chapter 4). Although the use of silence gives the helper much less control over the direction that topic development takes, it serves to increase the power of other types of responses. Thus, after you have remained silent for several moments, your next verbal response will have more influence in shaping the direction of topic development.

Minimal Verbal Activity

Minimal verbal responses are those verbalizations and vocalizations that people use when they are listening to someone else. The most common are "mm-hmm," "mmm," "yes," "oh," and "I see." They are unobtrusive utterances but have a significant reinforcing value. That is, when an utterance such as "mm-hmm" is used consistently following a particular topic or word, the future occurrence of that particular topic or word usually increases. Of course, minimal verbal responses can lose their reinforcing value if they are overused.

Paraphrase

Paraphrasing is the rephrasing of all or a selected portion of the client's previous communication, and it neither adds to nor detracts from the basic communication. It confirms for the client that the helper has heard the communication. Operationally, the paraphrase may be defined as a simple, compound, complex, or fragmentary sentence that mirrors the client's previous communication by using your own words. It is dependent in its grammatical structure on the grammatical structure of the client's previous response. The paraphrase can be used effectively as long as it is interspersed with other types of helper responses. Otherwise, it can produce a parrot-like effect that has an adverse effect on clients. When using a paraphrase response, it is helpful to use the most important words and ideas expressed in the content portion of the client's message. When you do this, your response lets clients know you have heard their message accurately and that you are able to respond to it in a way that does not simply copy or mimic their expression. Examples of paraphrases will help you understand this particular response:

CLIENT: I'm hoping to get a good job this summer.

HELPER: You're counting on getting the job you need this summer. (paraphrase)

CLIENT: It doesn't look like we'll get a vacation this summer.

HELPER: It looks like a vacation is not going to happen for you this summer. (paraphrase)

CLIENT: I like people, but I sure get tired of them.

HELPER: After a while, being around people can be fatiguing for you. (paraphrase)

Now try your hand with a few paraphrases:

CLIENT: This has been a really rough year for me.

YOU: _____

CLIENT: Probably the worst class I have is literature.

YOU: _____

Discuss your responses with someone.

Questions

In the last chapter, we discussed the use of questions as a tool to open an interview. Questions can also be a way to respond to content. Although most effective questions are usually open-ended—requiring more than minimal responses by the client—closed or clarifying questions are also occasionally useful for responding to client content messages. Recall that closed and clarifying questions usually focus on a specific piece of information. If you want to focus on one particular part of the client's content message, you may decide to use a closed question. For example, suppose the client says, "I seem to be having relationship problems with just about everyone in my life." You might want to focus on a specific related piece of information and could follow up with a closed question, such as, "Have these relationship problems started recently or have they been going on for a while now?" Similarly, a clarifying question may be used to help explore and clarify the meaning of the client's content message. In this same example, you could use a clarifying question, such as, "Can you elaborate on what you mean by 'relationship problems'?" Of course, remember that beginning helpers often rely on closed or clarifying questions, making them overused and less effective in the helping process.

In contrast to closed and clarifying questions, open-ended questions require more than a minimal one-word answer by the client. As noted in Chapter 5, you will find that it is very difficult to ask questions that clearly place the focus on your client. Typically, when you start asking questions, the client will give a minimal answer and then wait for the next question. In other words, the client has not assumed responsibility for the content of the interview. One purpose of the open-ended question is to prevent the client from answering questions with a "Yes" or "No" response. Open-ended questions also are useful for encouraging clients to elaborate and give information. They are introduced with *what*, *where*, *when*, or *how*. *Why* questions are usually avoided because clients rarely know the answer and because they appear intrusive. Some examples of open-ended questions include:

- "What do you like about it?"
- "What is keeping you from doing it?"
- "How do you feel about it?"
- "How is it helping you?"
- "When do you feel that way?"
- "Where does that occur for you?"
- "How does your wife enable you to keep doing this?"

Try a few open-ended questions for yourself:

CLIENT: It's hard to admit, but I really have wondered whether college is for me.

YOU: _____

CLIENT: I've gotten to the point where I can't do anything I'm supposed to do.

YOU: _____

Discuss your responses with someone.

Open-ended questions can easily be overused in an interview. A beginning helper often tends to bombard initial clients with questions. Extensive use of questions gives a ping-pong effect. The helper asks, the client answers, and so on; thus, the counseling resembles little more than an interrogation process. Cournoyer (2011) suggests that one way to avoid this is to intersperse your questions with active listening responses, such as paraphrasing. When helpers overuse questions, they may be acting more out of their own needs rather than trying to help the client in the form of structuring, clarifying, expecting, or soliciting information. Examples of situations in which questions are used to meet the helper's needs include:

- **Voyeurism:** Wanting to know certain things about the client to satisfy our own curiosity
- **Narcissism:** Wanting to make ourselves look good or look like the expert by the kinds of questions we ask
- **Sadism:** Bombarding the client with frequent or painful questions so much as to constitute harassment (Kottler, 1991, p. 160)

Murphy and Dillon (2008) recommended two questions a helper can ask when considering how to use questions selectively and effectively: "What is the purpose of my question?" and "How is this purpose therapeutic—how does it help the client?" These authors believe that clients have a right to be informed about the purpose of your questions, to know how the information will be used and by whom, and to understand that they can decline to answer any questions (pp. 151–152). Occasionally, beginning helpers resort to questions simply because they feel more comfortable with this type of lead. This is a good example in which silence may be used in lieu of another question. Ultimately, learning a variety of alternative verbal leads will help prevent overuse of questions.

It is also important to note that clients may have very different reactions to questions. Some clients may construe helper questions as a sign of interest on the helper's part. Other clients may view questions as intrusive and react by withdrawing. Questions can be culturally insensitive and offensive, particularly if they seek very personal information from clients in initial sessions or if they suggest a cause-effect orientation (Sue & Sue, 2008). Asking questions of a very personal nature may be perceived as lacking in respect by some Asian-American clients. Also, the worldview of some clients from other cultural groups, such as American Indians, reflects an intuitive and harmonious approach rather than a cause-effect approach. As with all verbal responses, helpers need to closely monitor the effects of their verbal leads—particularly questions—on new clients.

Summarization of Content Response

A summarization response is one that ties together multiple elements or key points of a client's message—either perhaps a long-winded message or a series of messages that occur over time, such as during an entire session. A *summarization of content* is a rephrasing of at least two or more different content or cognitive messages expressed by the client. This response is used to give focus and direction to an interview and to identify possible themes, narratives, or key ideas expressed within the client's communication. (Recall from Chapter 5 that summarization can also be used at the end of an interview to tie together the session and provide an ending for it.) Consider he following examples of the summarization of content response:

CLIENT: I've been pretty tired for the last few months. I just don't seem to have my usual energy. I am sleeping OK, but by early afternoon, I just run out of steam. Maybe it's because so much has happened around me lately—my partner just lost his job and my dog died about a year ago.

HELPER: Wow—it seems like a lot of pretty significant things have been happening in your life and you have noticed these affecting your energy level.

(summarization of content)

CLIENT (EARLY IN THE SESSION): I don't think I have a big problem with pot. I mean, I do smoke it every day, but it doesn't seem to interfere with anything I need to do. Well, sometimes I guess I do feel a little concerned because I like the feeling I get from it [pot], so I don't want to give it up.

HELPER: You have said a couple of things during this session about your smoking pot— that it doesn't interfere with anything you need to do and you don't want to give it up because of the effect it has on you.

(summarization of content)

In the next chapter, we will explore how summarization can be used to respond to affective messages as well in the summarization of feeling response. For now, try a few summarization of content responses on your own.

CLIENT: I find it easier to relate to my stepson than my own son. I think it's because we're not biologically related, if you know what I mean. There just seems to be so much less conflict between us.

YOU: _____

CLIENT: My partner confronted me about my drinking and got me to agree to come in here to see you, but I really don't want to be here. I don't think how much I drink is anyone else's business but my own.

YOU: _____

Discuss your responses with a colleague, supervisor, or instructor.

DIFFERENTIATION AND SELECTIVE RESPONDING

The emphasis in this chapter has been on the selective responding to some client messages as opposed to others. When the client presents you with a multiple message, you can respond to all the messages or to only some of them. If you respond only partially to the client's messages, that to which you do not respond may be dropped by the client in future communication, unless it is very important to him or her. In this case, the client may attempt to initiate discussion of the topic once again.

Selective responding involves a covert process on the counselor's part known as *differentiation,* which is the process of identifying all the different parts of the client's communication and making an intentional decision about which part to respond to and how. It also involves paying attention to or monitoring the effects of your choices on subsequent client communication.

The effects of selective responding require you to be much attuned to yourself and your own issues and ultimately to be comfortable with yourself, your issues, and your feelings. Effective responses to clients demand a sort of consciousness on your part about yourself. For example, if you are personally uncomfortable with issues such as sexuality, abortion, divorce, race, and so on, you may avoid responding to the mention of these topics by clients or if the expression of anger scares you, you may avoid responding to anything that might indicate the client is feeling angry. A major way that helpers become and stay conscious of themselves and their impact on clients is through consultation with a supervisor. We discuss this in greater detail in Chapter 10.

Because clients vary along many dimensions, the effects of your responses with clients will also vary in impact—positive and negative. Thus, it is erroneous to assume that all the responses and interventions presented in this book will work with all clients or will have the same meaning or results for all clients. Rarely does a "one size fits all" method work effectively in the helping process. Rather, helpers must assess each individual client and select responses and interventions that work best for the person sitting in front of them.

APPLICATION EXERCISE 6.2

Identifying and Responding to Cognitive Content

A. Identifying Cognitive Content

To give further practice in identifying cognitive content—thoughts or ideas pertaining to problems, situations, people, or things—carefully read the following client statements. Then, identify and list the different cognitive topics within each client response.

1. "I'm thinking about either going to graduate school or getting a job—whichever would be the better experience is what I'll do."

   _____

   _____

   _____

2. "When I was growing up, I never thought about being a CEO of an organization. I always thought I'd just be a stay-at-home mom. And people can say what they want to about it, but for me, this job is a very good fit, and I don't think my kids suffer just because I'm busy with work."

   _____

   _____

   _____

Feedback

The answers to the preceding exercises are as follows:

1. a. I'm thinking about going to graduate school.
   b. I'm also thinking about getting a job.
   c. I'll do whatever provides the best experience.

2. a. When I was growing up, I didn't think about becoming an organizational CEO.
   b. I always thought I'd be a stay at home mom.
   c. People can say what they want to about it.
   d. For me, this job is a good fit.
   e. I don't think my kids suffer just because I'm busy at work.

B. Responding to Cognitive Content

The following exercise will give you practice in using paraphrase, open-ended questions, and summarization of content. Read each client statement and then respond with the type of response indicated in parentheses:

1. **CLIENT:** I wish I had more friends here at school. People are in their own little cliques. I'd almost rather be alone than be in a clique and be a snob.
   You: (paraphrase) _____

   _____

2. **CLIENT:** I must admit I wasn't all that sure I'd enjoy being retired; after all, I've been used to working a pretty demanding schedule. But I find that the part I like the best is not really being that scheduled and being able to do what I want when I want.
   You: (open-ended question) _____

   _____

3. **CLIENT:** I don't want to be suspicious, but when I see my work colleagues going some-where and I'm not invited along, it does make me think that my performance review is going to get a negative evaluation.
   You: (summarization of content) _____

   _____

4. **CLIENT:** I wanted to go back to school mostly because of the fact that I thought that there would be someone to lead me because I just don't know which direction to go sometimes for a few things.
   You: (paraphrase) _____

   _____

5. **CLIENT:** Well, I know you're supposed to study every night, which I don't do, but I'm not the only one who hasn't studied this semester. A lot of other kids have lost interest too.
   You: (open-ended question) _____

   _____

6. **CLIENT:** Taking tests is real hard for me. Maybe it's because I came here from Mexico when I was younger. My English isn't that good. I can speak OK, but sometimes, I don't always understand the meaning of all the words, and that gets to be a problem on tests a lot.
   You: (paraphrase) _____

   _____

Discuss your responses with a colleague or supervisor.

To summarize the differentiation process of selective responding, consider these two key points:

1. The helper is able to generate a maximum number of ideas, words, and responses to communicate with a diverse group of clients.

2. The helper is able to observe the effects of the responses implemented in the session with a diverse group of clients and is flexible enough to modify these responses when the observations suggest they are not working.

The differentiation process and selective responding is particularly challenging in cross-cultural counseling. The temptation is to respond to the content or the affect of client messages in a way that is consistent with your own culture and yet may be inconsistent with the client's culture.

APPLICATION EXERCISE 6.3

Selective Responding

A. Anticipating Client Responses

Using your responses to the client in Part B of Exercise 6.2, write what you think would be the client's response to what you said. For example, with response 1, if you had asked, "What are the friends that you have made at school like?" the client would most likely have responded by giving you a description of the current friendships as they stand right now.

1. Your response: _____

_____

Client's next response: _____

_____

2. Your response: _____

_____

Client's next response: _____

_____

3. Your response: _____

_____

Client's next response: _____

_____

4. Your response: _____

_____

Client's next response: _____

_____

5. Your response: _____

_____

Client's next response: _____

_____

6. Your response: _____

_____

Client's next response: _____

_____

B. Observed Practice

One of you, designated as the speaker, will share a concern with the listener. As the speaker, make sure your initial statement contains several different ideas to which anyone could respond. For example, "I'm really having trouble in school. There's just so much work I can't keep up with it. I wonder if I can make good enough grades. I also need to keep my job to have enough money to pay for tuition, but I don't know if I'll continue to be able to work and study at the same time."

1. The respondent's task is to select one of the ideas or topics and respond to it by using a paraphrase, an open question, or a summarization of content. After your initial response, allow the speaker to continue and then respond with either silence or a minimal verbal response.
2. The observer's task is to track the way the speaker develops the topic and the course of future topics depending on the part of the communication to which the listener chose to respond.
3. After completing this in one triad, reverse the roles and then complete the same process two more times.
4. At the end of three practices, discuss what you have noticed about how the listener's choice of responses and topics influences the path of the speaker's communication.

EFFECTS OF RESPONDING TO COGNITIVE CONTENT

Responding to cognitive content can be an anxiety-reduction tool for clients easily threatened by feelings. Thus, there are times when rapport with clients is established more quickly by discovering how they think before wondering how they feel. It is also important to realize that behavior incorporates both feelings and thoughts. In order to solve problems and make decisions effectively, clients have to be able to think as well as feel. Responding to cognitive content assists clients in developing and expressing those thought processes involved in problem-solving and decision-making.

Although exploration of feelings is useful to most clients, it is often not sufficient for goal achievement. Once the helping goals have been established, action plans must be developed to produce goal attainment. Responding to cognitive content goes one step further than responding to affect in that it focuses directly on behavior change. On the other hand, responding primarily to cognitive content presents the following limitations:

1. It may reinforce the intellectualization process; that is, it may encourage the client to continue to abstract and deny feelings that are actually influencing his or her behavior.

2. It may not provide the opportunity that the client needs to share and express feelings in a nonjudgmental setting. The helping relationship may be the only one in which a client can feel that his or her emotions (and, consequently, the self) will not be misunderstood.

3. It may continue to repeat a pattern similar to the rules in the client's family of origin in which "feeling talk" is not allowed, encouraged, or explored.

Again, it must be stressed that the initial strategy in the differentiation process is an exploratory one. All clients will respond differently to your emphasis on feelings or on cognitive content. In the next chapter, we discuss client affective messages and possible helping responses to them in the differentiation and selective responding process.

Summary

In this chapter, we have shown that the helper has numerous response choices, and each choice has a corresponding effect on the client's following statement. In this reciprocal arrangement, both the helper and the client influence the path that will occur in the session. Most helpers would acknowledge the importance of the client's choices, which reflect how the client conceptualizes problems and solutions, self and others, success and failure, and responsibility and control. However, they do not always acknowledge that the helper similarly influences the session by choosing to respond to some messages rather than others and by exploring some issues rather than others—in short, by selecting what becomes the focus of the session.

These helper choices are made in rather commonplace ways, including silence, minimal vocal responses, questions, and paraphrases and summarization of content. The highly experienced helper makes these choices almost intuitively; the inexperienced helper must make these choices intentionally. If the inexperienced helper relies on intuition, the possibility of making bad choices is about equal to the possibility of making good choices. But the inexperienced helper who is unaware of and thus is not making intentional choices is very likely to lack a sense of what is happening in the helping process.

We also have indicated throughout this chapter that the effects of your responses will not only affect the focus and direction of each interview but will also vary among clients of various cultural groups. Both the helper's and client's worldview is an important determinant in this process.

Reflective Questions

1. What are some of the conditions that might work against you as you try to recognize the different messages in a client statement?
2. How does a helper shape or influence the topical direction of a session without even being aware that he or she is doing so?
3. Under what helping conditions might you want to have your clients talking about problems, events, situations, or people—as opposed to feelings?

Describe what you believe is your own natural tendency—to focus more on cognitive or on affective messages?

4. With yourself or a partner, reflect on ideas, beliefs, topics, or issues that are uncomfortable for you to discuss. How might this affect the way you respond to clients who present these issues and beliefs?
5. How might your own cultural affiliation and worldview affect what you focus on in a helping session?

My Helping Lab

For the following exercise, log on to MyHelpingLab at http://www.myhelpinglab.com and then click the Topics tab.

Click the Process, Skills, and Techniques tab to locate the Focused and Ongoing Assessment tab. Choose the

Video Lab for the Using Open and Closed-Ended Questions selection. After viewing this video clip, describe what you noticed about the use of both open- and closed-ended questions. How did these questions impact the session that you watched?

Recommended Readings

Cournoyer, B. (2011). *The social work skills workbook, 6th edition.* Belmont, CA: Brooks/Cole, Cengage.

Ivey, A., Ivey, M. B. & Zalaquett, C. (2010). *Intentional interviewing and counseling, 7th edition.* Belmont, CA: Brooks/Cole, Cengage.

Ivey, A. E., D'Andrea, M., Ivey, M. B. & Simek-Morgan, L. (2007). *Theories of counseling and psychotherapy, 7th edition.* Boston: Allyn & Bacon.

Johnson, D. W. (2009). *Reaching out: Interpersonal effectiveness and self actualization, 10th edition.* Upper Saddle River, NJ: Pearson.

Murphy, B. & Dillon, C. (2008). *Interviewing in action, 3rd edition.* Belmont, CA: Brooks/Cole, Cengage.

Responding to Affective Content

What are some of the ways you communicate how you feel? When you are "down in the dumps," how does your voice sound? When you are angry, what is your face like? Your mouth? Your eyes? Your jaws? When you are afraid, what are some of the expressions you use to communicate this feeling? Human beings have many ways of communicating their internal states. The set jaw is often associated with determination. The glaring eyes speak for anger, even in the small child. The trembling voices, the soft voice, the downcast eyes— all have their meanings. Clients use all the verbal and nonverbal modes to tell the helper their concerns. The emotions that accompany the narrative enrich and modify the message. They inform the helper about the events of the client's world and the client's reactions to those events. These cues are not always easy to read and can vary across cultures. Clenched teeth can mean more than one thing. The trembling voice only suggests the presence of an intense emotion. A part of being a helper is putting together the pieces or cues of clients' messages in such a way that you can make reasonably good guesses about the underlying emotion.

As indicated earlier, a client's communication presents alternatives. In addition to alternative cognitive topics, you will find that you are faced with choices between cognitive topics and affective topics. This chapter focuses on the affective message, how to recognize it, and how to reinforce its exploration by clients. To review briefly, client communications that deal primarily with people, events, or objects may be described as cognitive messages. Communications that reflect feelings or emotions may be described as affective messages. Many messages contain both cognitive and affective components. When this occurs, the affective message may not be obvious in the words of the client. Instead, the feelings may be expressed through nonverbal modes, such as vocal pitch, rapidity of speech, body position, and/or gestures.

THE IMPORTANCE OF RESPONDING TO AFFECTIVE CONTENT

Affective content represents feelings or emotions held by clients. Many clients are often either unaware of their feelings or afraid of them. Others—including those who learn to be helpers—do not want to feel feelings because of the rules those individuals have made about feelings. In fact, a major rule in dysfunctional families is "Don't feel"—sometimes made more specific such as "Don't feel angry" or "Don't feel sad." Little boys may hear "Don't feel sad or cry—you'll be a sissy"; little girls may hear "Be nice—be a good girl—don't say anything angry." Often, these rules have the effect of masking or interfering with how people truly feel. Fosha (2000) noted that a good part of the alienation from and fraying of family and social life can be traced to the fear of affect: "People disconnect from their emotional experience, afraid of being overwhelmed, humiliated or revealed as inadequate by the force of feelings, only to pay the price later in depression, isolation, and anxiety" (p. 13).

One of the most important functions in responding to client affect is to give clients permission to feel their feelings—to allow their feelings just to be—rather than stifling, controlling, or holding them back. In fact, persons who have held feelings for a long period of time may tend to hold the feeling in a particular musculature of the body, such as tight shoulders or neck, tense lower back, churning gut, and so on. When clients are given permission to reveal and release feelings, their energy and well-being are also often increased. This occurs because all the deep primary feelings have a survival value (Kelley, 1979). For example, anger allows an individual to protect his or her rights and establish personal boundaries or limits. The capacity to recognize and express anger is the basis for healthy assertiveness. As Kelley (1979) observed, "The person who cannot become angry, whose anger is deeply repressed, is severely handicapped . . . . These persons' assertions lack conviction and they are often at the mercy of or emotionally dependent on those who are capable of becoming angry" (p. 25). Moreover, the expression of anger is useful in close relationships to "clear the air" and prevent chronic boredom and resentment from building up. Anger and disgust that are expressed and released prompt subsequent expression of love; pain and sadness that are expressed promote later expression of joy and pleasure; and fear that is discharged allows for greater trust (Kelley, 1974). Fosha (2000) has elaborated on the healing power of affect: "To live a full and connected life in the face of difficulty and even tragedy requires the capacity to feel and make use of our emotional experience" (p. 13).

When a client's communication contains both cognitive and affective components, whether practitioners acknowledge *first* the affective or cognitive parts of the communication depends to some degree on the client, the presenting issues, and the practitioner's approach. For example, if a given client is in crisis or presents with a brain-based issue—such as substance abuse cravings or thought disorders—focusing on the affective communication may not be useful. If a client presents in "affective overload," such as a client in the grips of a major depression, focusing on the affective messages may make the client feel worse. In these instances, an initial cognitive focus may help to stabilize the client.

The practitioner's theoretical approach also impacts whether the initial and primary focus is on cognitive or affective communication. Cognitive-behavioral practitioners are more likely to focus on cognitive communication than person-centered practitioners. Teyber (2006)—who practices interpersonal therapy—believes that in all the indices a therapist has about how to respond to a client, the most productive response is to respond to the feeling as the client is currently experiencing it. Teyber also noted that another important function of responding to affective content is to help clients experience rather than simply talk about feelings. One way to help clients experience their feelings involves modeling or reflecting the feelings, as we discuss later in this chapter.

VERBAL AND NONVERBAL CUES ASSOCIATED WITH EMOTIONS

You may have wondered how you can identify another person's feelings. Although you cannot feel the client's feelings, you can infer what those feelings are and experience very similar feelings. To some extent, you may even be able to know what it is like to feel a certain way because you too have feelings. Most of the time, however, you will be able to identify the client's feelings by becoming aware of and sensitive to certain *leakage* because they communicate messages the client did not deliberately intend to have communicated (Ekman & Friesen, 1969). Other cues—primarily verbal—are more deliberately intended and are more easily recognized and identified. In the case of affective leakage, it is important to account for the inferences you draw. For example, when you say, "The client seems happy," that is an inference. If you instead say, "The client is smiling, and that may mean that he is happy," then you have accounted for your inference.

The total impact of a client's message includes both verbal and nonverbal elements. The verbal impact means that there are certain nouns, adjectives, adverbs, and verbs that express the client's feelings about something or someone, as shown here:

"I'm really worried about school."

The verbal element associated with the client's feelings in this example is the word *worried*. These kinds of words can be called *affect words*. They express some feeling that the client possesses. If an adverb such as *really* or *very* precedes the affect word, this indicates an even stronger intensity of emotion.

Nonverbal Cues to Affect

Not everything that follows an "I feel" client statement is necessarily an expression of affect. Usually, in one way or another, the body or some part of it is also involved in signaling and expressing affect. In other words, there is a "profoundly physical experience to the emotions (as in 'lump in my throat,' 'heavy heart,' or 'my blood is boiling')" (Fosha, 2000, p. 25). Nonverbal cues can be seen by observing the client's head and facial movement, position of body, quick movements and gestures, and voice quality. Although no single nonverbal cue can be interpreted accurately alone, each does have meaning as part of a larger pattern, or *gestalt*. Thus, there are relationships between nonverbal and verbal aspects of speech. In addition to the relationship between nonverbal and verbal parts of the message, nonverbal cues may also communicate specific information about the relationship of the people involved in the communicative process—in this case, the helper and the client. Nonverbal cues convey information about the nature and intensity of emotions, sometimes more accurately than verbal cues. The nature of the emotion is communicated nonverbally primarily by head cues; the intensity of an emotion is communicated both by head cues and body cues (Ekman & Friesen, 1967).

Close observation of the client's body, nonverbal behavior, and facial expressions in particular can offer important information to the helper about the nature and intensity of blocked feelings as well as feelings that are starting to emerge. For example, one of us recently saw a client who had been coming in weekly for the last few months. On this particular occasion, the helper noted that shortly after the client sat down, her face became contorted. She then began to describe a situation that had recently occurred involving a loss of an important relationship. The helper commented on her facial expression—the tightness of it—and inquired about what she might be holding back. She then immediately cried, and upon release of tears, her face softened and relaxed.

Culture and Nonverbal Affect Cues

It is very important not to assume the meaning of a nonverbal affect cue without checking it out with the client. In part, this is because the meaning may vary among persons and also among cultures. For example, there seem to be differences in cultures between contact and noncontact nonverbal behaviors, such as eye contact, touch, and physical distance between the helper and client (Watson, 1970). The one area of nonverbal expression that does not seem to vary among cultural groups involves facial expressions. The primary or basic emotions of anger, fear, sadness, and happiness do seem to be depicted in the same facial expressions across cultures, although the various norms of each culture may affect how much and how often these emotions are expressed (Mesquita & Frijda, 1992).

It is important for you as a helper to be aware of your own stereotypes and values that may bias your interpretation of nonverbal affect cues, particularly with clients who are from culturally diverse groups. For example, Western white helpers are accustomed to direct eye contact, but for some American Indian clients and for some Asian-American clients, lack of eye contact may be consistent with their cultural norms and values and does not suggest lack of attention or disrespect (Sue & Sue, 2008). Similarly, some African-American clients may also be misperceived on the basis of their nonverbal behavior. Some white mental health practitioners may describe an African-American client as hostile, angry, or resistant—simply because he or she is expressing oneself with nonverbal affect cues with which the white worker is unaccustomed, such as animated vocal expression, closer conversational distance, greater body movements, and prolonged eye contact when talking (Sue & Sue, 2008).

APPLICATION EXERCISE 7.1

Observing Behavior

Select a partner and then interact with him or her for about five minutes. Then, in turn, each of you describes your partner by using this phrase:

"I'm observing that you're ..."

Be sure to describe what you see, not how you think the other person feels or what the nonverbal behavior means.

TYPES OF AFFECTIVE MESSAGES

Although there are many different kinds of feelings, most distinct, universal feelings that are identified by words fit into one of four categories: joy, anger, fear, or sadness. There are now many lists of affect words available, but we continue to use the one that we believe was the original of all such lists (shown on the next few pages).

Positive Affect—Joy

Feelings of joy reflect positive or good feelings about oneself and others and indicate positive feelings about interpersonal relationships. Many of them can be identified by certain affect words. Affect word cues that communicate the general feeling of joy, well-being, affection, or satisfaction may be subclassified into five general areas:

Enjoyment	Competence	Love	Happiness	Hope
beautiful	able	close	cheerful	luck
enjoy	can	friendly	content	optimism
good	fulfill	love	delighted	try
nice	great	like	excited	guess
pretty	wonderful	need	happy	wish
satisfy	smart	care	laugh(ed)	want
terrific	respect	want	thrill	
tremendous	worth	choose	dig	

Source: T. J. Crowley: "The Conditionability of Positive and Negative Self-Reference Emotional Affect Statements in a Counseling-Type Interview." Unpublished doctoral dissertation. Amherst: University of Massachusetts, 1970. Reprinted by permission.

You can continue to add to this list of affect words related to positive affect. Can you begin to get the feeling for the message implicit in the usage of words such as these? Certain nonverbal cues often occur simultaneously with affection word cues. The most obvious of these cues are facial ones. The corners of the mouth may turn up to produce the hint of a smile. The eyes may widen slightly. Facial wrinkles disappear. Often, there is an absence of body tension. The arms and hands may be moved in an open-palm gesture of acceptance or the communicator may reach out and touch the object of the affection message. When the client is describing feelings about an object or event, there may be increased animation of the face and hands.

You might be wondering why we include positive affect, asking yourself, "Don't people who come to see helpers do so because of emotions such as anger, depression, anxiety, and so on?" Yes, that is partly the case. It is also true that intense positive affect can be as difficult as or even more difficult for some clients to own and tolerate than negative or disruptive feelings. Positive affect can make some clients feel "embarrassed, self-conscious, out of control, and vulnerable" (Fosha, 2000, p. 70). Moreover, it is all too easy in the helping process to bypass any positive feelings in the course of the counseling sessions to focus solely on negative or problematic feelings (p. 257). Finally, positive affect is important because clients can feel pride and joy in acknowledging and focusing on their ability to deal with and experience frightening or painful emotions. As Fosha has observed, "Joy, pride, self-confidence, and a new appreciation of one's abilities are some of the affective experiences that follow after the unbearable feelings become bearable" or, stated another way, "Joy can be the other side of fully faced and overcome fear" (p. 165).

Anger

Anger represents an obstruction to be relieved or removed in some way. Different kinds of stimuli often elicit anger, such as frustration, threat, and fear. Conditions such as competition, jealousy, and thwarted aspirations can become threats that elicit angry responses. Anger often represents negative feelings about oneself and/or others. Many times, fear is concealed by an outburst of anger. In such cases, the anger becomes a defensive reaction because the person does not feel safe enough to express fear. Anger is also a cover-up for hurt. Beneath strong aggressive outbursts are often deep feelings of vulnerability and pain. And anger can sometimes be hidden underneath smiles or verbal denials that anything could be wrong, such as an "I'm doing fine, thank you!" Verbal cues that suggest anger may be classified into four general categories:

Attack	Grimness	Defensiveness	Quarrelsomeness
argue	dislike	against	angry
attack	hate	protect	fight
compete	nasty	resent	quarrel
criticize	disgust	guard	argue
fight	surly	prepared	take issue
hit	serious		reject
hurt			disagree
offend			

Source: T. J. Crowley: "The Conditionability of Positive and Negative Self-Reference Emotional Affect Statements in a Counseling-Type Interview." Unpublished doctoral dissertation. Amherst: University of Massachusetts, 1970. Reprinted by permission.

You can continue to add to this list of affect words related to anger. Remember that anger covers a broad group of feelings and can be expressed in many ways. With the expression of anger, the body position may become rigid and tense or it may be characterized by gross changes in body position or movement. Sometimes, anger toward another person or the self may be expressed by hitting, which consists of fault-finding or petty remarks directed at the object of the anger. For example, one partner in couples counseling may express this sort of anger by continual verbal attacks on the other person or by incessant remarks of dissatisfaction with the partner. Hitting can also be expressed through nonverbal cues, such as finger drumming or foot tapping.

Certain vocal qualities can be associated with anger. Many times, the voice will become much louder as the person becomes more rigid in what he or she is saying; if the anger is very intense, the person may even shout. In some instances of intense anger, the feeling may be accompanied by tears. Many times, the expression of anger will cause vocal pitch to become higher. However, with some people, the vocal pitch actually is lowered, becoming more controlled and measured. This often means that the person experiencing the anger is attempting to maintain a level of control over his or her feelings.

Fear

Fear represents a person's reaction to some kind of danger to be avoided. Often, this reaction is a withdrawal from a painful or stressful situation, from oneself, or from other people and relationships. As such, the person experiencing the emotions of fear may also be isolated and sad or depressed. Fear can also be described as a negative set of feelings about something or someone that results in a need to protect oneself. Verbal cues that suggest fear may be classified into four general categories:

Fear	Doubt	Pain	Avoidance
anxious	failure	awful	flee
bothers	flunk	hurts	run from
concerns	undecided	intense	escape
lonely	mediocre	unpleasant	cut out
nervous	moody	uncomfortable	forget
scare	puzzled	aches	
tense	stupid	torn	
upset	unsure		

Source: T. J. Crowley: "The Conditionability of Positive and Negative Self-Reference Emotional Affect Statements in a Counseling-Type Interview." Unpublished doctoral dissertation. Amherst: University of Massachusetts, 1970. Reprinted by permission.

You can continue to add to this list of affect words suggesting fear. Remember that fear encompasses a broad category of feelings and can be expressed in a variety of ways.

Several facial cues are associated with fear. The mouth may hang wide open as in shock; the eyes may also dilate. Fear may cause a furrow to appear between the eyebrows. Fear of the helper or of the topic at hand may be reflected by the client's avoidance of direct eye contact; remember, however, that the meaning and use of eye contact varies among cultures.

Body positions and movements also are associated with the expression of fear. At first, the person experiencing fear may appear to be still in body position or may draw back. However, after this initial period, body movements usually become greater as anxiety increases, resulting in jerky and trembling motions. Although parts of the body may shake, the hands are often tightly clasped, as if giving protection. Tension also may be indicated through actions such as leg swinging, foot tapping, finger tapping, or playing with a ring or another piece of jewelry.

Voice qualities are also indicators of the level of anxiety the client is experiencing. As the level of anxiety increases, the breathing rate becomes faster and breathing becomes more shallow. As anxiety and tension increase, the number of speech disturbances increases. This yields a greater number of cues, such as errors, repetitions, and omissions of parts of words or sentences. The rate of speech also increases as anxiety mounts.

Sadness

Some of the more common conditions expressed by clients are feelings of sadness, loneliness, or depression. These emotions may be a response to a variety of client conditions, including unsatisfying personal relationships, environmental conditions such as disempowerment and oppression, physiological imbalances, or even poor nutrition. Sometimes, sadness can be a response to the helper's compassion and empathy. Having the helper's care and understanding can make the client more aware of not having it or not having had it in other life situations or with other people (Fosha, 2000, p. 227). Verbal cues that suggest sadness, loneliness, or depression include the

Sadness	Loneliness	Depression
unhappy	alone	depressing
adrift	abandoned	depressed
sorrowful	isolated	disillusioned
distressed	missing	weary
grieved	missed	listless
heartsick		discouraged
		despondent
		gloomy

Source: T. J. Crowley: "The Conditionability of Positive and Negative Self-Reference Emotional Affect Statements in a Counseling-Type Interview." Unpublished doctoral dissertation. Amherst: University of Massachusetts, 1970. Reprinted by permission.

following:
The intonation of a depressed person is also a departure from the normal intonation. The voice quality may become more subdued with less inflection, so the voice takes on more of a monotonic quality.

It is important to recognize that sadness has different meanings among cultures. In fact, in some societies, depression is not even recognized as an illness or a sign of something being wrong but rather an indication of spiritual insight (Castillo, 1997). In another example, O'Neill (1993) found that among Native Americans living on reservations, sadness had positive connotations because "it signified maturity and recognition of the tremendous loss they experienced through domination by Anglo American society" (Castillo, 1997, p. 208). Grief is also a phenomenon that is embedded in sociocultural contexts. For example, in Greece, a widow grieves for five years after her partner's death (Kramer, 1993). Moreover, while sadness in Western society is often characterized by a cognitive feature such as self-talk, in many non-Western societies, it is represented more by somatic symptoms (Castillo, 1997).

AFFECTIVE COMPETENCE

It is too simplistic to say that the helper communicates understanding of client feelings through attitudes such as empathy and positive regard. Although empathy and positive regard are necessary conditions in the helping relationship, the means for communicating these conditions also must be identified. Two primary reasons why the helper may not respond to client feelings are (1) the helper does not know appropriate ways of responding and/or (2) the helper "blocks" upon recognizing the client's feelings. Knowing how to respond to client feelings with empathy and positive regard takes more than the possession of these attitudes. The helper must make sure that these attitudes are communicated through words, statements, and timing that convey affective competence to clients. *Affective competence* means the helper is able to

APPLICATION EXERCISE 7.2

Identifying Affect Cues

To give you practice in identifying nonverbal and verbal affect cues, complete the following exercises:

A. Identifying Nonverbal Affect Cues

Select a partner. One of you will be the speaker; the other will be the respondent. The speaker should select a feeling from the following list. (Note how any cultural affiliations affect this process.)

- Contentment or happiness
- Puzzlement or confusion
- Anger
- Discouragement
- Disgust
- Worry or anxiety
- Embarrassment and self-consciousness
- Excited or thrilled

Do not tell the respondent which feeling you have selected. Portray the feeling through nonverbal expressions only. The respondent must accurately identify the behaviors you use to communicate the feeling and should infer the feeling you are portraying. After he or she has done so, choose another and then repeat the process. When you have portrayed each feeling, reverse roles and then repeat the exercise.

An alternative way to do this is in two small groups or teams. Each team picks one emotion to act out, and the other team has to guess what it is just from the nonverbal affect cues. If the other team guesses correctly, they get one point. If they do not, the first team can continue to try to act it out or they can pick another emotion to act out. As soon as the second team guesses the emotion accurately, it will be their turn, and they can pick an emotion to act out. If it is identified accurately by the other team, that team then gets one point. Try to continue until both teams have acted out all the different emotions on the list. Afterward, you can process this activity with the following sorts of questions:

1. Which feelings were easiest to act out? Easiest to identify?
2. Which feelings were hardest to act out? Hardest to identify?
3. What have you taken away with you from this activity about nonverbal affect cues?

B. Linking Body Cues and Emotions

Many emotions are expressed graphically by descriptions about the body. Smith (1985) has provided an excellent list of some of these. We have adapted his exercise, which is to enact each of them with your own body and note the feelings and body sensations that accompany each enactment.

- He holds his head high.
- She has a tight jaw.
- He turns away.
- She has shifty eyes.
- He sticks his chest out.
- Her shoulders are stooped.
- He stoops low.
- She sits tall and straight. (pp. 60–61)

C. Identifying Verbal Affect Cues

The speaker should select a feeling from the following list:

- Surprise
- Elation or thrill
- Anxiety or tension
- Sadness or depression
- Seriousness or intensity
- Irritation or anger

Do not inform the respondent which feeling you have selected. Verbally express the feeling in one or two sentences. Be certain to include the word itself. The respondent should accurately identify the feeling in two ways:

1. Restate the feeling by using the same affect word as the speaker.
2. Restate the feeling by using a different affect word but one that reflects the same feeling.

Here is an example:

SPEAKER: I feel good about being here.
RESPONDENT: You feel good?

or

RESPONDENT: You're glad to be here.

Choose another feeling and then complete the same process. When you have expressed each feeling, reverse roles and then repeat the exercise.

D. Identifying Affective Components

Read the following client statements taken from actual interview typescripts, and identify the affective component(s) in each statement by writing first-person sentences and by underlining the affect word of each client's communication. Here is an example:

CLIENT: I'm not the type that would like to do research or, uh, things that don't have any contact directly with people. I like to be with people, you know—I feel at home and secure with people.

In this statement, the affect word like is identified, and the following affective components are identified by written sentences by using the first person:

1. I enjoy being with people.
2. People help me feel secure.

If there is more than one affective component within a given client communication, place an asterisk (*) next to the one that you feel has the greatest bearing on the client's concern. In the preceding example, asterisk either 1 or 2 depending on which has the greater bearing in your opinion.

Client Statements

1. "Well, uh, I'm happy just being with people and having them know me."
2. "And, and, uh, you know, they always say that you know some people don't like to be called by a number; well, I don't either."
3. "In speech, I'm, uh, well, in speech, I'm not doing good because I'm afraid to talk in front of a bunch of people."
4. "I can't afford to lose my place on the honor roll and bring shame to my family."

simultaneously both feel personal feelings and deal with client feelings while still providing safety in the counseling relationship (Fosha, 2000, p. 42). Stated another way, it means that the helper is not so overwhelmed by personal or client emotions that he or she is immobilized and does not know what to do. It also means that the helper does not shut down feelings—whether personal or the client's—in order to proceed in the session, to cope with a difficult situation, or to run the session on "automatic pilot." As Fosha (2000) states, the simple definition of affective competence is to be able to both *feel and deal* while also providing a safe relationship for the client.

Teyber (2006) has observed how important it is for clients to receive from helpers a more satisfying response to their feelings than they have gotten from other persons in the past. In order to do so, when working with affective content from clients, helpers must be able to provide a safe and supportive atmosphere—often referred to as *a holding environment*. A holding environment simply means that the helper is able to allow and stay with or "hold" the client's feelings instead of moving away or distancing from the feelings or the client. In doing this, the helper acts as a container; that is, the helper's comfort in exploring and allowing the emergence of client feelings provides the support to help the client contain or hold various feelings that are often viewed by the client as unsafe.

This holding environment is usually dramatically different from what either the young client is experiencing or what an adult client experienced while growing up. If the child was sad or hurt, the parent often responded by withdrawing from the child, shaming the child for feeling that way, or denying the child's feelings (Teyber, 2006). In all these parental reactions, the child's feelings were not heard, validated, or "contained"; as a result, the child learned, over time, to deny or avoid these feelings or, even worse, to regard his or her feelings as bad and "deserving of shame, guilt, and punishment" (Fosha, 2000, p. 79). Children are developmentally unable to experience and manage feelings on their own without the presence of another person who can be emotionally present for them and receive and even welcome their feelings. If the parent was unable to help the child "hold" feelings in this manner, it will be up to the helper to do so. Helpers do this by verbal responses that convey understanding of the client's feelings and by nonverbal responses that convey support and compassion. In this way, the helper allows clients to know that he or she is not overwhelmed or threatened by their feelings, is not judgmental or rejecting of them, does not need to move away from them in any way, and is still fully committed to the relationship (Teyber, 2006). This corrective or reparative emotional experience helps clients to own their feelings so they do not have to deny them or push them aside. It also helps clients to tolerate and regulate their emotions without being overwhelmed by them.

Blocking refers to the helper's reaction to client feelings in ways that reduce or restrict his or her helpfulness. For example, the helper may accurately identify the client's feelings of anger but avoid responding to these feelings for several reasons. The helper might be afraid that the client will leave if the interaction gets too intense; the helper might not trust his or her own judgment and be afraid of turning the client off with an inaccurate response; the helper might fear that acknowledging the feeling would produce a flood of more intense feelings in the client that would be difficult to handle; or the helper might have similar feelings that might be aroused. Client feelings related to sex, self-worth, and achievement are also potential blocks.

As mentioned earlier, the primary problem with blocking is that the helper does not respond to the client's feelings in a more helpful way than the client received in the past. Blocking by the helper repeats the same aloneness that clients had to endure with their feelings as a child. As Fosha (2000, p. 83) noted, aloneness and loneliness—frightening and painful in and of themselves—only strengthen the painful experiencing of anything else a client may be going through or witnessing. Teyber (2006) has listed a variety of ways in which helpers may block dealing with client affect appropriately:

- Become anxious and change the topic.
- Fall silent and emotionally withdraw.
- Become directive and tell the client what to do.
- Interpret what the feelings mean and intellectually distance themselves.
- Self-disclose or move into their own feelings.
- Reassure and explain that everything will be all right.
- Diminish the client by trying to rescue him or her.
- Become overidentified with the client and insist that the client make some decision or take some action to manage the feelings. (p. 184)

When you find yourself responding in one of these ways, note what is happening to you and how you are feeling. This can be a useful topic to talk over with your supervisor (see also Chapter 10).

VERBAL RESPONSES TO AFFECTIVE MESSAGES

It is possible to identify certain helper responses that will assist you in discriminating among affective messages and communicating your understanding of the client's feelings at the same time. Two such responses are *reflection of feelings* and *summarization of feelings*. The most effective verbal responses to client affect messages are those that reflect the client's feelings and experiences in a spirit of empathy, compassion, authenticity, and helpfulness. This does not mean helpers will always be able to be perfectly empathic or make perfect reflective responses. However, it does mean that clients will know they exist not only in the "mind" of the helper but also in the "heart" of the helper (Fosha, 2000, p. 58).

Reflection of Feelings

The reflection of feelings response is distinctly different from the paraphrase response, but the two are often confused. As indicated earlier, a paraphrase is a rephrasing of all or a portion of the cognitive content in a client's response, whereas a *reflection* is a rephrasing of the affective portion. When the client's response contains both cognitive and affective components, the helper must differentiate between the two in order to reflect the affective content.

Reflection of feelings accomplishes precisely what its name indicates: a mirroring of the feeling or emotion present in the client's message. This response helps clients to own and express feelings. The value in this is helping clients to recognize their feelings and to accept those feelings rather than fear them. Initially, clients may defend against feelings because they seem dangerous. People who feel sad may do everything in their power to avoid feeling sad or blue. Ultimately, the client needs to learn to trust his or her feelings; it is the experiencing and expressing the sadness rather than the blocking or numbing out of it that is healing (Brammer, Abrego & Shostrom, 1993).

The reflection of feelings response can occur at different levels. At the most obvious level, the helper may reflect only the surface feeling of the client. At a deeper level, the helper may reflect an implied feeling with greater intensity than that originally expressed by the client. The more obvious level occurs when the helper reflects an affect message that is overtly present in the client's message by using a different affect word but one that captures the same feeling and intensity expressed by the client, as in the following example:

CLIENT: I feel really mad that you interrupted me.

HELPER: You're very angry about being interrupted.

The second kind of reflection occurs at a deeper level. This one mirrors an affect message that is only covertly expressed or implied in the client's message. For example, consider the implied affect message in "I think we have a really neat relationship." The feeling inherent in the words refers to a positive affect message of like, enjoys, pleased, and so forth. Thus, a reflection that picks up on the implied feeling in this communication might be among the following:

- "Our relationship is important to you."
- "Some good things are in it for you."
- "You're pleased with the relationship."

This reflection that occurs at a deeper level not only mirrors the covert feeling but also must at least match the intensity of the client's feeling and perhaps even reflect greater intensity of feeling. Furthermore, the most effective reflection is one that emphasizes what it is the client anticipates—in other words, one that acknowledges the implied admission of the client's message. Consider this sort of reflection in the following example. Note that the helper reflects back the covertly implied feeling with a greater intensity of affect and acknowledges the implied admission—that is, what the client would like to do or feel, as shown here:

CLIENT: I feel like I have to be so responsible all the time.

HELPER: Sometimes, you'd feel relieved just to forget all that responsibility— to say 'to hell with it'—and really let go.

Although empathy and understanding of feelings are not themselves panaceas, they do serve some useful functions in the helping process. For one thing, empathy enhances emotional proximity, creating an atmosphere of closeness and generating warmth. Also, empathy contributes to a sense of self-acceptance. When one person feels really understood by another, there is often a feeling of relief—"Gee, I'm not so confused and/or mixed up after all"—and a sense of acceptance about oneself—"This other person has understood me without condemning the way I think or feel."

Summarization of Feelings

Summarization of feelings is very similar to reflection of feelings in that it is a response that discriminates between different affective components of the client's communication and communicates understanding of the client's feelings by the helper. The basic difference in the two responses is one of number, or quantity. The reflection of feelings responds to only one portion of the client's communication, whereas the summarization of feelings is an integration of several affective components of the client's communication. Thus, summarization of feelings is really an extension of reflection of feelings. In this response, the helper is attending to a broader class of client responses and must have the skill to bring together seemingly diverse elements into a meaningful gestalt (Ivey et al., 2007). Like the reflection of feelings, summarization of feelings involves reflecting the feelings of the client in your own words. Again, this encompasses not just one feeling but a bringing together of several feelings into a significant pattern.

Although there are some instances in which clients present one predominant feeling, there are other instances in which clients have several feelings going on at the same time. Teyber (2006) noted that two common affective constructions with mixed components include anger-sadness-shame and sadness-anger-guilt. In the first sequence, the primary feeling is often anger, but it is a negative response to hurt or sadness. Often, the experiencing of the anger and sadness provokes shame. In the second sequence, the predominant feeling is sadness, but it is often connected to anger that has been denied because the expression of it produces guilt. These affective sequences are typically acquired in childhood and are a result of both family of origin rules and culture.

The summarization of feelings response can identify the various affective states the client describes or experiences. Consider the following examples:

CLIENT: I'm so pissed off at my mother and my wife. They're always on my back, telling me what to do, where to go, how to think—planning my whole life for me. It's been this way for years. I wish I could do something different, but I just feel hopeless about it. I wish for once I could be a man and stand up to them, but I just keep giving in and giving in.

HELPER: You seem to be feeling several things in this situation: First, you're obviously angry about their behavior. Also, you feel sad and perhaps ashamed about your powerlessness to effect any change—is that accurate?

CLIENT: I'm really feeling down and out about my job. It's so hard to find the energy to keep going in day after day. I don't really mind the work, but over the years, the people there have been so nasty that I don't want to be around them. I know if I weren't the nice person that I am I would probably really tell them a thing or two.

HELPER: You're feeling discouraged about your job. It also sounds like you're feeling pretty angry and fed up with your coworkers, but because of your own niceness, you feel a little guilty or reluctant to express your irritation with them.

Summarization of feelings is often used instead of reflection of feelings when a client's communication contains many different affective elements rather than just one or two. It can also be used effectively when the interview appears to be bogged down. For example, when one topic has been covered repeatedly or when a dead silence occurs during an interview, summarization can increase the interview pace. By tying together various feelings, summarization can identify a central theme. It also provides direction for the interview and may thus furnish the needed initiative to get the interview going again.

APPLICATION EXERCISE 7.3

Responses to Affective Components

A. Responses to Client Statements

For the following helper-client interactions, please observe the following directions:

1. Read each interaction carefully.
2. For each client statement, identify—by writing sentences—the various affective components of the communication.
3. For each client statement, write your own response to the affective portion(s). Use both a reflection of feelings and a summarization of feelings for each client statement.

> CLIENT: Uh, I'm unsure why I'm having such a hard time letting my family and friends know I'm gay. I mean, I watch TV now, and I see a whole sort of cultural revolution going on there. But when it comes to me, I feel very hesitant.

Affective components: _____

Reflection of feelings: _____

_____

Summarization of feelings: _____

_____

> CLIENT: My daddy won't want to meet you because you're black and I'm half black. And he treats my mom and me like dirt. And he thinks only white people deserve to be treated well. I just wish I had a dad who was good to me and my mom. I miss that.

Affective components: _____

Reflection of feelings: _____

_____

Summarization of feelings: _____

_____

B. Observed Practice

Complete the following exercise with two other people:

1. One of you—designated as the speaker—should share a personal concern with the respondent.
2. The respondent's task is to respond only to affective topics by using only the two responses covered in the chapter: reflection of feelings and summarization of feelings.
3. The observer will use the Observer Rating Chart (Figure 7.1) to keep track of the number and kinds of responses used by the listener. This feedback should then be given to the listener.
4. After interacting for approximately ten minutes, reverse the roles.

Helper	Type of Helper Response	
Response	*Reflection of Feelings*	*Summarization of Feelings*
1.		
2.		
3.		
4.		
5.		
6.		
7.		
8.		
9.		
10.		
11.		
12.		
13.		
14.		
15.		
16.		
17.		
18.		
19.		
20.		

FIGURE 7.1 Observer Rating Chart

In using both the reflection of feelings and the summarization of feelings responses, be careful to heed our earlier caution about the potential effectiveness of these two responses depending especially on the race, gender, and ethnicity of clients, particularly in initial sessions. Ivey, Gluckstern, and Ivey (1993) noted:

In White, North American and other cultures, men are expected to hold back their feelings. You aren't a "real man" if you allow yourself to feel emotion. While many men can and do express their feelings in the helping interview, some should not be pushed too hard in this area in the first phases of counseling. Later, with trust, exploration of feelings becomes more acceptable.

In general, women in all cultures are more in touch with and more willing to share feelings than men. Nonetheless, this will vary with the cultural group. Some cultures (for example, Asian, Native Americans) at times pride themselves on their ability to control emotions. However, this may also be true with those of British and Irish extraction.

African Americans and other minorities have learned over time that it may not be safe to share themselves openly with White Americans. In cross-cultural counseling situations, trust needs to be built before you can expect in-depth discussion of emotions. (pp. 73–74)

EFFECTS OF RESPONDING TO AFFECTIVE CONTENT

The importance of responding to client feelings as an anxiety-reduction tool has already been mentioned. Generally speaking, responding to affect diminishes the intensity of feelings. For example, responding to (accepting) strong feelings of anger expressed by the client will reduce the intensity of the feelings and assist the client in gaining control of them so the client is not overwhelmed by feelings. The expression of feelings may be an important goal for some clients. Some people have had so few opportunities to openly express their feelings that to find an acceptant listener provides highly beneficial relief.

Responding to affect with acceptance and understanding can also assist clients in incorporating personal feelings and perceptions into their self-image. In other words, the helper's acceptance of feelings that have been previously denied and labeled as "bad" by the clients suggests that they may have mislabeled these feelings and thus themselves. In this way, helpers model affective competence for clients. They help clients learn how to manage their feelings instead of denying them or shutting down and not functioning.

Finally, responding to affect is often the best way to communicate your warmth and involvement with clients. That is, responding to client feelings establishes a high level of trust between you and your clients. It is precisely this kind of trust that enables clients to own their feelings, behaviors, and commitment to behavior change. Fosha (2000) described this process in a very clear way:

> Why is it more effective to say something to somebody than merely to think it and feel it, even if the other does little more than listen? Why should it make such an enormous difference to communicate something to another person? In expression—and reception by the other—the full cycle of processing core affect is complete . . . . The difference between aloneness and the sense of being integrated in the mainstream of mutuality—community—is created by the act of affective communication with one other person, who is open and interested. (p. 28)

Although responding to affect early in the helping process can be the best strategy for reducing client anxiety, with some clients, your response to their affect message may only induce greater anxiety. With this kind of client, you will have to modify the strategy and respond to cognitive topics in order to find out how the client thinks and what kind of ideas he or she has. Helpers who always emphasize feelings to the exclusion of cognitive content impose certain limitations on the helping process. Some of the limitations of responding only to feelings include the following:

1. Responding only to feelings is unrealistic and therefore reduces the client's ability to generalize aspects of the helping relationship to other relationships. For most clients, it is highly unlikely that any of their friends or family would take only their feelings into account.

2. Responding only to feelings fosters an internal focus to the exclusion of the world around the client. Clients may become so preoccupied with themselves that the level of their other relationships deteriorates even more. Also, responding to an internal focus reflects a European-American worldview that will not be compatible with the worldview of some clients from other cultural groups.

3. Responding to affect induces catharsis—the ventilation of pent-up feelings and concerns. For some clients, this may be all that is necessary. For other clients, this is not a sufficient goal. With catharsis, there is a greater possibility of reinforcing "victim mythology"; that is, the helper's responses to feelings may only generate more client negative self-referent statements.

In this chapter, we discussed the process by which the helper makes discriminations or differentiations—sometimes subtle ones—that affect the outcome of a session. Choosing to respond to the cognitive dimension of a client's problems leads the session in one direction. Choosing instead to respond to the affective dimension leads in a quite different direction. The cultural affiliations of both helper and client help to shape this process.

Summary

The expression and development of affect is naturally assumed to be part of the process of helping. However, this does not mean that the beginning helper will be either comfortable with or sensitive to affective messages. Nor are clients always comfortable with affective messages and experiences either. Sometimes, affect is implicitly expressed in the client's communication. At other times, one type of affect masks a different and perhaps more significant affect, such as anger masking fear. When these conditions exist, it is easy to miss the affective message. When client affective messages are missed, clients may feel as though the helper has blocked their emotional experience in the same way a caregiver did. Helpers need to be attuned not only to client affect but also to ways in which their own experience makes them more likely to block the expression of affect by clients.

In this chapter, we introduced verbal and nonverbal cues that suggest the presence of affect, the nature of affect, and how to respond selectively to affect. We also emphasized that the meaning of affect cues varies among clients and cultures. The development of these helping responses is closely related to the client's perception of helper empathy. In other words, as you become more accomplished at recognizing affect accurately and responding to it, your behavior will be perceived as increasingly empathic. According to Fosha (2000, p. 58), clients experience the helper's empathy when they know they exist not only in the mind of the helper but also in the helper's heart. Reflecting and summarizing client feelings are two particularly helpful counseling responses in communicating your understanding to clients and in promoting affective competence in clients. This is not to suggest that you would want to respond to every perceived feeling. In Chapters 6 and 7, we considered the process of selective responding to cognitive or affective messages and the effect of your choices on the progress of the interview.

Once your exploratory objective has been achieved and you have chosen when to emphasize affective content and when to emphasize cognitive content, it is time to develop and implement strategies for each of these areas. There are some strategies that are more productive in working with affective material. Other strategies are best implemented when the focus is on behavior and cognitions rather than feelings. These strategies are presented in the following chapters.

Reflective Questions

1. When a client's message contains both cognitive and affective components, what conditions might lead you to respond to the affective element? How might this be influenced by the client's culture?

2. If you were a client, would you prefer a helper whose natural inclinations were toward feelings or toward rational thinking? What would be the advantages for you if you had the helper you preferred? What would be the disadvantages for you with such a helper?

3. Often, clients are less aware of their feelings than of their thoughts. How might you assist clients to become more aware of their feelings by the way you choose to respond?

4. One of the things we discussed in this chapter is the issue of helper blocks—that is, ways in which a helper may deliberately or inadvertently avoid responding to client affect. Considering the primary emotions of anger, fear, sadness, and happiness, what affect area do you think you would be most likely to block? How does your history contribute to this?

My Helping Lab

For each exercise, log on to MyHelpingLab at http://www.myhelpinglab.com and then click the Topics tab.

1. Click the Process, Skills, and Techniques tab to locate the Establishing the Therapeutic Relationship tab. Choose the Video Lab for the Challenging Clients to Think about Feelings selection. After watching these clips, describe how the helper, Dr. Hardy, reflected the client's feelings of hurt and disappointment and what effect this had on the progression of the helping session.

2. Click the Theories tab and then click the Multimodal tab. Choose the Video Lab for the Exploring Feelings and Themes with Clients selection. Could you identify Dr Lazarus's use of summarization of feelings response with this client? What functions did this response serve in this helping session?

Recommended Readings

Fosha, D. (2000). *The transforming power of affect.* New York: Basic Books.

Knapp, M. L. & Hall, J. (2010). *Nonverbal communication in human interaction, 7th edition.* Belmont, CA: Wadsworth.

Mesquita, B. & Frijda, N. (1992). Cultural variations in emotions: A review. *Psychological Bulletin, 112,* 179–204.

Smith, E. (1985). *The body in psychotherapy.* Jefferson, NC: McFarland.

Teyber, E. (2006). *Interpersonal process in psychotherapy, 5th edition.* Belmont, CA: Wadsworth.

Conceptualizing Issues and Setting Goals

It is appropriate now to consider some of the larger issues of counseling—namely, the nature of client concerns and the establishment of goals that are realistic antecedents to the solution of those concerns. There are philosophical questions that underlie these issues because there is no one way of conceptualizing human problems. We will not be able to resolve the philosophical problems for you. In fact, it may require the greater part of your career to do that. But we will present a viewpoint that represents our stand at this time. We find it useful because it focuses not only on our clients but also on the world that they return to after each helping session—a world in which the problems are real.

THE CLIENT'S WORLD

What brings clients to counseling? The answer to this—more than any other question—will reveal your role as helper. It is a disarmingly simple question but not one to be taken lightly. We begin with this response: Clients enter counseling when they experience issues and needs that they alone are unable to understand or to meet or when their particular coping strategies to meet needs or resolve issues no longer work.

All human beings share certain basic needs. These include the need for security, nourishment, survival, affiliation, love, and self-esteem. In a classic article, Jourard (1963, pp. 33–38) has conceptualized these needs in a way that is useful for counseling. They include the following:

1. *Survival needs:* All people are concerned with self-preservation and safety. This includes psychological safety as well as physical safety. Although people may not always recognize threats to their psychological safety, they do recognize their responses to those threats—namely, increased anxiety, inaccurate or restricted perceptions of the world, and increasingly inappropriate behavior.

2. *Physical needs:* These include the needs for nourishment, shelter, income, freedom from pain, rest, and replenishment of energy. When these needs go unmet or become distorted (e.g., overeating or migraine headaches), people's responses may inhibit the satisfaction of still other needs (e.g., the migraine sufferer finds it difficult to achieve love and sex needs). As another example, clients whose physical needs are eliminated as a result of a natural or manmade disaster are necessarily so focused on survival and basic physical needs that higher level needs—such as attachment, ambition, mental health, freedom and so on—are overtaken by this basic, almost instinctual preoccupation with safety and survival.

3. *Love and sex needs:* These are the needs to become involved in a close personal way with another human being. People grow in their development of these needs and often recognize their intensity only when they have suddenly experienced the loss of a close personal relationship. When these needs are unmet, people question their potential to love and to be loved, to be in an extended relationship, or to be able to give to or take from another person. When such loss occurs, it is not hard to understand why grief theorists discuss loss as rejection.

4. *Status, success, and self-esteem needs:* These are the needs that motivate people to achieve in the eyes of their peers and to gain respect, confidence, or admiration. When these needs are unmet, people lack self-respect and self-confidence or overreact with excessive and manufactured self-respect and self-confidence.

5. *Mental health needs:* When these needs are met, people feel like functional human beings. When they are unmet, people are incongruent, disillusioned, disoriented, and vulnerable to despair.

6. *Freedom needs:* These are the needs to feel autonomous, free to make personal choices, or free not to choose. When these needs go unmet, people feel restricted, undervalued, or unappreciated.

7. *Challenge needs:* These are the needs for activity, future orientation, and opportunity. When they are missing, people are vulnerable to boredom, meaninglessness, or emptiness.

8. *Cognitive-clarity needs:* These needs reflect the drive to resolve the conflicts in values, ideas, and commitments that exist in people's lives and the need to live one's life with honor and integrity.

Perhaps you would add to or take away from this list, according to your view of human experience. However, the point is that all human beings experience needs as a part of living. To experience a need does not set a person apart as unusual, inadequate, or in some other way lacking. On the other hand, human beings are not always adept at recognizing (comprehending) experienced needs nor do they necessarily possess the skills required to meet needs once the needs are recognized. To recognize and meet one's needs is not necessarily a natural part of the process of living; it must be learned.

The place where people learn or do not learn what their needs are and how to get them met is in their family of origin. This is where needs are either affirmed and met or shamed and rejected. Teyber (2006) noted:

> Many enduring psychological problems begin when basic childhood developmental needs are not met . . . and once the need gets consistently or repetitively blocked, the child in growing up will either block the need in the same way his or her environment blocked it to avoid reexperiencing the need or will to try to rise above the need to have it met indirectly or to partially gratify it by a particular style of coping. . . .

> Children's unmet childhood needs do not dissipate or go away as they grow up. The need may be repressed or defended against, but it continues to seek expression. As a result, clients do not give up trying to have the need met. At the same time, the unmet need remains too anxiety-arousing to be expressed directly. So clients try to rise above the unmet need and indirectly, fulfill it by adopting . . . a particular interpersonal coping style. (pp. 246–249)

For example, an adult client whose early needs for affection were shamed may block current needs for affection and claim, "I don't need anybody's love. I can make it on my own." Yet, at some level, the unmet need for affection will still try to seek expression, and when it does, the client will try to cope with it in a particular way but usually in an unsatisfying or troublesome way. In addition to this intrapsychic view of needs, we also need to recognize the role of external stressors and environmental events in creating needs. For example, clients also experience needs in terms of current life events and may enter therapy when various life stressors or developmental issues become too hard to handle. For example, consider an adult woman who is coping well with her partnered relationship and her job. But as her aging father unexpectedly develops Alzheimer's disease, her world starts to fall apart, and she experiences needs now that were either not there or not apparent to her before this event.

Current life events and environmental stressors are particularly important in shaping needs of clients who feel marginalized because of race, gender, sexual orientation, religion, health/disability status, ethnicity, or socioeconomic status and who experience the effects of stereotyping, discrimination, and oppression on a frequent and repetitive basis. In these situations, emotional distress resulting from current needs is often more the result of a lack of both real and perceived power in a client's everyday, current life rather than unmet developmental childhood needs (Brown & Ballou, 1992). For example, consider the situation of a financially challenged Latina woman who is raising her three children single-handedly. She has no living parents to help her in child-rearing, and her two brothers were shot and killed in an urban gang fight. She has a part-time job with no benefits and is in danger of losing it because she has needed to take days off to care for her sick children. Furthermore, in riding the subway to her place of work, she is met with racial taunts. Clearly, the context of her current world is a major factor in her presenting needs.

Thus far, we have drawn a picture of the client as a person who is (1) continually experiencing issues and needs, (2) not always understanding or even recognizing some of those issues and needs, and (3) seeking your assistance when unrecognized and/or unmet issues and needs become the bigger issue of living. Although this may be an adequate description of the person entering counseling, it fails to embrace the total situation of the client. Any description of clients must also include the world in which they live, including significant others, employment or the setting in which they spend the major portion of the day, expectations for self and others, habits and routines, dreams and fantasies of the future, attitudes toward the past, values and the meanings of life, and methods developed for survival (survival of responsibilities, tensions, disappointments, expectations of others, dashed hopes, etc.). You might wish to refer to our discussion of the initial interview in Chapter 5 for a review of all of these components, as conceptualizing client issues begins in the initial session. In addition to this review, consider the following issue-oriented questions posed by Sperry, Carlson, and Kjos (2003):

- What concerns brought you here?
- Why now?
- How has this been affecting your daily functioning? (p. 67)

Sometimes, clarity about these questions and the client's real presenting issues does not come quickly or easily. For example, a young man comes into the helper, and at the end of the session, it is still unclear what led him to seek the services of a helper, although he is speaking generally about his family stress. In fact, not until the third session does the client allude to his sexual orientation. Finally, by session five, he discloses that he is bisexual and has been thrown out of his house by his parents, who have told him they never want to see him again. He now has to support himself financially but is not really prepared to do so yet. As a result, he has been living for the last six weeks in his car, unaware of any community resources that may be available to him. In addition, he is starting to feel tremendous guilt about his bisexuality because of his parental reaction and his religious upbringing. In this case, it has taken about six weeks for the client to feel safe enough with the helper to get to the heart of what is really bothering and troubling him.

THE ROLE OF THE HELPER IN ASSESSING CLIENT CONCERNS

Based on what we have said about the client who is entering counseling, it follows that you would have some fairly clear responsibilities. These responsibilities are above and beyond creating a favorable climate for counseling—even beyond being a good and caring listener. It is your role to hear the issues as clients describe their concerns and to also help them hear those needs and issues, recognizing from our earlier example that such clarity may be ambiguous at first. Next, it is your role to help clients formulate goals that will help meet the needs or resolve the issues. From these goals, plans of action may be constructed, implemented, and evaluated. Finally, you must help clients recognize that they are making progress. When clients have lived with problems too long or they seem too overwhelming to clients, it is difficult to trust any progress.

The helping process may often be viewed as an unfolding process in which the outer, more obvious issues precede the more subtle, less obvious concerns. As an example, consider an Asian-American man who comes to counseling with an obvious dilemma: He cannot fall asleep at night. He has a physical need to sleep. After the insomnia problem has been addressed and the goals and strategies have been formulated to help with this, focus is then directed toward those pressures that led to the insomnia in the first place. This could be the result of old wounds or unmet needs that have become recently reactivated as well as cultural and environmental factors that are overlaid on top of these. For example, this client reports that he recently lost his job as a result of layoffs; he now feels lacking in self-respect and self-confidence and may have esteem needs, wanting to be respected, valued, and appreciated by himself and by others. He does not want to "lose face" among his family and culture. These may be carryover needs from family and culture that are now being felt again because of a major loss. He also faces survival needs related to loss of income in his current life.

As you attempt to conceptualize or understand client issues, it is important that you keep in mind that client issues and needs are complex and multidimensional, consisting of multiple elements. In other words, it is the exception rather than the rule for a client to come in and say, "I'm just having one problem with my best friend. That's it." And even in the case of children, an issue with a best friend usually has many more layers than what appears at first. The child may be angry with the friend or may feel betrayed by the friend. The child may have concluded that he or she is unlikable. The child may be acting in ways that put barriers between the friendship. The child may have a learning disability that contributes to misperceptions about or miscommunications with the friend or to troubles in the classroom. Or the child may be reacting to a breach in the friendship as a result of something that happened at home, school, or in the larger community or cultural network.

These multiple dimensions of client issues involve the following six:

1. *Contextual factors:* Time, place, concurrent events, and cultural and sociopolitical issues
2. *Beliefs:* The client may already have beliefs that contribute to the problem, impede the solution, or become the problem.
3. *Feelings*: The emotional responses to the problem that often exaggerate the problem, impede the comprehension of the problem, or become the problem
4. *Behavior:* The habits and routines that are inappropriate responses and perhaps contributors to the problem
5. *Interactional and relational patterns:* Those established ways of reacting to familiar others, including the miscommunication channels, expectations, self-fulfilling prophesies, coping styles, and so on
6. *Language patterns:* The narratives and stories the client constructs about self, others, and the world as well as the literal and evaluative use of language

These six dimensions of client issues derive from orientations to counseling that we call theoretical approaches or counseling theories. (We summarize the major theoretical approaches in Chapter 9.) Some of these approaches emphasize the role of feelings or beliefs and cognitions in the development and maintenance of client issues, whereas others emphasize the role of behaviors, language, systems, and cultural factors. We take an integrative position that emphasizes the importance of all six dimensions. We will return to this six-component formulation again in Chapter 9, in which we discuss the use of counseling strategies to promote change in these six dimensions.

As noted earlier, conceptualization of client issues does not come quickly. It comes progressively. After your first session with clients, you will begin to have some hunches about them, their world (and how they view it), and their concerns (and how they view them). In subsequent sessions, these initial hunches will be modified as you understand your clients better and as your clients understand and report their world to you. There will be mistaken hunches along the way. These are to be accepted as part of the process too. Acknowledge and discard them. The remainder of this chapter is an extension of the conceptualizing process—that is, conceptualizing the client's goals.

PROCESS AND OUTCOME GOALS

The helping process involves two types of goals: process goals and outcome goals. *Process goals* are related to the establishment of therapeutic conditions necessary for client change. These are general goals, such as establishing rapport, providing a nonthreatening setting, and possessing and communicating accurate empathy and unconditional regard. They can be generalized to all client relationships and can be considered universal goals. Process goals are your primary responsibility; you cannot expect your clients to help you establish and communicate something like unconditional regard.

Unlike process goals, outcome goals will be different for each client. *Outcome goals* are the goals directly related to your clients' changes—to be made as a result of the helping process. As you are able to help your clients understand their concerns, you will want to help them understand how counseling can be used to respond to these concerns. The two of you will begin to formulate tentative outcome goals together. As counseling continues, the original goals may be modified through better understanding of the issues and through the development of new attitudes and behaviors that will resolve them. Goal-setting should be viewed as a flexible process, always subject to modification and refinement. Most importantly, outcome goals are shared goals that both you and your clients agree to work toward achieving.

Outcome goals that are visible or observable are more useful because they allow you to know when they have been achieved. However, not all outcome goals are stated as visible goals. For example, consider these two outcome goals:

1. To help your client develop more fully his or her self-actualizing potential
2. To increase the frequency of positive self-statements at home and at work by 50 percent over the next six weeks

Both of these could be considered to be outcome goals. They might even be so closely related as to be the same in terms of outcomes. Your clients may be much more attracted to such goals as developing their self-actualizing potential. You may want to view the development of self-actualizing potential as a composite of many smaller and more specific goals. To state it a little differently, self-actualizing is a hypothetical state that cannot be observed. It can only be inferred through certain visible and audible behaviors. Using this goal, you have no way of knowing the types of activity that your clients will enter into while proceeding toward the goals. As a result, you and your clients will know very little about what they could be doing in the relationship, and you will have no way of assessing progress toward the desired results. Consequently, the first goal listed is not as satisfactory as the second in that it does not provide you or your clients with specific guidelines for change.

When outcome goals are stated precisely, both you and your clients have a better understanding of what is to be accomplished. This better understanding permits you to work more directly with your clients' problems or concerns and reduces tangential efforts. Equally important are the benefits you are able to realize in working with specific behavioral goals. You are able to enlist the cooperation of your clients more directly because they are more likely to understand what is to be done. In addition, you are in a better position to select viable techniques and strategies when your clients have specific objectives. Finally, both you and your clients are in a better position to recognize progress—a rewarding experience in its own right. It is also important to realize that specific observable statements of outcome are now required as part of treatment planning by almost all counseling agencies that receive both state and federal funding because they are clues to client progress and effectiveness of the helper's strategies and interventions. Outcome goals form the basis of *treatment plans* in counseling. A treatment plan describes the client's presenting issues, outcome goals and ways to measure such goals, and intervention strategies. It also includes a projected timeline of treatment and is required by most health care insurance companies for third-party reimbursement.

CULTURALLY APPROPRIATE HELPING GOALS

Clients who feel marginalized from the mainstream culture may find mental health services based on long-range goals irrelevant. Clients faced with financial challenges, discrimination, and disempowerment may be far more concerned with survival and physical needs and short-term goals that are oriented toward resolution of current life issues (Rosado & Elias, 1993).

Sue and Sue (2008) noted that culturally diverse clients do not always share many of the values evident in both the goals and the processes of the helping process. It is important for

APPLICATION EXERCISE 8.1

Goal-Setting

Aaliyah is a young Muslim woman who is a junior in college in the United States. She requests a female counselor, and in the first few helping sessions, she expresses great reluctance to seek help because her Muslim parents—who still live in Turkey—do not approve of seeking help outside their extended family for problems, believing instead that they are "tests from Allah." She is hesitant to describe her pressing concerns; however over time, she does reveal that has a non-Muslim live-in boyfriend. Her parents are coming to the States to visit her, and she is very afraid of having them find out about this relationship. She is fraught with anxiety about their upcoming visit and is experiencing ambivalence about disclosing or concealing the relationship from them. She is experiencing some sleeplessness and some general "aches and pains" that are new for her.

Identify a few goals that you think might be appropriate in working with Aaliyah, given what you know about her and her cultural affiliation so far.

_____

_____

_____

Are your goals specific or vague? How would you and she know when you had achieved these goals? Are your goals process or outcome goals? If they are outcome goals, how would achieving them affect Aaliyah? Are your goals consistent with Aaliyah's cultural affiliation? How do you know? Discuss your goals with your instructor or supervisor.

helpers to identify their own cultural biases and values and to ensure that they do not steer clients in a direction that disavows the beliefs and values of the client's culture. To do so is to enact a form of racism, sexism, ageism, and so on, because it suggests the helper is in a superior position, while the client is in an inferior position (Sue & Sue, 2008).

In addition, the duration of helping goals also plays a role in culturally sensitive goal formation. Many clients from culturally diverse backgrounds do not return to counseling or end the helping process early because they feel the helper is committed only to the pursuit of long-term counseling goals. Long-term goals are often less suitable for some diverse clients, such as those from lower socioeconomic levels or those who want short-term, concrete, direct action results (Sue & Lam, 2002; Sue & Sue, 2008).

THREE ELEMENTS OF GOOD OUTCOME GOALS

Perhaps you have noticed from our previous examples that outcome goals are different from process goals in several respects. A well-stated outcome goal includes the following elements: the behavior to be changed, the conditions under which the change will occur, and the level or amount of change. These elements apply to any outcome goal, whether it is to modify eating patterns, reduce negative self-appraisal, or increase saying no to unreasonable requests.

The first element of an outcome goal specifies in behavioral terms what the client will do differently as a result of counseling. In other words, determine what unmet needs will become the targets of change and in what specific ways. The second element of an outcome goal indicates the conditions under which the desired change will occur. It is important to weigh carefully the situations or settings in which the client will attempt a new behavior. You would not want to set your client up to fail by identifying settings in which there was little hope for success. The client might agree to modify alcohol use at home during the evenings but not to attempt to modify alcohol use when going out on Saturday nights. The third element of outcome goals involves the choice of a suitable and realistic level or amount of the new behavior. That is, how much of the new behavior will the client attempt? Remember that for treatment plans, the amount or level of the outcome goal is very important because the goals need to be measurable. Consider the following examples of good outcome goals—good in the sense that they incorporate the three elements we described above, the behavior, conditions, and level.

APPLICATION EXERCISE 8.2
Outcome Goals

In the following exercise, examples of client outcome goals are presented. Determine which of the three elements of an outcome goal—behavior, condition, or level—may be missing. After each example, list the missing parts by using B for behavior, C for condition, and L for level. Feedback will be provided to you at the end of the exercise.

The following example is provided as an illustration: to increase job placement (behavior) of clients with physical challenges seen in a rehabilitation agency (condition) by 30 percent during a one-year time period (level).

Identify the missing parts in the following six outcome goals:

1. To decrease temper tantrums
2. To increase exercise to two times a week over a six-week period
3. To decrease the number of nightly arguments at home with your (the client's) partner
4. To decrease tardiness
5. To reduce aggressive behavior with a sibling by 50 percent
6. To make three positive comments about the strengths of each member of your (the client's) family during a one-week period

Feedback

1. The missing elements are the condition (C) and level (L) of the goal.
2. This goal specifies the behavior and the level; the condition (C) is missing.
3. The level (L) of the goal is missing.
4. This goal specifies the behavior; the condition (C) and level (L) are missing.
5. The behavior (B) is missing; "aggressive behavior" is a label and does not specify what the person would reduce.
6. This is a complete outcome goal! "Making positive comments" is the behavior; "three of them in one week" is the level; "to each family member" is the condition.

Marquita's goals for counseling: Marquita indicates at the outset she wants to take better care of her body. This intention—worked through with the helper—yields the following outcome goals:

1. To get at least seven hours of sleep at home on four or more nights during a given week.
2. To test her blood sugar levels (she is diabetic) at work once a day five days a week.
3. To do some kind of exercise activity at least thirty minutes a day in a gym she belongs to at least three days a week.

TRANSLATING VAGUE CONCERNS INTO SPECIFIC GOALS

Rarely does a client begin by requesting assistance in achieving specific behavior changes. Instead of saying, "I want to be able to talk to people without getting nervous," the client is likely to say, "I'm shy." In other words, a personal characteristic has been described rather than the ways in which the characteristic is experienced. It then becomes the helper's job to help the client describe the ways in which the characteristic could be changed.

Taking nonspecific concerns and translating them into specific goal statements is no easy task for the helper. You must understand the nature of the client's concern and the conditions under which it occurs before the translation can begin. Even then, there are difficulties. Egan (2010) has suggested the use of certain future-oriented questions to help guide clients in the goal-setting process:

- What would this problem situation look like if I were managing it better?
- What changes in my present lifestyle would make sense?
- What would I be doing differently with the people in my life?
- What patterns of behavior would be in place that are not currently in place?
- What current patterns of behavior would be eliminated?
- What would I have that I don't have now?
- What accomplishments would be in place that are not in place now?
- What would this opportunity look like if I developed it? (pp. 314–315)

What can you expect of yourself and your clients in terms of setting specific goals? First, the goals that are set can never be more specific than your understanding and the client's understanding of the problem. This means that at the outset of counseling, goals are likely to be nonspecific and nonbehavioral. But nonspecific goals are better than no goals at all. As you and your client explore the nature of a particular concern, the type of goal(s) appropriate to the problem should become increasingly clear. This clarification will permit both of you to move in the direction of identifying specific behaviors that—if changed—would alter the problem in a positive way. These specific behaviors can then be formulated into goal statements; as you discuss the client's problems in more detail, you can gradually add the circumstances in which to perform the behaviors and how much or how often the target behaviors might be altered.

After you and your client have established the desired outcome goal together, you can identify some action steps that might help the client achieve the overall goal or target. These action steps can be thought of as subgoals. Subgoals consist of a series of smaller or intermediate steps or tasks that help the client perform the desired behaviors gradually. When several subgoals are identified, these are usually arranged in a sequence or hierarchy. The client completes one subgoal successfully before moving on to another one. By gradually completing the activities represented by subgoals in a successful manner, the client's motivation and energy to change may be reinforced and maintained. Successfully completing subgoals may also reduce potential failure experiences by giving the client a greater sense of control and empowerment and by helping the client achieve the overall desired change in a more gradual manner.

APPLICATION EXERCISE 8.3

Outlining Goals

Assume that Brent has come to you for counseling, complaining of insomnia. As you and Brent probe the facets of his concerns, you can consider the specific changes Brent would like to make. Gradually, these changes can be developed into an outline of desired goals. We refer to this as an outline because the major headings (I and II) represent the two overall or primary outcome goals for Brent; the subheadings reflect the subgoals or activities Brent might perform to achieve the overall goal gradually. Remember that goal-setting is a flexible process and that the goals listed in this outline might change as counseling with Brent progresses.

OUTCOME GOAL I: To be able to go to sleep within an hour of going to bed at least four nights of the week at home

    A. To identify in writing all his prior solutions for trying to go to sleep (counting sheep, day-dreaming, eating a snack, etc.)

    B. To substitute these "trying to go to sleep" activities with "trying to stay awake" activities

OUTCOME GOAL II: To increase (by 50 percent) Brent's positive feelings and thoughts about himself over the time in which he receives counseling

    Complete the goal outline for this second outcome goal listed above. You might begin by establishing the criteria that Brent would consider important. You might also consider having Brent describe some of the situations in which he feels good about himself. You may also want to explore how he felt about growing up as a young boy in his family and his cultural referent group. What could Brent do to achieve his short- and long-term goals? From this kind of information and using your own imagination, construct the specific types of subgoals that would help Brent implement this second outcome goal. Continue this process for outcome goals II and III for Brent.

OUTCOME GOAL II: _____

    A. _____

        _____

    B. _____

        _____

    C. _____

        _____

    D. _____

        _____

OUTCOME GOAL III: To acquire another job at a higher salary range within the next year

    A. _____

        _____

B. _____

_____

C. _____

_____

D. _____

_____

Notice the process by which outcome goals are established:

1. They begin as overall goals that are directly related to the client's specific or general concerns or descriptions of a set of problems and that are consistent with the client's culture.
2. Specific and observable subgoals are established that—if achieved—permit the realization of the overall goals.

Thus, goal-setting moves from general to specific goals; the specific goals are directly related to the general goal, and the general goal is a reflection of the problems and needs presented to the helper.

CLIENT RESISTANCE TO GOAL-SETTING AND THE STAGES OF CHANGE MODEL

Occasionally, a client may be hesitant about setting goals or reluctant to work toward change. For instance, after completing a helping session with her client, a helper said, "This was the fifth interview, and I still can't get him to talk about goals." When this happens, the helper must deal with the question "What's the client resisting?"

In working with clients who are resistant to goals, it is helpful to realize that such behavior is purposeful. That is, what the client does or avoids doing achieves some desirable result for the client. Consequently, you may find that the client who resists setting goals may be protecting the behavior that is in need of modification because that behavior is doing something desirable. An example is the chronic smoker. Although an individual may recognize the negative consequences of smoking, he or she also clings to the habit, believing that it is a helpful way to deal with a tense situation, that it is relaxing, that it increases enjoyment of a good meal, and so forth. Almost all addictions to substances are examples of this. Another example of this is avoidance. Although some clients may wish to change something, their avoidance of the very thing they want to change can feel so protective that the negative consequences engendered by the avoidance outweigh the potential positive consequences of change.

It becomes your task to get clients to identify what they gain from their current behavioral and interpersonal patterns. In so doing, you may determine whether that gain or outcome can be achieved in more desirable ways. For example, a young student may throw paper airplanes out the school window in order to receive attention from peers. Gaining attention may be a desirable outcome. It is the method that is the problem. Therefore, you and your client may consider more appropriate means for gaining increased attention other than throwing paper airplanes out the school window! In a more complicated scenario, consider the student or worker who engages in procrastination, missing critical deadlines, resulting in poorer grades or negative job evaluations. While for some clients such real or imagined negative feedback may motivate them to meet deadlines, for others, the gain of putting off the task once again may actually mask the potential pain of a lower grade or lower evaluation. Some clients may present with interpersonal patterns that may seem problematic, such as nagging their friends or partner, yet the control they seek from such behavior stops them from thinking seriously about changing the pattern.

A useful way to think about client resistance to goal-setting is to reflect on how resistant most people are to change itself. Outcome goals request clients to change. Prochaska, DiClemente, and Norcross (1992) developed a well-tested model of change called the *stages of change model* that helps to explain client resistance to change. Essentially, the stages of change model represents "specific constellations of attitudes, intentions, and behaviors related to an individual's readiness in the cycle of change" (Prochaska & Norcross, 2010, p. 492). In their model, there are six stages of change a person progresses through:

1. Precontemplation: The client is either not aware of a need to change or does not want to change; he or she often views the "problem" as belonging to someone else. When clients at this stage of change present to helpers, it is often at the request of someone else. Clients at the precontemplation stage are not only not aware of their problems but also unaware of any risks of their behaviors. A large number of persons who engage in risky or unhealthy behaviors fall into this category. Clients at this stage of change need to acknowledge there is an issue and increase their awareness of the negative aspects of the issue in order to move ahead to the next stage (Prochaska & Norcross, 2010, p. 493).

2. Contemplation: The client becomes aware of a need to change and thinks about it but has not decided to do anything about it. Some people can stay "stuck" in contemplation for years, often because in weighing the pros and cons of change, they feel ambivalent about change itself, and such ambivalence keeps them stuck. In order to move ahead to the next stage, clients in contemplation "must avoid the trap of obsessive rumination for years—what we call chronic contemplation—and make a firm decision to take action" (Prochaska & Norcross, 2010, p. 494). One of the ways that practitioners can help clients do so is through the use of little action steps. Sometimes, a life crisis such as a poor health diagnosis or the death of a loved one can also spark a move out of chronic contemplation.

3. Preparation: The client has decided to take some action in the near future, perhaps as soon as the next month or two. Also in this stage, perhaps the client has tried some action in the past but was unsuccessful. Helpers can detect clients who are in this stage because they report some small behavioral changes already made and because they have started to move out of ambivalence about change as they recognize that the advantages of change outweigh the risks of not changing. As Prochaska and Norcross (2010, p. 494) observe, "Like anyone on the verge of momentous actions, individuals in the preparation stage need to set goals and priorities. In addition, they need to dedicate themselves to an action plan they choose." As you can see, clients at the preparation stage are more likely to be able to set outcome goals, while those clients still stuck in precontemplation and contemplation tend to benefit more from process goals.

4. Action: The client is ready to change and has usually begun to take some action toward the desired outcome, although the issue has not yet been successfully resolved. However, clients in this change are highly motivated to do the work and make the commitment necessary to change the problem. The stages of change model assumes that clients are in the action stage if they have successfully altered a problem behavior by reaching a specific criterion—that is, a specific level of the outcome goal that we described above. Clients in the action stage often terminate the helping process quickly but appropriately because they implement action quickly and effectively. Moreover, clients at this stage tend to "recognize the pitfalls that might undermine continued action, whether these are cognitive, emotional, and/or environmental" (Prochaska & Norcross, 2010, p. 495).

5. Maintenance: The client reaches his or her goals through various action plans. Moreover, the client maintains the change for a period of at least six months. Now the focus is on consolidating the gains that have been made and on preventing relapses. However, maintenance is not a "static stage" but rather "a continuation, not an absence, of change" (Prochaska & Norcross, 2010, p. 495). For some individuals, especially those with chronic issues, maintenance becomes a lifelong stage—or at least needs to become a lifelong stage lest these persons fall into relapse mode.

6. Relapse and Recycling: As Prochaska and Norcross (2010) indicate, many persons taking action do not successfully maintain the change on the first or even second attempt. Often, clients maintain a gain for a short time, but the gains do not endure for the six-month period required by the maintenance phase we discussed earlier. This is especially evident in the treatment of serious clinical disorders and addiction issues. When relapse occurs, many of these clients return to helpers for "recycling"—also referred to by some as "booster sessions." For example, in the couples counseling we do, it is not uncommon for couples to come back for refresher sessions when starting to lose ground on changes they have made in prior sessions.

It is important to note that the change model is not presumed to be a linear model in which people move through one stage to the next in a progressive fashion but is instead a cyclical model in which clients spiral through change. For example, when clients relapse, they may recycle back to a much earlier stage of change, such as precontemplation—or, more likely, contemplation or preparation. As Prochaska and Norcross explain this process, they note that "[t]he spiral pattern suggests that most relapsers do not revolve endlessly in circles and that they do not regress all the way back to where they began. Instead, each time relapsers recycle through the stages, they potentially learn from their mistakes and can try something different the next time around" (2010, p. 496). As you can imagine from this spiral pattern, when clients do relapse and regress to an earlier stage, the goals of helping will usually shift back with them. For example, this process may mean that the helper has to become more attentive once again to process goals in order to help the client recover from the distress of falling back. It may also mean that the client and helper revisit the outcome goals and devise altered or new ones.

As an example of this model, consider a person who has felt consistently anxious for the last few years. This anxiety is chronically debilitating in that it prevents her from doing certain things that are anxiety-arousing. She comes to a college or mental health practitioner and reveals that she has been feeling this way for several years. During this time, she has sought out a lot of information on the web and from books about anxiety. But it has taken her two years to decide to seek out the help of a helper and to inquire about the use of medication. When this client was in precontemplation, she was not aware of having an issue with anxiety nor was she aware of its consequences for her. When she did become aware of this but did not yet do anything about it, she moved into the contemplation stage. As she sought information from books and the web and as she thought about what the information meant to her, she moved into the preparation stage.

When she visited the practitioner and sought help and wondered about using medication, she had moved into the action stage. When—through the assistance of the helper—she engages in behaviors to resolve the anxiety, she will move into the maintenance stage, in which her task will be to continue her action plans to reduce the anxiety.

Research on the stages of change model has the following implications with respect to client resistance to change (Prochaska & Norcross, 2010):

1. The stages of change model can predict client dropout from counseling across a variety of client issues. Most of the clients who drop out early are in the precontemplation stage (Prochaska & Norcross, 2010).

2. The amount of progress clients make during counseling depends on the particular stage of change they are in at the beginning of the helping process. Clients in precontemplation and contemplation have not yet made a commitment to change. Clients in the preparation stage have made a tentative commitment to change but are only ready for small steps toward the desired goal. As Prochaska and Norcross observe, "the further along clients are in the stages of change at the beginning of therapy, the more quickly they can be predicted to progress" (p. 497).

Unfortunately, although people in the action stage are ready to work quickly toward an outcome goal, they represent a minority of those clients actually seeking help. As a result, to work effectively with clients in the precontemplation, contemplation, and preparation stages, helpers must be more proactive in the change intervention strategies they use, and they also need to match their change strategies to each client's stage of change (Prochaska & Norcross, 2010; see also Chapter 9). It is also useful to help clients set goals that are both realistic and feasible so they may be more able to move from one stage of change to the next (Prochaska & Norcross, 2010).

Sometimes, clients resist attempts to establish goals because they feel that the helper (either overtly or subtly) is pushing them in a certain direction. As we mentioned earlier, this may be a particular issue with clients who feel marginalized. Unless clients can determine some personal goals of counseling, the probability of any change is minimal. You can avoid creating client resistance to goals by encouraging active participation by clients in the goal-setting process.

APPLICATION EXERCISE 8.4
Stages of Change

Review the stages of change model we presented in the prior section. Select two or three current issues in your own life. Apply the stages of change model to each of these issues. What do you notice about the stages of change with respect to these two or three issues? What conclusions can you draw from this activity? You may want to complete this activity by yourself, with a partner, or in a small discussion group in your class.

CLIENT PARTICIPATION IN GOAL-SETTING

Often, goal-setting is construed to mean that you listen to the client, make a mental assessment of the problem, and prescribe a solution or goal. In fact, such a procedure is doomed to failure. The nature of the helping process is such that the client needs to be involved in the establishment of goals. Otherwise, the client's participation is directionless and renders the client a nonparticipant. As difficult as change is for human beings, it is compounded when clients are left out of the change process! An example will illustrate this idea. A beginning helper was seeing a client who was overweight, self-conscious about her appearance, reluctant to enter into social relationships with others because of this self-consciousness, and very lonely. The helper informed the client that one goal would be for her (the client) to lose one to three pounds per week under a doctor's supervision. With this, the client became highly defensive and rejected the helper's goal, saying, "You sound just like my mother."

Goal-setting is highly personal. It requires a great deal of effort and commitment on the client's part. Therefore, the client must select goals that are important to the client. In the preceding example, the client's resistance could have been prevented if the helper had moved more slowly, permitting the client to identify for herself the significance of her weight and the importance of potential weight loss for herself. The helper also needs to remain open to the possibility that there are other outcomes desired by this client. The helper presumed that the goal or desired change involved weight loss. In this particular situation, after several sessions, the client disclosed that she was being sexually molested by her father and still living at home. Then, she identified resolution of this situation and related trauma as her desired goal for counseling.

Sperry, Carlson, and Kjos (2003) suggested some useful questions to elicit client participation in the goal-setting process:

- How have you tried to make things better—and with what results?
- How do you think the issue is best handled—what do you see as your part in this change process? As my part in this process?
- When will things begin to change and get better for you?
- What will your life look like when things get resolved for you—and how does this feel? (p. 68)

Finally, we stress again the importance of the client's cultural beliefs and values in deciding what goals to pursue for counseling. In the preceding example, consider the fact that most European-American girls and women in the United States are preoccupied with weight and body image in a way that many men and girls and women of color are not. It is up to the client, not the helper in the mainstream culture, to decide what goals are relevant and appropriate.

Summary

In this chapter, we entered into the therapeutically active portion of the helping process. In addition to the interactive process that takes place between helper and client, the helper begins to establish an internal conceptualization process in which the client's world is studied. That study is both within the client's context and in the larger context of the family, the culture, and the society in which the client lives. Clients will become involved in this study—often quite naturally—as they unfold their experiences, feelings, and thoughts about themselves, others, and their current world. Interwoven in this process is an emerging awareness of a different or perhaps better set of conditions, which become translated into goals. Some of these goals are related to the helping relationship. Others are more related to the client's world. Through the recognition and establishment of these goals, the helper begins to understand the direction counseling will take and can begin to help the client reach that same awareness. In conceptualizing client issues and goals, it is useful to remember the stages of change model (Prochaska, DiClemente & Norcross, 1992). Not all clients are ready for change or for change in big ways. We continue this exploration of the process of change in the following chapter, where our focus turns to the use of helping intervention strategies.

Reflective Questions

1. Both the client and the helper bring their worlds into the helping session. We indicated that goal-setting evolves out of an understanding of the client's world. How might the helper's world affect that process of goal-setting? Should the helper be concerned about this issue? Why?

2. With yourself or with a role-playing partner, identify a current problem in your life. Consider the list of Egan's eight questions found on page 131. How do these questions help you (or your partner) develop goals and future scenarios for this concern?

3. In the beginning of this chapter, we discussed how unmet childhood needs can be reactivated in adult life. As an exercise—first for yourself and then with a client—consider completing the following question posed by Steinem (1992): "Write down on [a piece of paper] ... the things you wish you had received in your childhood and did not" (pp. 104–105). When you have completed this exercise, you have discovered what your needs for yourself are now.

4. How might the needs of a financially challenged low-income client differ from the needs of a client with a high-paying and secure job? What about the needs of a company manager who was recently laid off due to downsizing? How would these needs affect the outcome goals?

5. Discuss the stages of change model with respect to several different client issues. For example, consider this model with a child who is afraid to come to school, an adolescent who became pregnant after a night of intoxication and does not know what to do, an adult who is addicted to painkillers after suffering a severe back injury at work, and an elderly person who is starting to suffer from dementia and does not want to move out of her home.

My Helping Lab

For each exercise, log on to MyHelpingLab at http:// www.myhelpinglab.com and then click the Topics tab.

1. Click the Theories tab to locate the Integrative tab. Choose the Video Lab for the following selections: Exploring the Problem, Identifying Barriers, Working Toward Goals, and Goal-Setting. After watching these four video clips, respond in your class or with a partner to the following questions:

   a. Given these video clips, what can you say about this client's world? Can you identify specific needs of this client (based on page 124 in the text)? Can you also identify various dimensions of the client's presenting problems (based on page 127 in the text)?

   b. Based on these scenarios, which of the five stages of change model does the client appear to be in at this time? Why?

c. How would you describe the client's overall readiness to change?

d. What do you think about this client's level of participation in the goal-setting process?

e. What kinds of process goals were evident to you between this helper and client in watching these clips?

f. What client outcome goals were evident to you after watching these clips?

g. What actions steps or subgoals were evident to you after watching these clips?

2. Staying with the Theories tab, click the Transtheoretical tab and then choose the Video Lab. Watch the following three selections:

a. Assessing the Stage: How does Dr. Norcross assess which stage of change the client presents with in his cocaine addiction?

b. Preparation: What does Dr. Norcross do to help the client stay in the maintenance stage and avoid the relapse stage for his cocaine addiction?

c. Client Responsibility: How does Dr. Norcross enhance the client's motivation to change with respect to his alcohol use? Can you determine from this clip an outcome goal that the client commits to pursue?

Recommended Readings

DiClemente, C. C., Doyle, S. R. & Donovan, D. (2009). Predicting treatment seekers' readiness to change their drinking behavior in the COMBINE study. *Alcoholism Clinical and Experimental Research, 33,* 879–892.

DiClemente, C. C., Schumann, K., Greene, P. & Earley, M. (2011). A transtheoretical model perspective on change: Process focused interventions for mental health and substance abuse. In D. Cooper (Ed.), *Principles of intervention in mental health-substance use.* London: Radcliff.

Egan, G. (2010). *The skilled helper, 9th edition.* Belmont, CA: Brooks/Cole, Cengage.

Prochaska, J. & Norcross, J. C. (2002). Stages of change. In J. C. Norcross (Ed.), *Psychotherapy relationships that work* (pp. 303–314). New York: Oxford University Press.

Prochaska, J. & Norcross, J. C. (2010). *Systems of psychotherapy: A transtheoretical analysis, 9th edition.* Belmont, CA: Brooks/Cole, Cengage.

Sperry, L., Carlson, J. & Kjos, D. (2003). *Becoming an effective therapist.* Boston: Allyn & Bacon.

Sue, D. W. & Sue, D. (2008). *Counseling the culturally diverse.* New York: John Wiley & Sons.

Young, M. E. (2009). *Learning the art of helping, 4th edition.* Upper Saddle River, NJ: Pearson.

Using Integrative Helping Strategies and Interventions

In the previous chapter, we mentioned a variety of factors that contribute to client issues, including feelings, behaviors, beliefs, language, interactional patterns, and cultural factors. To deal effectively with such complex issues, helpers need to equip themselves with a variety of strategies and interventions designed to work with all the various ways in which concerns are manifested. We believe that helpers who have a variety of tools to use with clients are in a better position to address client issues than those who are limited in their knowledge and experience to a single approach.

In this chapter, we examine a number of helping strategies or interventions. Those that are presented here have been selected because they are used by helpers of varying theoretical orientations and because—when used in conjunction with each other—they treat the whole person. The strategies we describe are used to help clients (1) work through feelings, (2) work with behaviors, (3) work with beliefs and attitudes, (4) work with language and narratives, (5) work with interactional patterns and relationships, and (6) work with cultural and social systems. Table 9.1 illustrates a variety of counseling strategies that are based on various theoretical orientations to helping. This table also shows manifestations, or "markers," of six dimensions of client issues. The theoretical orientations reflected in Table 9.1 constitute the major approaches to counseling practices and interventions. Although these theoretical orientations have different views regarding the helping process, the helping relationship, and specific helping interventions, each theoretical orientation has "useful dimensions" (Corey, 2009, p. 4).

Sharf (2007) has concluded that in this day and age, practitioners use different parts of various theories in actual practice and have become much more integrative in their work. Efforts to integrate theoretical approaches stem primarily from the increased awareness that each singular approach may be inadequate in and of itself and the recognition that each approach offers something of potential value to clients. Although we touch briefly on varied theoretical approaches in

TABLE 9.1 Treatment Strategies and Corresponding Manifestations of Client Problems

Affective	Behavioral	Cognitive	Language	Systemic	Cultural
Person-centered therapy; Gestalt therapy; body awareness therapies; psychodynamic therapies; experiential therapies:	*Skinner's operant conditioning; Wolpe's counter-conditioning; Bandura's social learning; Lazarus's multimodal therapy:*	*Rational-emotive therapy; Beck's cognitive therapy; transactional analysis; reality therapy:*	*Acceptance and commitment therapy; social constructivism; narrative therapy: solution-focused brief therapy:*	*Structural therapy; strategic family therapy; intergenerational systems:*	*Multicultural counseling; cross-cultural counseling; gender-sensitive therapy:*
Active listening: empathy; positive regard; genuineness; awareness techniques; empty chair; fantasy; dreamwork; bioenergetics; biofeedback; free association; transference analysis; dream analysis; focusing techniques.	Guided imagery; roleplaying; self-monitoring; physiological recording; behavioral contracting; assertiveness training; social skills training; systematic desensitization; contingency contracting; action planning; counterconditioning.	A-B-C-D-E analysis; homework assignments; counter-conditioning; bibliotherapy; media-tapes; brainstorming; identifying alternatives; reframing; ego grams; script analysis; problem definition; clarifying interactional sequences; coaching; defining boundaries; shifting triangulation patterns; prescribing the problem (paradox).	Cognitive defusion; metaphors; mindfulness; behavioral tasks; commitment to valued actions; identification of self narratives; re-storying and restructuring of symbolic meaning of narratives and resulting conclusions.	Instructing about subsystems; enmeshment and differentiation; addressing triangulation, alliances, and coalitions; role restructuring; clarifying interactional systems; reframing; prescribing the problem (paradox); altering interactional sequences; genogram analysis; coaching; defining boundaries; shifting triangulation patterns.	Meta-theoretical, multimodal, culturally based interventions; focus on world views, cultural orientation, cultural identity; liberation and empowerment perspectives; culturally sensitive language, metaphors, rituals, practices, and resources; collaboration; networking; consciousness raising; advocacy.

(continued)

TABLE 9.1 (Continued)

Affective	Behavioral	Cognitive	Language	Systemic	Cultural
Manifestations Emotional expressiveness and impulsivity; instability of emotions; use of emotions in problem solving and decision making; sensitivity to self and others; receptive to feelings of others.	*Manifestations* Involvement in activities; strong goal orientation; need to be constantly doing something; receptive to activity, action, getting something done; perhaps at expense of others.	*Manifestations* Intellectualizing; logical, rational, systematic behavior; reasoned; computer-like approach to problem solving and decision making; receptive to logic, ideas, theories, concepts, analysis, and synthesis.	*Manifestations* Cognitive fusion; evaluative and comparative language; experiential avoidance; overreliance on reasoning; overidentification with one's story or narrative to construct a particular sense of self or a single "truth."	*Manifestations* Enmeshed or disengaged relationships; rigid relationship boundaries and rules; dysfunctional interaction patterns.	*Manifestations* Level of acculturation; type or worldview; level of cultural identity; bi- or trilingual; presenting problems are, to some degree, culturally based.

Source: Adapted From Harold Hackney, Sherry Cormier, *The Professional Helper: A Process Guide to Helping* (6th ed.). Table 7.1, pp.160–161, 2009. Reproduced by permission of Pearson Education, Inc.

this chapter because they are linked intrinsically to different helping strategies and interventions, for thorough explorations of the major theoretical approaches to helping, we urge you to consult a number of useful texts (see Brooks-Harris, 2008; Corey, 2009; Corsini & Wedding, 2010; Prochaska & Norcross, 2010; Rochlen, 2007; Sharf, 2007).

WORKING WITH CLIENT FEELINGS

Why do people have feelings, and how do they relate to well-being? In discussing this topic, Greenberg (2002) offered the following perspective: Feelings and emotions (also referred to as affect in Chapter 7) are important to our well-being. Rather than being an inconvenience, feelings are "signals" that give us clues about our relationships and communication with others. Unfortunately, we don't know how to handle our feelings very well, and as a result, we disappoint both ourselves and others. "Without the skills for dealing with emotional storms, some persons develop the belief that controlling their emotions is the best solution . . . still others embrace spontaneity and follow their feelings without deliberation . . . and some grow not to trust their own emotional signals, trying not to have emotions at all!" (Greenberg, 2002, p. x).

A big part of working with client feelings involves the recent concept of *emotional intelligence* (EQ)—that is, the art of learning when and how to express a feeling and when expression of a feeling will not help (p. 14). Emotional intelligence is rooted in the brain, particularly the prefrontal cortex, a sizable part of the brain located just behind the forehead (Miller, 2006). Emotional intelligence forms the basis of the interventions we suggest here for working with client feelings. These interventions support clients' work with their feelings in three ways that specifically promote EQ:

1. To identify and assess feelings
2. To elicit and express feelings
3. To understand and regulate feelings (Greenberg, 2002)

The strategies we present are derived primarily from experiential theoretical approaches to helping, such as gestalt therapy, and from psychodynamic and interpersonal therapies.

Identifying and Assessing Feelings

Helping clients become aware of their feelings enables them to identify what they are really feeling deep down in their "core" and helps them in problem-solving. We describe two strategies to help clients identify and assess their feelings: verbal leads and emotion logs.

VERBAL LEADS FOR IDENTIFYING FEELINGS.   One strategy to encourage clients to identify feelings is often simply accomplished by using *verbal leads* or open-ended questions that focus on client feelings and that help clients elicit different facets of their emotions. The following examples suggested by Teyber (2006, p. 165) are particularly helpful:

- Can you bring that feeling to life for me and help me understand what it is like for you when you are feeling that?
- Do you have an image that captures that feeling or goes along with it?
- Is there a particular place in your body where you experience that feeling?
- Is this a familiar or old feeling? When is the first time you can remember having it? Where were you? Who were you with? How did the other person respond to you?
- How old do you feel that you are when you experience that emotion? Can you attach an age to it, such as seven years old or thirteen years old?

EMOTION LOGS.   Greenberg (2002) has recommended the use of a daily *emotion log* to help clients identify feelings. You can easily construct an emotion log for a client. List the days of the week across the top of the page or in the horizontal direction. In the vertical direction on the left side of the page, from top to bottom, list a number of different affect words. You can obtain these affect words directly from our affect word lists in Chapter 7. When the clients have identified and tracked their feelings on this log, they can bring the completed log to the next session. Together, the helper and client can explore the following questions to assess the feelings recorded on the log, as recommended by Greenberg:

1. What is your name for the emotion?
2. Was it a more sudden onset emotion or a more enduring mood?
3. Did you have body sensations with your emotion?
4. Did thoughts come into your mind?
5. Did you act or feel like doing something or expressing something?
6. What brought on the emotion or mood?
7. What information is your emotion giving you? (pp. 128–129)

As Greenberg (2002) has pointed out, changing emotion requires experiencing it: "To change in therapy, clients cannot just talk intellectually about themselves and their feelings, they need to viscerally experience what they talk about . . . as total suppression of emotion is unhealthy" (pp. 8, 10). We describe three interventions to help clients elicit and express their emotional experience.

Eliciting and Expressing Feelings

INCREASING BODY AWARENESS OF FEELINGS.   Clients can also learn to get in touch with their feelings through the use of strategies that encourage greater awareness of what is occurring within one's body. When a person feels tense, it is usually seen or experienced in the contraction of a muscle or group of muscles. Continued tension results in pain, such as a headache or numbness, which occurs from nerve pressure accumulated from the tension. Smith (1985) has recommended the following intervention to help clients acquire body awareness:

> Close your eyes and just relax for a few moments. Breathe comfortably. (Pause.) (Repeat the directions to relax and the pauses until the client seems to be involved in the exercise.) Check out your body to see what you find. Note anything in your body which calls attention to itself. Just monitor your body, inch by inch, from the tips of your toes to the top of your head and down to the tips of your fingers. In particular, note any hot spots, cold spots, tight or tense muscles, pains, tingling, or anything happening in your body. Don't try to edit or change anything; just be aware and note what is happening. (Pause for a minute or two.) Take your time. When you are finished, open your eyes. (Wait until client opens her or his eyes.) (p. 107)

Following this, the helper asks the client to describe whatever he or she noticed.

Perls (1973), a gestalt therapist, suggested that clients also can identify and express feelings by being asked to exaggerate a particular body action. This strategy is useful because people often make bodily movements that suggest an action that reflects a current and present emotion; it is considered a "slip of the body," much in the way a person says something unintended yet meaningful, as in a verbal "slip of the tongue." As Smith (1985) noted, by inviting the client to repeat the action in an exaggerated form, the meaning of the body action usually becomes apparent. Smith (1985) gave the following illustration:

An example of this is the patient who, while talking about her ex-lover, begins slightly swinging her leg which is crossed over the other leg, knee on knee. The therapist asks her to be aware of her leg and she says, "Oh, I'm just nervous today." So the therapist asks her to exaggerate the movement. She swings her leg in a larger arc, with more force, and declares, "I must want to kick him. But I didn't know I was angry today. Oh, I just remembered what he said last week. I am mad at him!" (p. 110)

By asking the client to exaggerate the body movement, the helper encourages the client see that she has both repressed and inhibited a feeling of anger. When a client's movement is directed toward oneself—for example, if she has been chewing her cheek—the exaggeration of this would also illustrate how she had taken the feeling of anger toward the ex-lover and directed it back toward herself. Additional strategies to promote body awareness in clients can be found in a primer on gestalt counseling and therapy by Joyce and Sills (2010).

BREATHING. Another way to help clients get in touch with and express feelings is through work on *breathing*. According to Lowen (1965), a bio-energetics therapist, every emotional problem is manifested in some sort of disturbance in breathing. Perls (1969), the founder of gestalt therapy, connected shallow breathing and sighing with depression, yawning with boredom, and restricted breath with anxiety. Smith (1985) observed that effective breathing is necessary for vitality; that insufficient breathing leaves the person in a state like "a fire with an inadequate draft" (p. 119). Healthy breathing involves the entire body (p. 120).

There are numerous ways to work with breathing. The first is to note to the client the occasions on which he or she holds a breath or breathes in a shallow or constricted manner. For some clients, it may be useful to teach them the art of deep breathing, in which the breath is started (inhaled) in the abdomen, moves up through the chest, and is released thoroughly in the exhalation, often with the aid of a vocal sound. When clients can breathe deeply and do not hold back or interrupt the breathing cycle, they are more likely to experience what they feel. Another way to increase breathing awareness is to instruct the client to count the "in" breath and the "out" breath (Gilligan, 1997). For example, you might say, "As the breath comes in through the nostrils, filling up the lower diaphragm, say silently, 'Breathing in, one.' As the breath goes out, say silently, 'Breathing out, one'" (p. 76). The next breath is counted as two, then three, and so on. Other clients may use word mantras with their breath, such as "let in" on the "in" breath and "go out" on the "out" breath.

Gilligan (1997) noted that the restriction of breathing is often such a chronic activity that it becomes unconscious or without awareness. He has suggested asking clients to recall an "antagonistic image, thought, or a feeling" and whether they sense it "inside" or "outside" their breath (p. 76). He observed that usually "difficult processes are experienced outside the breath" (p. 76). When the difficult experience is brought inside the breath, an important shift in relationship to the troubling experience usually occurs.

One of the advantages of breathing interventions is that breathing is a universal phenomenon. All people—regardless of differences in race, gender, age, class, religion, sexual orientation and so on—breathe. Many have learned, over time, to shut down their breathing, resulting in a variety of somatic and emotional symptoms. At the same time, certain medical conditions, such as low blood pressure, insulin-dependent diabetes, recent surgery, or pain, may make breathing interventions contraindicated without the expressed approval of the client's health care provider (Cormier, Nurius & Osborn, 2009).

INCOMPLETE SENTENCES.   Another possible intervention to help clients elicit and express feelings is with the use of *incomplete sentences*. Usually, after some work has been done on breathing, the helper "feeds" the client with an incomplete sentence stem and then the client finishes the sentence with the first thing that comes to mind, continuing to say the same root of that sentence with different completions until there is a point at which the client seems finished. Then, another sentence stem is "fed" by the helper.

Examples of incomplete sentences developed by Branden (1971) to elicit feelings include:

- Something I'm feeling is . . .
- When I look at you, I feel . . .
- As you look at me, I feel . . .
- If I felt mad (or scared or shy or happy, etc.) . . .
- One of the things that I do when I feel mad is . . .
- One of the things that might make me feel mad is . . .
- One of the ways that feeling mad helps me is . . .
- A good thing about feeling mad is . . .
- A bad thing about feeling mad is . . .
- The rule we had in my family about feeling mad was . . .

Understanding and Regulating Feelings

The expression of feelings is useful, but such expression needs to be accompanied by making sense of these feelings and learning how to integrate them effectively into daily life and relationships with self and others. Emotional arousal or expression of emotions alone is insufficient for good therapeutic outcomes; expression needs the added component of reflection about the feelings (Warwar & Greenberg, 2000). Reflection or making meaning of emotional experience helps clients to understand their feelings and to regulate them. Emotion diaries are a way for clients to write a narrative about their emotional experiences. Emotion logs, which we described earlier, are a visual tool clients can use to help them recognize and record selected aspects of their emotional experiences.

EMOTION DIARIES.   *Emotion diaries* help clients understand feelings by writing a narrative account or story about one's emotional experience of a traumatic event. Pennebaker (1990) found that writing about the feelings associated with an upsetting event for twenty minutes at a time—with at least four different entries in the diary—had a significant effect on improving health and immune system functioning as well as a reduction in the disturbing memories of the event. The positive effects of emotion diaries include not only writing about current incidents as a client experiences them but also about events that occurred at an earlier time that still elicit painful feelings for the client. Emotion diaries are a good way to help clients cope with and understand the sad and tragic events of everyday life, including but not limited to terrorism and disasters (Greenberg, 2002; Halpern & Tramontin, 2007).

In addition to understanding feelings, regulating affect is a way for clients to contain feelings so they are not overwhelmed by them. *Affect regulation* has an increasingly important role in the modern world, which is filled with both natural and manmade disasters. Disturbing emotions, such as sadness, shame, fear, anger, and powerlessness, can overwhelm a client. Many clients believe the only way they can regulate these overwhelming feelings is to shut them down, but as Greenberg (2002) and others have found, this strategy is not useful in the long run. Other clients try to avert experiencing these feelings by self-medicating through the abuse of substances or by self-harming, such as cutting themselves. These clients in particular can benefit by learning to regulate undesirable emotions with more self-soothing feelings. The following strategy described by Greenberg is useful for helping clients learn affect regulation skills.

Dealing with Difficult Emotions

1. Imagine a situation or personal interaction that produces this difficult emotion. This might be a conversation with a parent or partner that leaves you feeling difficult emotions of rage, worthlessness, or undesirability.
2. As the emotion emerges, shift your attention to the process of sensing. Describe the sensations. Describe their quality, intensity, and location and any changes in these. Breathe.
3. Pay attention to accompanying thoughts. Describe the mental process in which you are engaging, whether it be thinking, remembering, or criticizing. Breathe.
4. Focus on another softer, good feeling, such as love, joy, or compassion. Imagine a situation or personal interaction in which you feel this. Feel it now. Allow the feeling to fill you.
5. Talk to the old, difficult feeling from your space in your new, healthier feeling. What can you say to the bad feeling that will help transform it to a better feeling? Say this. (Greenberg, 2002, p. 214)

Increasingly, data are suggesting the importance of cultivating positive emotions, which support health and well-being—specifically decreased pain and increased longevity, especially among older clients (Pressman & Cohen, 2005). The emotions of joy and happiness promote resilience. Activities associated with the cultivation of positive emotions include writing down things that go well during the day, noting gratitude, encouraging someone to go on a "strength date" where they show off a skill or talent, and writing forgiveness letters (Seligman, 2000).

In using interventions to work with client feelings, it is important to recall the cautions we mentioned in Chapter 7 regarding culture. Some clients from some cultural groups may feel uncomfortable with these kinds of strategies because their cultural group does not focus on feelings or on revealing feelings to a nonfamily member. Other clients may be much more concerned with survival, class, and social issues, so focusing on affect seems irrelevant to them.

WORKING WITH CLIENT BEHAVIORS

There are a variety of strategies designed to help clients modify their behaviors. Behavioral interventions are based on the assumption that behavior is learned; therefore, inappropriate or maladaptive behavior can be unlearned, while more adaptive behavior can be acquired (Wilson, 2010). Behavioral approaches also rely heavily on a scientific method (Wilson, 2010). This means that the therapeutic interventions and their outcomes are tested in some empirical way to establish the efficacy of the strategy or strategies being used. In this section, we describe three strategies designed to work with client behaviors: skills training, self-management, and exposure therapies.

Behavioral Skills Training

Behavioral skills training is used to help clients acquire skills to perform particular tasks in particular situations. For example, a client comes in to see you because she falls silent in many interpersonal situations. She reports having difficulty expressing her opinions in group settings and with her husband. She would like your help in increasing her frequency and range of assertiveness skills. Another client comes in and reports that he has yet to ask someone out on a date, spends most of his time alone, and is feeling very lonely because he does not know how to use the inter-personal skills necessary for the development of relationships. He would like your help in acquir-ing some effective social skills. A child's parents come in to see you and report that they feel like failures because they cannot find effective ways to parent their child who is acting out at home and in school. They need your help in developing useful parenting skills and strategies. On an-other day, you see a couple who is in frequent conflict. They tell you that they spend much of their precious time together arguing, even though they cannot recall the next day what the con-tent of the argument was about. They know how to argue very well. They both grew up in fami-lies where arguing was a common occurrence. Yet, they do not know how to be friends with each other, and sadly, they suggest they simply do not know much about listening and communicating with one another. Expressing positive feelings to the other person is just about unheard of for this couple. They want your assistance in developing effective communication skills to enhance their relationship. In all these situations, and more, helpers can use behavioral skills training to help clients develop skills that are not yet in their repertoire or, at the least, may be known to the client but not used in necessary contexts and situations. Skills training promotes freedom for clients by providing them with an increased range of responses and with alternative ways of responding and behaving across a variety of contexts (Spiegler & Guevremont, 2010).

SOCIAL MODELING.   An important part of behavioral skills training is social modeling. *Social modeling* is based on observational learning and imitation (Bandura, 1969). From early child-hood, children learn to watch and imitate—a fact that parents who speak too freely in front of their small child know all too well. In modeling, the helper demonstrates a skill or a set of skills to the client, who observes what the helper does. Sometimes, symbolic models—such as films, stories, DVDs, and movies—are also used with clients as very cost-effective methods. In addi-tion, helpers can encourage clients to find natural models or people in the client's everyday envi-ronment who exhibit behaviors and skills the client needs to learn and practice (Spiegler & Guevremont, 2010). Modeling can promote significant change in and of itself in a very brief time—often in one or two counseling sessions. Most often, it is combined with other modalities, such as behavior rehearsal, in a skills training package.

BEHAVIOR REHEARSAL.   *Behavior rehearsal* literally means what it says. It involves having the client practice performing or demonstrating newly learned or newly expressed skills. In prac-tical terms, behavior rehearsal consists of a series of graduated practice attempts in which the client rehearses the desired behaviors, starting with a situation that is manageable and not likely to backfire. Often, the practice attempts are arranged in a hierarchy according to level of difficul-ty. For example, the client described previously whose concern was social skills deficits may practice social skills with persons he does not care about before he practices with persons whose opinion matters to him. Adequate practice of one situation is important before moving on to re-hearse a more difficult or complex skill or situation.

FEEDBACK.   An important part of behavior rehearsal and behavioral skills training is *feedback*. Feedback is a way for the client to recognize both the problems and successes encountered in the rehearsal and practice attempts as well as a way of observing and evaluating one's performance and of initiating corrective action. However, feedback used indiscriminately in skills training may be ineffective. Feedback is most helpful when the client is willing to change, when the type and amount of feedback given is adequate but not overwhelming, and when the feedback helps the client discriminate between effective and ineffective skills and performance of such skills. Feedback can be supplied by the helper, by persons in the client's environment, by the client, and by videotapes. Because much of skills training is based on *shaping*—or the idea that skills are learned when successive approximations of the desired behavioral responses are reinforced—feedback that focuses on gradual improvement and stresses client strengths is most effective. A final aspect of behavioral skills training involves promoting transfer and generalization of the newly learned skills to settings in which the effective use of the skills is important. This is often accomplished with homework assignments or in vivo tasks in which the client practices the skills in situations in the natural environment. One important overall caveat in behavioral skills training is to make sure both the skills selected and the training itself are culturally relevant to the client. For example, there may be situations in which clients from some cultural groups would not feel safe being assertive. For example, as Sue and Sue (2008) point out, clients from traditional Hispanic and Asian cultures—depending on their level of acculturation—often value restraint in expressiveness of strong feelings and opinions. In these cultural groups, "subtlety" rather than assertiveness is a "highly prized art" (p. 143).

Self-Management

Many people are legitimately concerned about the long-term effects of helping. In an effort to promote enduring client changes, helpers have become more concerned with client self-directed change. This interest has led many counseling researchers and practitioners to explore the usefulness of a variety of helping strategies called *self-control* or *self-management* (Wilson, 2010). The primary characteristic of a self-management strategy is that the client administers the strategy and directs the change efforts with minimal assistance from the helper. Like modeling, self-management strategies are cost-effective. One of the most commonly used self-management strategies is self-monitoring.

SELF-MONITORING.   *Self-monitoring* involves having clients count and/or regulate given habits, thoughts, or feelings. Self-monitoring seems to interfere with the learned habit by breaking the stimulus-response association and by encouraging performance of the desired response, which is then often reinforced by the individual's sense of progress following its accomplishment. In implementing the procedure, you will need to consider what, how, and when to self-monitor.

  • **What to Monitor:**   An initial step involves selecting the behavior to monitor. Usually, individuals will achieve better results with self-monitoring if they start by counting only one behavior—at least initially. For example, clients may count positive feelings about themselves, or thoughts of competency, or—as we saw earlier in this chapter—feelings and emotions. The counting encourages greater frequency of these kinds of thoughts and feelings. Clients may count the number of times they tell themselves to do well on a task or they may count the number of behaviors related to goal achievement (e.g., the number of times they tell their partner "I love you," the number of times they initiate conversations or participate in class discussions, etc.). Clients also can monitor both process and outcome behaviors. For example, a client could monitor the outcomes of a study program, such as grades on tests, reports, and papers. Equally—if not more—important is the act of self-recording the processes involved in studying, such as going to the library, finding a quiet study place, preparing for a test, researching a report, and so on. As Watson and Tharp (2007) stated, "You may want to keep track of your progress toward some goal, but the important thing to pay attention to *via* recording is the *process* you are going through... . Pay attention to the *process* so you can improve the process, and the goal will happen" (p. 90). In other words, noting the processes involved in changing the behavior is as useful as noting the behavioral outcome itself. For example, consider the client we described who failed to express important opinions and was engaging in self-monitoring. In addition to monitoring the *outcome* of self-expression, monitoring the *processes* involved in assertive self-expression— such as finding contexts or situations for self-expression, practicing phrases of self-expression, watching other people successfully engage in self-expression, and any other behaviors that lead to assertive self-expression—would be just as helpful. Clients also need to select behaviors to monitor that they care about and that are consistent with their values and their cultural affiliations and identities.

• *How to Monitor:*   The particular method the client uses to count the target response will depend on the nature of the selected response. Generally, clients will count either the frequency or duration of a response. For example, if they are interested in knowing how often the response occurs, they can use a frequency count to note the numbers of times they smoke, talk on the telephone, initiate social conversations, or think about themselves positively. Sometimes, it is more useful to know the amount of time the behavior occurs. A person can count the duration or length of a behavior in these cases. For example, clients might count how long they studied, how long they talked on the telephone, or the length of depressed periods of thought. Often, it makes sense to use frequency counts if it is easy to count the number of separate times the behavior is performed and to use duration counts if separate occasions are not easy to count or if the target behavior continues for several minutes at a time. Obviously, there are some times when a client may monitor both frequency and duration—for example, the number of cigarettes smoked in a day as well as the amount of time spent smoking cigarettes in a day. Sometimes, it is also important to know something about the *intensity* of a target response. In these instances, clients can also monitor the intensity or severity of a response on a rating scale, such as a 1 to 10 or a 0 to 100 rating scale. For example, with a client who reports a lot of daily stress, this client could rate his or her stress level at several points (at least four) during each day on a 1 to 10 point scale, with a 1 representing no stress and a 10 representing severe, incapacitating stress.

In addition, it is important to balance the self-monitoring with attention to *both* positive and negative behaviors. Having a depressed or anxious client self-monitor only depressed or anxious thoughts or feelings can lead the client to feel worse and more discouraged. And for clients who are having ideas of self-harm or suicide, self-monitoring may be contraindicated (Watson and Tharp, 2007, p. 102). Similarly, clients who only record the number of times they binge-eat or drink or smoke cigarettes may decide—after noticing all these negative behaviors—that change is too difficult after all. An antidote is to have clients also self-monitor positive behaviors—for example, times when they feel happy or calm rather than depressed or anxious. With clients who overeat or smoke, they can record the times they had the urge to eat or smoke but resisted the urge. Even small and infrequent successes need to be recorded in order to have this type of balance in an effective self-monitoring plan.

Clients will need to record with the assistance of some recording device. These can range from simple devices—such as note cards, logs, and diaries for written recordings—to more mechanical devices—such as a golf wrist counter, a kitchen timer, a wristwatch, a tape recorder, or a handheld computer. The device should be simple to use, convenient, portable, and economical.

• ***When to Monitor:*** It is important to self-record the target as soon as it occurs for several different reasons, as summarized by Watson and Tharp (2007). First, immediate recording is more accurate. When we wait until a later time to record a response, our delayed recall is usually not as accurate. Second, immediate recording is more complete. In waiting to record a response, we often omit important information. Finally, if a client waits until the end of the day to engage in self-recording, his or her emotional state may be different at this time and his or her recordings may be positive or negative. Also, it is the actual act of recording itself—not just thinking about recording—that seems to produce change—through a process called *reactivity*. Reactivity simply means that behavior is reactive or responsive to the process of self or other observation; for example, when we are told we are going to be observed—either by someone else or by ourselves—our behavior usually shifts. And if the behavior is something we really value, the shift is usually in the positive direction. Watson and Tharp (2007) note that this effect is so predictable that "clients in psychotherapy may be assigned to observe themselves as part of their therapy, a first step in changing problem behavior" (p. 93).

A critical issue in the effective use of any self-management strategy has to do with encouraging the client to use the strategy consistently and regularly. Clients may be more likely to do so when they can see the advantages of self-management and when the helper maintains some contact with the client during the self-management process.

Exposure Strategies

Many clients who benefit most from behavioral strategies present to helpers with problems of anxiety and trauma. For example, a female college student was raped while walking from the parking lot to her dorm and now she does not want to walk to the parking lot again. A person in the military involved in a war or natural disaster zone witnesses the death of a comrade and does not want to go back into the war or disaster zone. Another client develops a fear of flying and avoids airplanes even when required by work to travel quickly. One of the most common ingredients of anxiety- and trauma-related concerns involves *avoidance* or the act and process of staying away from a feared object, person, or situation. Unfortunately, the act of avoidance greatly strengthens and reinforces the client's anxiety. You are probably familiar with the old saying "get back in the trenches." This saying underscores the idea of *exposure therapies*. While exposure therapies are varied in type and duration, the common underlying process is that they all work to get the client "back in the trenches" by helping the client engage in the behaviors and situations that have been avoided, "under carefully controlled and safe conditions" (Spiegler & Guevremont, 2010, p. 206).

IMAGINAL AND IN VIVO EXPOSURE. Exposure strategies can be imaginal or in vivo and brief or prolonged. In *imaginal exposure,* a client imagines encountering the avoided, feared, or traumatic situation(s) with the helper's guidance. Clients are asked to imagine the events on a repeated basis in some kind of a consecutive or chronological narrative. Often, imaginal exposure sessions are taped for the client to listen to at a later time. With *in vivo exposure,* clients reduce learned fear and avoidant responses by confronting the feared, avoided, or traumatic situations and objects in the actual environment (hence, the phrase "in vivo"). Sometimes, the helper—or preferably, for safety reasons, two or more helpers—accompanies the client in the in vivo situations. The goal of in vivo exposure strategies is for clients to become so accustomed to the feared objects or situations (referred to as "habituated," defined as a 50 percent reduction in anxiety to the feared object or situation) that they no longer need to avoid the situation or object. In vivo exposure is frequently used in treating phobias and panic.

BRIEF EXPOSURE.   In *brief exposure,* clients are exposed to the threatening event(s) both for (1) a short period of time—usually ranging from a few seconds to a few minutes—and (2) incrementally—beginning with the aspects of the situation producing the least anxiety or threat proceeding to the aspects producing the greatest amounts of anxiety or threat (Spiegler & Guevremont, 2010, p. 206). To accomplish this, the helper and client usually first generate an anxiety hierarchy—that is, a list of the feared events/objects graded by either amount of emotional distress, time, or some other variant related to the event. For example, a client who presents with a fear of driving would generate an anxiety hierarchy based around distance and setting, starting with the idea of driving a short distance—perhaps only out of one's driveway. At the top of the hierarchy, the client would be driving a long distance, perhaps on an unfamiliar highway. This type of exposure was developed in the 1950s by Wolpe (1958) in a procedure referred to as *systematic desensitization.*

PROLONGED EXPOSURE.   More recent developments in exposure are credited to Foa (see Foa, Keane & Friedman, 2009). In *prolonged exposure,* the client is exposed to the threatening object or situation for (1) a more lengthy period ranging from ten minutes to one hour and (2) directly and immediately rather than gradually (Spiegler & Guevremont, 2010, p. 207). Prolonged exposure—also referred to as *flooding*—maximizes the client's anxiety with large rather than small doses of the feared object or situation at the outset. The core condition of prolonged exposure is that the client is exposed to a highly aversive situation long enough for the client's discomfort to peak and then decline (Spiegler & Guevremont, 2010). In prolonged and intensive exposure, the helper is always present during all exposure assignments, either imaginal or in vivo.

All forms of exposure are accompanied by a strong rationale with informed consent and lots of homework practice. As McNeil and Kyle (2009) observe, while informed consent is necessary in any form of helping, it is especially important in exposure therapies because the process of exposure can be "highly emotionally evocative" and can seem "counterintuitive" to clients (p. 507). These authors and clinicians stress to clients that exposure is "an investment of anxiety at the present time for greater calmness in the future" (McNeil and Kyle, 2009, p. 507). Additionally, exposure may also be used in conjunction with breath work, cognitive coping, and muscle relaxation. Brief and graduated exposure has some advantages over prolonged and intense exposure. Because clients typically experience less distress with brief and graduated approaches, they are more likely to consent to this strategy and more likely to stay the course and not drop out of counseling. Smyth (1999), who has generated an exposure-based CBT treatment for post-traumatic stress, recommends the following guidelines for helpers who use exposure-based strategies:

1. Start with brief and graduated exposure before using any prolonged and intensive exposure.
2. Avoid using prolonged and intensive exposure until brief and graduated exposure has yielded strong cognitive coping effects and moderate anxiety reduction effects.
3. Use imaginal exposure before using in vivo exposure, with either brief or prolonged exposure strategies.
4. If using prolonged and intensive exposure seems to overwhelm the client emotionally, return to brief and graduated exposure strategies. (pp. 77–78)

In conclusion, the essence of exposure-based strategies is to help clients approach rather than avoid a feared object or situation in the absence of any real threat and to reduce the client's emotional distress through repeated practice, passage of time, and cognitive coping (Smyth, 1999, p. 65).

Many behavioral strategies have been used quite effectively with diverse groups of clients, perhaps because these strategies focus on action and change rather than insight and exploration (Hays and Iwamasa, 2006). Still, it is important to remember that some of the notions underlying behavioral interventions are decidedly Eurocentric in that they focus on an internal locus of control and responsibility.

WORKING WITH CLIENT BELIEFS AND ATTITUDES

Beliefs and attitudes represent meanings, interpretations, or thoughts a client has about a situation—sometimes referred to as *cognitions*. Beliefs are potent because they affect clients' perceptions about themselves, others, and their lives. Clients encounter all sorts of difficulty based on their beliefs and attitudes because they may be distorted and based on incomplete information. For example, clients who are depressed or highly anxious tend to view themselves, others, and the world in a negative way (A. T. Beck, 1976; J. S. Beck, 1995; A.T. Beck, 2005; A.T. Beck and Alford, 2009; Clark and A. T. Beck, 2010).

A major focus of these interventions is on changing the way the client thinks. *Cognitive therapists* believe that by changing the way a client thinks, his or her emotional distress and problematic behavior also can be changed (Dobson, 2010). There is now a substantial body of research that shows the effectiveness of cognitive therapy in reducing both symptoms and relapse rates—with or without medication—in a number of different kinds of mental health disorders (A. T. Beck, 2005). There is also recent research supporting the notion that cognitive therapy does help some clients regain emotional control (Siegle, Carter & Thase, 2006). In this section of the chapter, we describe two related but somewhat different ways of working with client feelings: A-B-C-D-E analysis and cognitive restructuring.

A-B-C-D-E Analysis

A-B-C-D-E analysis is an intervention strategy based on a cognitive counseling approach known as *rational-emotive therapy* (RET), developed by a psychotherapist named Albert Ellis. (Ellis has relabeled RET as REBT, or rational-emotive behavior therapy.) According to Ellis, emotional distress is created by faulty, illogical, or irrational thoughts. In other words, if someone feels emotionally upset, it is not a person or a situation that creates the emotional upset but rather the individual's beliefs or thoughts about the situation. Reduction in emotional distress is brought about when the individual's irrational thinking is changed to rational thinking through interventions such as A-B-C-D-E analysis.

In the first part of this strategy, the client learns to recognize the activating event (A), usually a situation or person that the client finds upsetting. The activating event is often what prompts the client to seek counseling ("My relationship is on the rocks," "I lost my job," "My partner is a jerk," "I don't have any friends," "Why don't boys like me?" "I got passed over for the team," etc.). The most important aspect of this part of the strategy is to refocus clients from attributing their distress to this activating event to their thoughts about it. For example, the helper might respond with: "I realize it's upsetting to you not to make the team; however, it's not this situation in and of itself that's making you feel so bad but rather your thinking about this situation." In the next part of the strategy, the client's specific thoughts or beliefs (B) about the activating event are explored and identified. The client may have both rational and irrational thoughts, but it is the irrational thoughts that contribute to the emotional distress and that need to be targeted for change. Rational thoughts are ones that are consistent with reality, are supported by data, and result in moderate levels of emotional upset (e.g., "I didn't play as well as other people in the tryouts, and they got picked and I didn't"). Irrational thoughts are not based on facts or evidence and lead to high levels of emotional distress (e.g., "Because I didn't make the team, I am a jerk"). Irrational beliefs often take the form of either catastrophization ("It will be awful when . . .") or "musturbation" ("I must . . . "; "I should . . . "; "I have to . . .").

The helper then links the irrational beliefs with the resulting emotional and behavioral consequences (C)—that is, what clients feel and how they act as a result (e.g., "I feel so bad. I just can't seem to snap out of it. I didn't want to go back to school because I'm so ashamed of not making the team."). The helper shows the client how his or her specific irrational beliefs led to these consequences. For example, the therapist might respond with: "You're feeling awful and staying away from school because you now view yourself as a nobody—it's not that you got passed up that is making you feel and act this way; it's the way you're now thinking about yourself."

The real work of the strategy comes next in the disputation (D) phase. Disputation involves disputing or challenging the client's irrational beliefs with the intent of eliminating them and helping the client acquire more rational thinking. The helper uses questions to dispute the client's irrational beliefs. Some examples of questions suggested for cognitive disputation by Walen, DiGiuseppe, and Wessler (1992) include:

- Is that true? Why not?
- Can you prove it?
- How do you know?
- Why is that an overgeneralization?
- Why is that a bad term to use?
- How would you talk a friend out of such an idea?
- What would happen if . . . ?
- If that's true, what's the worst that can happen?
- So what if that happens?
- How would that be so terrible?
- Where's the evidence?
- How is a disadvantage awful?
- Ask yourself, can I still find happiness?
- What good things can happen if X occurs?
- Can you be happy even if you don't get what you want?
- What might happen?
- How terrible would that be?
- Why would you be done in by that?
- What is the probability of a bad consequence?
- How will your world be destroyed if X happens?
- As long as you believe that, how will you feel?
- "Whatever I want, I must get." Where will that get you?
- Is it worth it? (pp. 97–99)

Dryden (2009) notes that the disputation process (which she refers to as the examination process) can occur through a variety of methods and helper styles, including not only these Socratic-like questions listed above but also with didactic, declarative psycho education, humor, and metaphors or stories.

When the disputation process has been effective, it will be apparent in new effects (E), such as lessened emotional distress and changes in behavior (e.g., "I still don't like the fact I didn't make the team, but I know I'm not a jerk just because of that"). It is important for the helper to help clients recognize when and if these emotional and behavioral shifts in effects occur. Some recent research has suggested that for individuals who ruminate (the maladaptive tendency to focus repetitively on the causes and consequences of negative moods), the acts of identifying and disputing negative cognition may actually increase rather than decrease rumination (Joorman and Gottlib, 2008). This effect was found to be particularly evident with college students who ruminated and felt stressed and received the A-B-C-D-E model via a self-help workbook. The author of this study concluded that "self taught cognitive skills such as identifying and disputing negative cognitions may render cognitive interventions ineffective (or potentially harmful) for college students, particularly those who ruminate" (Haeffel, 2010).

Cognitive Restructuring

Cognitive restructuring is based in theory on the work of Aaron T. Beck, a cognitive therapist, and on the practice of Donald Meichenbaum, a cognitive-behavioral therapist. *Cognitive restructuring* is based on the notion that clients generate emotional distress due to the problematic and inflexible ways they interpret the events of their lives (A. T. Beck, 1976). The procedure helps clients to recognize and alter or to loosen and change troublesome thoughts, beliefs, and *schemas*—schemas being rather core or basic dysfunctional beliefs that clients regard as "truths." Cognitive restructuring involves not only helping clients learn to recognize and stop self-defeating thoughts and beliefs but also to substitute positive, self-enhancing, or coping thoughts and beliefs. Beck (1976) suggested three approaches to restructuring self-defeating thoughts, beliefs, and schemas:

1. What is the evidence?
2. What is another way of looking at it?
3. So what if it happens?

In the first part of cognitive restructuring, clients learn to stop obsessive, illogical, or negative thoughts as they occur. This involves discrimination training in which they are made aware of what "they tell themselves" before, during, and after problem situations. Clients might be instructed to note and record their negative thoughts and beliefs before, during, and after stressful or depressing situations for one or two weeks. As Newman (2003) noted, "[S]pecifically, clients are asked to notice their episodes of excessive anger, despair, fear, and the like, and to choose not to accept them at face value. Rather, clients are instructed to ask themselves, What could be going through my mind right now that could be triggering or worsening how I'm feeling right now?" (p. 92). This sort of discrimination process will yield themes and patterns that provide clues about the cognitive schemas or core "truths" the client believes, such as failure or rejection or abandonment.

After clients are aware of the nature and types of their self-defeating thoughts and belief systems, the helper helps them work toward identifying more positive or coping thoughts and beliefs that can replace the negative ones. These coping thoughts and beliefs are considered to be incompatible with the self-defeating thoughts and beliefs.

Coping thoughts are designed to help clients picture dealing with problem situations effectively, although not perfectly. In this way, they are considered better than mastery thoughts, which focus on perfection, because they expose the clients to possible mistakes and prepare them to recover from errors they may make in life (McMullin, 2000). It is best to personalize these coping thoughts for each client. Clients also need to learn coping thoughts to use before, during, and after problem situations. For example, a client who fails tests due to anxiety might concentrate on thoughts such as "I will be calm" or "Keep your mind on your studies" before an exam. During an exam, clients learn to concentrate on the exam and to stay calm instead of worrying about flunking or thinking about their nervousness. After using some coping thoughts, clients can be taught to reward or congratulate themselves for coping—instead of punishing themselves for worrying.

When clients have identified some possible alternative coping thoughts to use, they can practice applying these thoughts through overt (role-play) and covert (imaginary) rehearsal. The rehearsal may take the form of a dialogue or a script and may be read aloud by the client or put on index cards or audiotape. McMullin (2000) observed that for most clients, a period of at least six weeks is necessary for the practice of coping thoughts.

A sample cognitive restructuring dialogue used for rehearsal by a high school client who feared competitive situations is provided by Cormier, Nurius, and Osborn (2009):

> OK. I'm sitting here waiting for my turn to try out for cheerleader. Ooh, I can feel myself getting very nervous. (*anxious feeling*) Now, wait, what am I so nervous about? I'm afraid I'm going to make a fool of myself. (*self-defeating thought*) Hey, that doesn't help. (*cue to cope*) It will take only a few minutes, and it will be over before I know it. Besides only the faculty sponsors are watching. It's not like the whole school. (*coping thoughts*) Well, the person before me is just about finished. Oh, they're calling my name. Boy, do I feel tense. (*anxious feelings*) What if I don't execute my jumps? (*self-defeating thought*) OK, don't think about what I'm not going to do. OK, start out, it's my turn. Just think about my routine—the way I want it to go. (*coping thoughts*) (p. 398).

Identifying and internalizing coping thoughts and beliefs seem to be crucial in order for clients to really benefit from cognitive restructuring. Gradually, clients should be able to apply their newly found coping skills to the in vivo situations as these occur. If cognitive restructuring is successful, clients can detect an increased use of coping thoughts and a decreased level of stress in their actual environment. In vivo practice seems crucial for the efficacy of this strategy in order to promote the clients' confidence in their newly learned beliefs (Meichenbaum, 2007).

The use of cognitive strategies with diverse groups of clients has received increased attention in the last few years. However, as Hays and Iwamasa (2006) have pointed out, the values inherent in cognitive interventions reflect those of the mainstream culture. Also, as Brown (1994) asserted, there are instances for some clients in which the supposedly irrational beliefs may be reasonable or even lifesaving, given the individual's life and environmental context (p. 61). However, the process of challenging or disputing these beliefs may not fit with some clients from particular cultural groups. Therefore, a useful caveat is to cultivate awareness in using cognitive strategies. Be flexible in the way you implement these strategies, and be sensitive to the client's reaction.

WORKING WITH CLIENT LANGUAGE, SYMBOLIC MEANING, AND STORIES

In the preceding two sections of the chapter, we discussed intervention strategies that focus on client behaviors and cognitions. These types of strategies have been referred to as the first wave and second wave of behavior therapy—the *first wave* being interventions that focus primarily on reducing maladaptive behaviors and on establishing more effective behavioral responses, with the *second wave* including interventions that focus primarily on reducing maladaptive cognitions and on establishing more effective ways of thinking. Currently, there is a *third wave* of behavior therapy that includes a variety of approaches, such as DBT, or *dialectical behavior therapy* (Linehan, 1993), which is used to treat a disorder called "borderline personality disorder"; *mindfulness-based cognitive therapy,* or MBCT (Segal, Williams & Teasdale, 2001; Williams, Teasdale, Segal & Kabat-Zinn, 2007), which is used to treat depression; and an approach we will focus on in this chapter called *acceptance and commitment therapy*, or ACT (pronounced as one word rather than letters), developed by Hayes and colleagues (Hayes, Strosahl & Wilson, 1999; Hayes, 2004; Luoma, Hayes & Walser, 2007).

Acceptance and Commitment Therapy Strategies

To some degree, ACT interventions share some commonalities with behavioral and cognitive approaches. For example, ACT also focuses on the use of science or research to collect data about positive and negative therapy outcomes and currently has a well-supported empirical basis for its model (Hayes, Luoma, Bond, Masuda & Lillis, 2006). Also, like traditional cognitive-behavioral approaches, ACT focuses on the function of both behaviors and private events, such as thoughts, feelings, and body sensations. ACT interventions are based on an approach to human language in which literalization, evaluation, and comparison are viewed as contributors to psychopathology. In the opinion of ACT therapists, clients become fused or overidentified with beliefs and schemas that are created and maintained by language. For example, a client with an eating disorder becomes fused with the role of being bulimic or anorexic.

DEFUSION.   What do ACT helpers do in these situations? First, they employ a series of processes designed to tackle the fusion to literal language, called *defusion techniques* ("defusion" being a word they made up). One of the major ways they do this is through the use of language metaphors. Defusion aims to help clients look *at* their thoughts rather than *from* their thoughts (Hayes & Smith, 2005; Luoma, Hayes & Walser, 2007). Stated another way, defusion techniques are "methods for learning how to get present in the here and now in a broader and more flexible way, with the point being to break through the illusion of language" in order to notice the process of thinking (p. 21). In the previous example, the client would be encouraged to defuse by stating "I'm having the thought that I'm bulimic" instead of "I'm bulimic." Hayes and Smith (2005, p. 21) explain it this way: "When you think a thought, it structures your world. When you see a thought you can still see how it structures your world, but you also see that you are doing the structuring…. It would be as if you always wore yellow sunglasses and forgot you were wearing them. Defusion is like taking off your glasses and holding them out, several inches away from your face; then you can see how they make the world appear to be yellow, instead of seeing only the yellow world" (notice the metaphor in this description). Defusion methods are used in ACT to deal with problems linked to language but not with situations such as abuse that require action and are based on client values.

EXPERIENTIAL AVOIDANCE.   ACT helpers also note and focus on *experiential avoidance*—that is, the private events or experiences that clients try to avoid, such as the sadness and despair a client may feel as a result of her eating disorder. However, unlike the cognitive therapist who uses disputation processes to challenge faulty beliefs and negative emotions, ACT endeavors to help clients develop acceptance of these private or internal experiences. If the client says "I'm a terrible person," the ACT helper may respond by saying "Notice the thought you're having. Thank it. Don't give your life over to it if it plays a negative role in your life." This is because ACT has found that by trying to eliminate a particular thought or belief, it actually takes greater hold and becomes more central. In ACT, acceptance helps clients move out of the narrowing process that comes as a result of experiential avoidance and aversive control with the goal of increasing psychological flexibility. ACT methods focus on changing the *function* or *context* of the thought rather than the specific form of the thought or even the frequency of the thoughts and beliefs.

MINDFULNESS.   ACT also promotes awareness of the present moment through *mindfulness*. Based on the work of Kabat-Zinn (2003; 2005), mindfulness simply means having the client get in touch with experiences as they occur on a moment-to-moment basis (note that it is also useful for helpers because we need to model this for our clients). Sometimes, it is referred to as simply "being in the moment." In ACT, the purpose of mindfulness is to help clients separate or defuse from literal, evaluative language and thoughts. Mindfulness is also a major component of other therapeutic interventions (such as DBT and MBCT), and mindfulness mediation has as host of positive effects on the body, ranging from increased immune function to decreased hypertension. A useful way to teach mindfulness to clients is with the mnemonic ONE MIND (Marra, 2004, pp. 105–106):

O̲ne thing

N̲ow

E̲nvironment—what is happening out there?

M̲oment—immediate

I̲ncrease senses—touch, taste, vision, hearing

N̲onjudgmental—not good or bad, right or wrong

D̲escribe—descriptive rather than evaluative or comparative language

While there are many ways to be mindful, a basic one is to simply sit quietly for an extended period of time and follow your breath—notice it coming into the body and notice it going out of the body.

VALUES AND COMMITMENT.   A final aspect of ACT that is somewhat unique is the emphasis it places on values and commitment. ACT practitioners help clients get in touch with what they deeply want in their lives. In ACT, unlike a goal—which is something you can obtain and has a beginning and an end—a value is more of an ongoing process. A value is what and who you want to be about in your life. A typical ACT homework assignment might be to have the client develop narratives about what they want to be about in specific life domains, such as intimate relationships, family, social networks, employment and work, education and training, spirituality, and citizenship and community. After exploring this question, ACT practitioners help clients enact actions to support these values and anticipate barriers that may impede the actions. A particular area of focus in counseling would be when clients indicate that something is important to them and yet they have limited success in that domain. For example, a client may want to be in a loving relationship but is living alone. When clients discover what they deeply value, they may experience strong emotions and also a renewed sense of vitality. ACT is a rather comprehensive approach that encompasses a variety of interventions, much like DBT. For more information, you may wish to consult the ACT website (http://contextualpsychology.org).

Narrative Therapy Interventions

Not dissimilar to the ACT approach are interventions based on social constructivism called *narrative therapy*, or NT. Like ACT, NT also has been referred to as a "third wave" in psychotherapy. Both ACT and NT stress the symbolic meaning resulting from clients' literal language processes and narratives or stories they have developed about themselves and their lives. For example, a client who is afraid to leave the house has usually constructed a narrative or story that is titled "I'm an agoraphobic." This story gets told, retold, and repeated so many times that the client identifies with it and believes it represents a single "truth" about himself or herself. In NT, a "story" is something that has a recognizable structure, a beginning, middle, and end, and also a plot. The story contains events that occur in sequence in time, and the plot accounts for this sequence. Stories may be past, present, or projected into the future. They may be held by clients in secret or repeatedly shared to others. The aim of constructivist and narrative therapy interventions is to help clients engage in "restorying" so there are alternative stories available in addition to the one they brought to the helper's door. White and Epston (1990), who are associated with the development of narrative therapy, believe that clients' identities become fused with their initial story.

EXTERNALIZING QUESTIONS.   In a collaborative way, the narrative therapist uses a series of questions to help clients deconstruct this narrative. These kinds of questions include *externalizing questions* to help the client separate from the problem. For example, with the client who self-identifies as agoraphobic, examples of externalizing questions used in NT would be:

> What does your anxiety require of you, and how do you adjust to meet these requirements?
> Or
> What's the mission of your anxiety in your life? How do you participate in this mission?

In this example, these externalizing questions make the anxiety or the agoraphobia an occurrence rather than the way the client self-defines.

QUESTIONS OF UNIQUE OUTCOMES.   These externalizing questions are followed by questions exploring *unique outcomes*—because it is in the account of unique events or memories of "forgotten exceptions" that alternative stories and narratives are developed. In the previous example, a question of unique outcomes would be:

> Were there ever times in your life when you resisted, not allowing the anxiety to take over? How? What was your experience then?

Basically, NT assumes that the client's presenting and primary story is a "first draft," and the task of the narrative strategy is to help the client create additional drafts that are more accurate, accepting, and inclusive. This is accomplished through a series of questions such as those noted previously over a period of time—often requiring repetition, patience, and time to allow a newer version of the old story to emerge. NT also requires careful listening by the helper. As Sedney, Baker, and Gross (1994) noted, helpers listen to the sequences in the story, how the story is started, hints of feelings and emotions, the client's understanding of one's role in the story, and even what is missing in the story. For additional information about this approach, consult the NT website at http://www.narrativeapproaches.com.

One of the things that ACT and NT have in common is their emphasis on the client's fusion to literal language. Like ACT, NT also uses a lot of metaphors to introduce new language to clients. And also like ACT, NT questions clients' definitions of themselves as "abnormal" and promotes self-acceptance. Another thing ACT and NT share in common is their emphasis on client knowing. ACT helpers encourage clients to trust themselves and their experiences. Narrative therapists emphasize to clients that they—not others—are the authors of their stories and they have the power to revise them because they hold the "privileged position" as the story's author and creator (White, 2007).

Currently, narrative approaches are valuable for clients with trauma issues. Clients are encouraged—with the support of the helper—to construct a conscious narrative of their traumatic experience so their story of it is complete, without gaps, from beginning to end. The purpose of the narrative in trauma therapy is to help clients gain access to memory stored in the nonverbal mind, to organize traumatic memory fragments into a coherent nonverbal narrative, and to bring closure to the experience by translating the nonverbal narrative into a conscious historical memory.

Narrative approaches are also very useful in career counseling. Savickas (1993) described the role of the career helper as one of an editor. In this role, the career helper helps clients identify and describe their life stories, find meaning in them, and construct stories about their future that encompass their careers. Because one's career is viewed as more than one's job, narrative approaches to career counseling help clients discover the interrelationship of life roles in their stories—both current and future.

Finally, although many clients arrive in counseling with individual stories, many others have stories connected to families and cultures. NT is a predominant approach in family therapy as well as in individual counseling (Bitter, 2009). One of the things that NT can do is help enlarge the space of the dominant story to allow room for marginalized perspectives and narratives that get squeezed out by the dominant story. NT has been referred to as an approach of social justice. In the following two sections of this chapter, we describe interventions that specifically address strategies for working with client systems and cultural groups.

In some ways, the ACT and NT approaches have much in common with effective multicultural counseling. Both approaches employ an accepting rather than an evaluative position. ACT has generated several studies of its efficacy with diverse kinds of clients (Hayes et al., 2006). NT is essentially a pluralistic approach that values diverse and multiple realities and underscores the importance of inclusion for marginalized perspectives. A potential limitation of these approaches cited by Corey (2009) is that the "not knowing" stance of the helper and the "client-as-expert" stance for the client may engender a potential lack of confidence in the helper's ability to be helpful with clients from some cultural and ethnic groups.

WORKING WITH CLIENT INTERACTIONAL PATTERNS AND RELATIONSHIPS

With any individual client who seeks counseling, the client is part of a larger interpersonal network, sometimes referred to as an *interpersonal system*. In any interpersonal system such as a marriage, a family, a work department, or a peer group, all segments of the system are interrelated, and change in one part affects the entire system. In those interpersonal systems to which the client belongs, the client typically interacts in predictable patterns. These patterns can be seen within the context of the helping system as well as within the various systems to which the client belongs. In other words, the helper can see the client's typical interpersonal pattern not only in the kinds of interactions the client reports with other persons but also in the way this interpersonal pattern is re-enacted within the helping relationship. Thus, in working with interactional patterns of the client, the helper can intervene at two different levels: use of interventions that deal directly with the helper-client system and use of interventions that have an impact on the client's interactional style with other persons.

Re-enactment of Interactional Patterns in the Helping Process

Clients begin to develop predictable interactional patterns in their family of origin. *Interactional patterns* are affected by many factors, including family construction and birth order (Adler, 1958), family rules and communication patterns (Watzlawick, Beavin & Jackson, 1967), and general level of health or dysfunction of the family system (Haley, 1997; Miller, 1981). For many people who become clients, their family of origin experience was problematic in three major ways:

1. There was a lack of a strong bond between the parents—sometimes referred to as a lack of a "primary parental coalition" (Minuchin, 1974).
2. There were disruptions or interruptions in the ways parents met children's developmental needs for nurturance, structure, separateness, and attachment.
3. There were child-rearing practices that were either too authoritarian or too permissive in nature.

To cope with this, children—as they grow older—develop a characteristic way of interacting with others. People who use an Adlerian counseling model refer to this as a "lifestyle" (Adler, 1958); those who use a transactional analysis model refer to this as a "script" (Woolams & Brown, 1979). We will talk about three characteristic interpersonal patterns from a developmental/dynamic model (see also Horney, 1970). Clients generally cope in interpersonal systems by (1) moving toward people, (2) moving away or withdrawing from people, or (3) moving against or resisting other people.

People who move toward others are likely to be perceived by others as understanding and accommodating. These sort of people are usually helpful and cooperative but have trouble being appropriately assertive, direct, and, above all, angry. This sort of lifestyle or interpersonal pattern is designed to elicit from others the support and nurturing that was missed as a child. With a client who behaves like this toward the helper, the helper must be careful not just to provide acceptance but also to focus on the general interpersonal style of the client—what the client has missed from his or her family and is trying to elicit from the helper as well as—no doubt—from numerous other people.

Clients who characteristically move away or withdraw from people will demonstrate the same behavior in the counseling relationship. They may seek help, but they will attempt to maintain as much emotional distance as possible and to remain emotionally unconnected from the counseling per se. Although at one level these clients are trying to push the helper away, at another level, they want desperately for the helper to stay connected to them. These clients pose quite a challenge for helpers. To respond reflexively and give up on the client is nontherapeutic. At the same time, if the helper attempts to become too emotionally connected, these clients will feel alarmed and anxious because this is so unfamiliar. The helper will need to stay present and engaged at a pace that follows the client's lead; but above all, the helper must not give up on these individuals.

Clients who move against people are likely to try to directly intimidate the helper or to passively resist the helper's efforts. They may behave in ways either to take control of the session or to "push the helper's buttons" and make the helper feel inadequate. These kinds of clients may be especially difficult for beginning helpers who may respond counter-therapeutically with fear, competition, or counter-hostility (Teyber, 2006). Again, as in other instances, it is important for the helper not to respond reflexively and give these clients what they are trying to elicit. With these individuals, the helper must avoid getting involved in a battle or power struggle and focus instead on what the clients may be trying to get and/or avoid with their interpersonal styles and the likely impact on their lives. These three interpersonal coping styles create challenges because they are used in all types of situations, including life choices such as careers and partners, in a rigid or inflexible way (Teyber, 2006). Lack of psychological flexibility is a major reason why clients come to see helpers.

Why do clients act out their typical interactional pattern with helpers? Quite simply, it is a form of a test. They feel that the helper will respond in the same old way as most everyone else, but they hope against hope that the helper will provide a different and more helpful response. When the helper does, they will not have to keep re-enacting their same old pattern and can move beyond the point at which they become "stuck"—not only with the helper but also with other people. Teyber (2006) presented the following brief illustration of this process.

> Suppose a rather passive and dependent woman says to her male therapist, "Where should we start today?" Even though he has the best of intentions, the therapist will fail this test and reenact a maladaptive relational pattern if he says, "Tell me about _____." . . . The therapist is likely to pass this test and disconfirm this faulty belief if he repeatedly looks for ways to encourage her own initiative and actively supports her when she takes it. (p. 289)

Teyber (2006) also noted, "The therapist can fail the client's test by responding in a way that reenacts maladaptive relational patterns and confirms pathogenic beliefs. Alternatively, the therapist can pass the test and provide a corrective emotional experience by behaviorally demonstrating that, at least sometimes, some relationships can be different" (p. 288). Shifts in these interpersonal patterns we have discussed form the basis of a therapeutic approach known as interpersonal therapy.

Interpersonal Therapy

Originally developed by Klerman and Weissman (1992), interpersonal therapy is now an evidence-based helping approach for the treatment of depression. Interpersonal therapy or ITP emphasizes that client issues do not occur in a vacuum but rather an interpersonal context. ITP therapeutic strategies are designed to help clients respond more effectively to this interpersonal context and particularly interpersonal issues that are associated with the onset of clinical symptoms. Specific ITP strategies used to help clients achieve this goal focus on interpersonal disputes, role transitions, and interpersonal deficits.

INTERPERSONAL DISPUTES. These strategies help clients to identify interpersonal disputes and choose a satisfactory plan of action to address them, including modification of expectations or communication patterns. The helper works to promote client understanding of how role expectations can relate to interpersonal disputes (Weissman, Markowitz & Klerman, 2007). Questions to help clients understand this process include the following:

- What are the issues in the disputes?
- What are the differences in the expectations and values?
- What options do I have in this dispute? (Klerman and Weissman, 1992)

In addition, the helper explores with the client whether there are also any parallels in other relationships (including the therapeutic one). For example, what is the client gaining by this interpersonal dispute? What are the unspoken assumptions behind the client's behavior, and how is the dispute perpetuated? (Klerman and Weissman, 1992)

ROLE TRANSITIONS.   These strategies help clients to mourn and accept any loss of an old or former role (such as spouse, employee, sibling, child, partner, etc.) as well as to regard a new role as something that can be a positive force. The helper assists clients in reviewing positive and negative aspects of both old and new life roles and in exploring feelings about what has been lost and what can be gained. The helper also attends to any appropriate expression of feelings or affect related to role change and encourages development of new social support systems and new skills (Klerman and Weissman, 1992). For example, consider the client who feels lost, abandoned, and blue after his or her last child gets married and leaves home. While the primary role of parent is no longer primary, the helper helps the client explore other opportunities for new roles with increased leisure time and fewer responsibilities for one's family. Perhaps it is a time in the client's life for some new skills training, a new job focus, or new learning that may lead to a new path or greater creativity.

INTERPERSONAL DEFICITS.   These strategies help clients explore issues of social isolation or deficits in social support systems. The helper assists the client to explore prior significant relationships, including both negative and positive aspects of such relationships. Additionally, the helper and client explore any repetitive patterns that crop up in the client's interpersonal relationships. For example, as we discussed above, perhaps the client withdraws socially from opportunities to meet new people. Or perhaps the client has difficulty in initiating social contacts and events and relies on invitations and contacts only if initiated by others. This category also includes exploration about the therapeutic relationship. The helper provides the client with opportunities to discuss the client's positive and negative feelings about the helping relationship and the helper and how these feelings may be reflections of other relationships in the client's life (Klerman and Weissman, 1992). For additional information about the IPT approach, we encourage to consult the source guide developed by Weissman, Markowitz, and Klerman (2007). In addition, Teyber (2006) has written about an extensive, integrative approach to interpersonal therapeutic interventions. You will note some similarities between this third focus of IPT and the material we discuss in the following section on working with client social systems.

WORKING WITH CLIENT CULTURAL AND SOCIAL SYSTEMS

Almost all the interventions we have presented in the preceding part of this chapter are drawn from counseling theories, such as interpersonal, self-in-relations, gestalt, rational-emotive, cognitive-behavioral, Ericksonian, and family systems. These theories have been developed by founding fathers and, as such, have been critiqued by multicultural theorists as reflecting a Eurocentric bias and value system and as being somewhat culturally irrelevant for clients who feel marginalized from the mainstream.

When issues of cultural salience—such as race, gender, religion, sexual orientation, and social class—are considered, some of the classic therapeutic interventions we have described may even be culturally contraindicated. According to Brown (1994), it is important to ask these questions in selecting a helping strategy:

1. Will this strategy oppress my client even more?
2. What does my strategy need to offer in working with a "multiply oppressed" client?

For those clients whose worldviews (i.e., basic perceptions and understanding of the world) do not reflect the "rugged individualism" of the Eurocentric tradition, other interventions that are more culturally appropriate are needed that address group, community, and sociopolitical causes as well as the individual causes the client presents.

The Community Genogram

Clients and their issues are connected to and impacted by the cultural and social systems to which they belong. Helpers are also affected by their own cultural and social systems. The impact of communities and social groups can be positive, negative, or mixed. The concept of a genogram was originally developed as a tool used in family therapy to view the chronology of a family's life cycle—that is, the effect of family generations on the client over time and over various developmental stages (Carter & McGoldrick, 2005).

Ivey (1995; Ivey et al., 2010) has developed the *community genogram* as a way to depict the interaction between a client and the community and cultural systems. As Ivey and colleagues (2002) noted, "One major community event can change the individual's total culture. In turn, one individual can affect the total culture as well" (p. 18). A genogram is a tool to "ensure that individual issues are seen in their full contextual background" (p. 10). Ivey and colleagues describe four goals of the community genogram:

1. to generate a narrative story of the client in a community context;
2. to help the client generate an understanding of how we all develop in community;
3. to understand the cultural background of the client; and
4. to focus on personal, family, and group strengths. (pp. 10–11)

(*Note:* We agree with Ivey and colleagues that before developing this sort of story and understanding with your clients that it is important to first develop this awareness with yourself, the helper of clients.)

There are two basic processes to using the community genogram. The first process involves developing a visual picture of the client's culture and community. The second process involves developing a strengths- or asset-based story or narrative of several positive images reflected in the visual picture. For specific guidelines within these two processes, refer to Figure 9.1.

Ecomaps

Another intervention that is useful for working with client cultural and social systems is the *ecomap*. An ecomap is a visual tool used to map the "ecology" (hence, *eco*), or the client's relationship to social systems in his or her life, including relationships, resources, and systems that may be strong, stressful, or unavailable or tenuous (Hepworth, Rooney, Rooney, Strom-Gottfried & Larsen, 2010). For example, Lott (2002) described how social institutions involving education and housing distance, exclude, and discriminate against poor and low-status persons. In general, social support systems—or lack thereof—play a crucial role in the social functioning of clients. A sample ecomap for a couple (dyadic) client is shown in Figure 9.2. In this figure, note that the

Part One

Develop a Visual Representation of the Community

1. Consider a large piece of paper as representing your broad culture and community. You should select the community in which you primarily were raised, but any other community, past or present, may be used.

2. Place yourself or the client in that community, either at the center or other appropriate place on the paper. Represent yourself or the client by a circle, a star, or other significant symbol.

3. Place your own or the client's family or families on the paper, again represented by the symbol most relevant. The family can be nuclear or extended or both.

4. Place the important and most influential groups on the community genogram, again representing them by circles or other visual symbols. School, family, neighborhood, and spiritual groups are most often selected. For teens, the peer group is often particularly important. For adults, work groups and other special groups tend to become more central.

5. Connect the groups to the individual, perhaps drawing heavier lines to indicate the most influential groups.

Part Two

Search for Images and Narratives of Strength

1. Focus on one single community group or the family. You or the client may want to start with a negative story or image, but do not work with the negative until positive strengths are solidly in mind.

2. Develop an image that represents an important positive experience. Allow the image to build in your mind, and note the positive feelings that occur with the image. If you allow yourself or the client to fully experience this positive image, you may experience fears and/or strong bodily feelings. These anchored bodily experiences represent positive strengths that can be drawn on to help you and your clients deal with difficult issues in therapy and in life.

3. Tell the story of the image. If it is your story, you may want to write it down in journal form. If you are drawing out the story from a client, listen sensitively.

4. Develop at least two more positive images from different groups within the community. It is useful to have a positive family image, spiritual image, and cultural image. Again, many will want to focus on negative issues, but maintain the search for positive resources.

5. Summarize the positive images in your own words and reflect on them. Encourage clients to summarize their learning, thoughts, and feelings in their own words. As you or your client thinks back, what occurs? Record the responses, for these can be drawn on in many settings in therapy or in daily life.

FIGURE 9.1   The Community Genogram: Identifying Strengths
Source: From Allen E. Ivey, Mary Bradford Ivey & Carlos P. Zalaquett. *Intentional Interviewing and Counseling, 7th edition.* Copyright 2010 by Wadsworth, a division of Cengage Learning, Inc. Reproduced by permission.

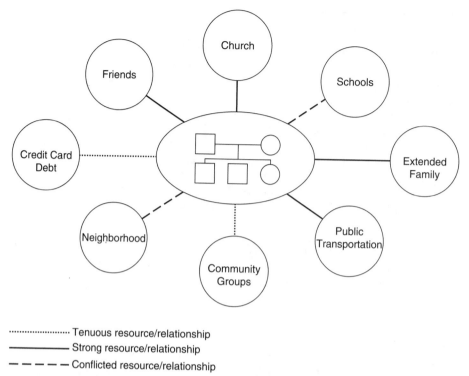

.... Tenuous resource/relationship
——————— Strong resource/relationship
— — — — Conflicted resource/relationship

FIGURE 9.2 **Sample Ecomap**
Source: Adapted from Dean H. Hepworth et al. *Direct Social Work Practice: Theory and Skills, 8th edition.* Copyright 2010 by Wadsworth, a division of Cengage Learning, Inc. Reproduced by permission.

clients—depicted in the middle of the map—are connected to various social systems by different types of lines:

1. A solid line (_____) connects the couple to systems that are strong.
2. A broken line (_ _ _ _ _) connects the couple to systems that are negative or stressful.
3. A dotted line (.............) connects the couple to systems that are unavailable or tenuous.

A helper uses an ecomap in conjunction with discussion of cultural and social support systems for the client, noting areas where social support systems are positive, negative, or lacking. The ecomap is a useful tool for meeting the challenge of assessing how these systems "interact, fail to interact, or are needed to interact in response to clients' needs" (Hepworth et al., 2010, p. 220).

Helping Roles and Indigenous Practices

In working with cultural and social client systems, a variety of roles are used to complement and extend the traditional role of helper/helper. These additional roles are described by Atkinson, Thompson, and Grant (1993) and Atkinson and Hackett (2004) as follows:

• *Adviser:* One who provides information and guidance and who engages in problem-solving with clients
• *Advocate:* One who represents and advocates for clients to other people and organizations

- *Change agent:* One who actively tries to impact the client's social and cultural environment, especially aspects of it that are discriminatory and/or oppressive
- *Facilitator of indigenous support systems and practices:* One who recognizes and actively uses the support people and systems indigenous or belonging to the client's culture. This may include the use of extended family or kinship, community elders, and religious and spiritual resources, such as a shamanic healer. This also may include the use of or the referral to someone trained and skilled in using healing methods indigenous or belonging to the client's culture, such as a *currandismo* (Mexican folk healer) or a tai chi instructor.

Many of the helping traditions from non-Western cultures are centered in spiritual and religious beliefs and systems. Often, the healers within these cultural systems are religious or spiritual leaders. For example, a client who has lost a significant family member or who is faced with a life-threatening illness may participate in a healing ritual to grieve the loss or to cleanse the body of impure thoughts, deeds, or spirits. For example, in some cultures, the healer—such as a shaman or a medicine man—makes a journey to this spirit world on behalf of a client who may be ill. Often, this journey is made to the sound of a drum or another percussion instrument or to a chant or song. For example, in the autobiography of Lori Arviso Alvord (Alvord & Van Pelt, 1999), she described the ritual of a Navajo blessing ceremony over the new intensive care unit in the traditional hospital in which she worked as a physician:

> The hataalii (medicine man) stood next to his wife. They were both dressed in traditional clothing . . . . In his hand the hataalii held a feather and a bowl of sacred water. He began to sing . . . . He stepped over to the row of doctors and waved an eagle feather. Over each of our bodies, he twirled the feather and sprinkled us with water. His voice rang out, rhythmic and atonal, that familiar sound of Navajo chant . . . . This ceremony medicine could make it possible for Navajo patients to feel safe being treated in the new ICU. (p. 105)

This sort of healing ceremony reflects the notion that for many non-Western cultures, healing is holistic, with "little distinction between physical and mental well-being. Many indigenous healers perceive human distress as an indication that people have fallen out of harmony with both their internal and external environment" (Lee, 1996, p. 90). This is especially important when one considers that the word *healing* means "wholeness."

An important concept in using helping strategies to effect change is that of *self-efficacy*, a cognitive process that mediates behavioral change (Bandura, 1997). When self-efficacy is high, clients feel a sense of personal agency, confidence, and empowerment. High self-efficacy not only influences feelings, beliefs, behaviors, and interactions but also a person's biochemistry. Increasingly, self-efficacy is also being identified as a significant factor both in the use of prevention and risk programs and in the academic and career performance of diverse groups of clients (Cormier, Nurius & Osborn, 2009). Self-efficacy seems to be an important factor in promoting change for female clients and for clients of color, especially when it is paired with some of the strategies that focus on external social systems as well as an internal sense of confidence in oneself.

APPLICATION EXERCISE 9.1

Intervention Strategies

In this exercise, three hypothetical client cases are described. After reading over each case, describe what you believe the client's probable counseling goals would be and the related intervention strategies that could be used to help each client reach these goals. Consider goals and strategies for all five areas we discussed in this chapter: feelings, beliefs, behaviors, language, interactional patterns, and cultural/social systems. You may do this activity alone, with a partner, or in a small-group discussion. You may wish to exchange your responses and ideas with other helpers or share your thoughts with your instructor.

A. CASE 1

Asani is an Asian American at a large university; she is overwhelmed by the size of the university, having lived in a small town all her life. She is concerned about her shyness and feels it is preventing her from making friends. Asani reports being uncertain about how to reach out to people and reports feeling very lonely but deeply longing for close friendships. She is also concerned about her performance on tests. Although she believes her study habits are adequate, she reports that she "blows" the tests because she gets so uptight about them. Asani believes her grades are a reflection of herself and her family. She is worried about bringing dishonor to her family if she gets low grades.

Probable Outcome Goals

1. _____

   _____

2. _____

   _____

3. _____

   _____

Possible Helping Strategies

1. _____

   _____

   _____

2. _____

   _____

   _____

3. _____
_____
_____

B. CASE 2

Mr. and Mrs. Yule have been married for seven years. Both are in their sixties, and this is the second marriage for each; their previous spouses died. Mr. and Mrs. Yule are concerned that they rushed into this second relationship without adequate thought. They report that they argue constantly about everything. They feel they have forgotten how to talk to each other in a civil manner. Mrs. Yule states that she realizes her constant nagging upsets Mr. Yule; Mr. Yule discloses that his spending a lot of time with his male buddies irritates Mrs. Yule. Mr. Yule calls Mrs. Yule a "nagger," and she refers to him as an "SOM—selfish old man."

Probable Outcome Goals

1. _____
_____

2. _____
_____

3. _____
_____

Possible Helping Strategies

1. _____
_____
_____

2. _____
_____
_____

3. _____
_____
_____

(continued)

C. CASE 3

Michael is a thirteen-year-old boy attending a middle school in an urban area. He is constantly starting fights and getting into trouble. He says he finds himself suddenly punching other kids—and that he does not know how or why. Only after the fights does he realize his temper has gotten out of hand. He reports that he considers himself to be "hotheaded" and that he likes that about himself. He reports spending a lot of time on the streets, and he feels this greatly helps him survive. He says that although he is close to his mother, he rarely sees her, as she works two to three jobs to support the family. He has had no contact with his father since he was a young boy.

Probable Outcome Goals

1. _____

_____

2. _____

_____

3. _____

_____

Possible Helping Strategies

1. _____

_____

_____

2. _____

_____

_____

3. _____

_____

APPLICATION EXERCISE 9.2

Construction of Summary Cases

This activity asks you—by yourself or with a partner or in a small group—to create several scenarios of cases and examples. Describe each case by using the questions below. The purpose of the activity is to help you pull together various aspects of what you have learned in this book and apply them to various helping situations.

1. Construct a helping situation that involves a client who in some way is culturally different from you—different gender, race, age, ethnicity, religion, sexual orientation, health/disability status, socioeconomic level, and so on.
2. Describe the cultural dimensions of the client and the cultural dimensions of the helper.
3. Describe any potential therapeutic, cultural, and ethical issues arising from this scenario.
4. Describe ways the helper should handle the situation or respond to this client, including any specific helping strategies and interventions that are needed.

Summary

In working with clients—all of whom present unique concerns and circumstances—you may find the strategies described in this chapter useful. However, there are several cautions to consider in using a helping strategy effectively. The first caution in strategy implementation is to avoid oversimplification of the procedure. Although a procedure may seem relatively simple to implement, even with little experience, any therapeutic endeavor can be effective or ineffective depending on how it is administered. Second, you must practice using strategies. You will not be an expert when you first start using them, but your skills will grow as you practice. Also, remember that strategies are rarely used in isolation. Several different strategies or combinations of procedures may be necessary to deal with the complexity and range of concerns presented by a single client. As an example, suppose a helper treats a client's alcoholism but ignores the anxiety for which alcohol is used as a tranquilizer. The strategies used to decrease the drinking behavior may not be too effective unless the helper and client also use strategies to deal with the client's limited coping skills, self-defeating thoughts, and environmental issues that maintain the drinking.

Remember that the effectiveness of helping strategies depends—to some degree—on the strength and trust of the helping relationship as well as the degree to which these strategies are used in a gender- and culture-friendly way. Responding to a client's social and environmental milieu is as important in strategy implementation as responding to a client's presenting feelings, beliefs, and behaviors.

Also, it is important to realize the limitations of helping objectives and strategies and of helpers. One of the most frustrating experiences that helpers report is the experience of being thwarted in their attempts to help clients change and grow. Beginning helpers often approach the counseling process with a lot of zest, zeal, and unwavering idealism. Although a certain amount of this is useful, it can also lead to discouragement with oneself and with clients. Almost all clients will resist your attempts to help in some way. Some clients who see you at the request of someone else may be openly oppositional. Other clients may desire to change but because of biochemical imbalances may require medication for such things as depression or anxiety management. Clients with addictions may also find the process of recovery especially difficult. Clients from very dysfunctional family systems may find the weight of the system working against their own individual efforts to change. So, as you approach your growth and development and your own efforts in working with clients, it is important to remember that there are some limits to what happens in the counseling process and that almost all client resistance to change is about fear. As clients become more able to trust themselves and you, your efforts and theirs will be rewarded.

Reflective Questions

1. In this chapter, we discuss a variety of interventions to work with the whole person (e.g., the client's feelings, beliefs, behaviors, language, interactional patterns, and cultural/social systems). As you have read and worked with these interventions, which ones feel most natural and comfortable for you? Which ones do you believe would cause the most trouble? Why?

2. Where in your own body do you consistently hold in feelings? How do you become aware of these? What do you do to release them?

3. Can you identify situations in which your beliefs have affected the way you feel and act?

4. Which persons have you used in your life for role models? Do characters in books, TV shows, or movies also serve as role models for you? What are their characteristics that appeal to you?

5. How do you apply self-management to everyday behaviors for yourself?

6. What would your life be like if you simply noticed your thoughts rather than judging them?

7. Can you identify labels you have constructed for yourself from your stories about yourself? How have these labels helped you? Limited you?

8. What is your characteristic interactional pattern? Can you trace it back to your family of origin? How do you think this pattern will affect the way you interact with your clients?

9. Refer to Figure 9.1, and with a partner or in a small group, construct a community genogram for yourself, your family, and your own cultural reference groups. Discuss what you learn or glean from this process with your partner or group members.

My Helping Lab

For each exercise, log on to MyHelpingLab at http://www.myhelpinglab.com and then click the Topics tab.

1. Click the Theories tab to locate the Gestalt tab. Review the Video Lab segment for Child-Body Awareness. If you were the helper, what kinds of suggestions would you offer to this client to help him become more aware of his body and its relationship to his feelings?

2. Next, click the Theories tab to locate the Cognitive tab. Choose the Video Lab for the following selections:

   a. *Identifying Specific Beliefs about the Problem:* In this segment, how did the therapist help the client explore his beliefs about himself? In your opinion, was this cognitive approach helpful or not helpful in this cross-racial dyad and with this client's presenting issue?

   b. *Identifying Positive Beliefs for Recovery:* How effective were the therapist's attempts to help the client develop some useful, adaptive beliefs in this segment?

   c. *Cognitive Intervention:* Do you agree with the therapist's assertion in this segment that "the only thing stopping this client is his thinking"? Why or why not?

   d. From the cognitive intervention that you saw, can you construct an A-B-C-D-E analysis? Share your thoughts of it with your classmates or instructor.

3. Continuing with the Theories topic, locate the Cognitive-Behavioral tab and then choose the Video Lab for the following selections:

   a. *Exploring Feelings, Thoughts, and Behaviors:* What did you see Dr. Meichenbaum doing to help this client identify her core beliefs and feelings?

b. ***Shedding Light on Automatic Thoughts:*** How did Dr. Meichenbaum identify the relationship between what this client says to herself and her resulting feelings?

c. ***Using Empty Chair in CBT:*** In this segment, Dr. Meichenbaum uses a gestalt, affective strategy to help the client identify her feelings and the impact of these feelings. How did his use of this strategy help the client stay connected to her emotions?

d. ***Connecting Thoughts to Behavior/Feelings:*** What does Dr. Meichenbaum do to help connect thoughts, feelings, and behaviors for this client? What impact do you think this will have on the client's behaviors outside of this session?

e. ***Summarizing Options:*** In this segment, can you detect how Dr. Krumboltz helps the client identify goals, subgoals, and action steps, as we discussed in Chapter 8?

f. ***Helping Clients Become More Assertive:*** How does Dr. Krumboltz make use of modeling and behavior rehearsal in this segment? How did you feel about the impact of these strategies for the client?

g. ***Using Support to Empower Clients:*** What impact does providing positive feedback have on this client's commitment to the action plan they developed?

4. Continuing with the Theories tab, click the Narrative tab. Then, explore the following segments under the Video Lab:

a. ***Mother/Son Preferred Roles:*** How does the therapist elicit the client's problem story and the preferred story in this segment? How does the therapist relate the client's problem story to his resulting behavior and consequences? What do you note about the helper's use of language in this segment?

b. ***Mother/Son Externalizing the Problem:*** What do you think of the way the therapist externalizes the problem in this segment? With what effect?

c. ***Family: Exception:*** What did you think about the use of exception questions in this segment? How effective do you think they were?

5. Click the Theories tab again to locate the Object Relations tab. Watch both the Individual: Language of Relationships and the Individual: Interpretation of Patterns segments. In these segments, how does Dr. Scharff explore the nature of the relationship with the client? What relationship struggles does the client identify? How might these familial relationship struggles get reenacted with the helper?

6. Click the Process, Skills, and Techniques tab to locate the Practical Issues: Ethical Dilemmas tab. Next, choose the Video Lab for the Cultural Considerations in Counseling Sessions selection. How did these therapists use the cultural background of the couple to explore the couple's interpersonal patterns in their marriage? Can you identify what the primary interpersonal pattern in this marriage seems to be? Do you see any evidence of this interpersonal pattern getting replayed in the helping session between the couple client and the helpers?

7. Click the tab for Counseling Children and Adolescents to locate the Multicultural Considerations tab. Then, select the Case Archive to read and explore the case of When I Look into the Mirror: The Case of Tiffany. Respond to the three questions following this case on the MyHelpingLab site.

Recommended Readings

Beck, A. T. (2005). The current state of cognitive therapy: A 40-year retrospective. *Archives of General Psychiatry, 62,* 953–959.

Bitter, J. (2009). *Theories and practice of family therapy.* Belmont, CA: Brooks/Cole, Cengage.

Carter, B. & McGoldrick, M. (2005). *The expanded family life cycle: Individual, family, and social perspectives, 3rd edition.* Boston: Allyn & Bacon.

Cormier, S., Nurius, P. & Osborn, C. (2009). *Interviewing and change strategies for helpers: Fundamental skills and cognitive-behavioral interventions, 6th edition.* Belmont, CA: Brooks/Cole, Cengage.

Dobson, K. S. (Ed.). (2010). *Handbook of cognitive-behavioral therapies, 3rd edition.* New York: Guilford.

Dryden, W. (2009). *Skills in rational emotive behaviour counselling and psychotherapy.* Thousand Oaks, CA: Sage.

Greenberg, L. S. (2002). *Emotion-focused therapy: Coaching clients to work through their feelings.*

Washington, DC: American Psychological Association.

Greenberg, L. S. (2006). *Emotion-focused therapy for depression*. Washington, DC: American Psychological Association.

Hackney, H. & Cormier, L. S. (2009). *The professional helper, 6th edition*. Upper Saddle River, NJ: Pearson.

Hayes, S. C. (2004). Acceptance and commitment therapy, relational frame theory, and the third wave of behavioral and cognitive therapies. *Behavior Therapy, 35,* 639–665.

Hays, P. A. and Iwamasa, G. (2006). *Culturally responsive cognitive-behavioral therapy*. Washington, DC: American Psychological Association.

Hepworth, D. H., Rooney, R. H., Rooney, D. G., Strom-Gottfried, K. & Larsen, J. A. (2010). *Direct social work practice: Theory and skills, 8th edition*. Belmont, CA: Brooks/Cole, Cengage.

Kabat-Zinn, J. (2003). Mindfulness-based interventions in context: Past, present, and future. *Clinical Psychology: Science and Practice, 10,* 144–156.

Prochaska, J. & Norcross, J. (2010). *Systems of psychotherapy, 7th edition*. Belmont, CA: Brooks/Cole, Cengage.

Spiegler, M. D. & Guevremont, D. C. (2010). *Contemporary behavior therapy, 5th edition*. Belmont, CA: Wadsworth/Cengage.

Teyber, E. (2006). *Interpersonal processes in psychotherapy, 5th edition*. Belmont, CA: Brooks/Cole, Thomson.

Watson, D. L. & Tharp, R. G. (2007). *Self-directed behavior: Self-modification for personal adjustment, 9th edition*. Belmont, CA: Wadsworth.

Weissman, M., Markowitz, J. & Klerman, G. (2007). *Clinician's quick guide to interpersonal psychotherapy*. New York: Oxford University Press.

Common Challenges for Beginning Helpers*

Beginning helpers often experience fears and worries about their new role (Bernard & Goodyear, 2009). As most faculty and supervisors know, these feelings are normal and are experienced more intensely as beginning helpers move closer to their initial practicum and internship experiences. It is not a stretch to conclude and be comforted by the idea that even psychotherapy giants such as Albert Ellis, Carl Rogers, Alfred Adler, Fritz Perls, Carl Jung, Rollo May, Karen Horney, Virginia Satir, and Sigmund Freud struggled with many of the same fears and worries that you may be currently experiencing. They were also faced with developing and applying new skills, testing out unfamiliar environments, meeting new clients for the first time, applying confusing and sometimes convoluted theories to practice, and responding to the feedback and evaluation of others (which was not always favorable or kind). Biographical information about these key figures and their journey as clinicians and imperfect individuals is available on the web. You also may be surprised to know that although these fears and worries typically decrease over time, remnants may linger as you face new challenges, are confronted with old fears, navigate unfamiliar terrain, and learn and try out new skills. Thus, a discussion of these issues benefits not only beginning helpers but also helpers who know the value of retooling. This chapter provides an overview of some of these fears and worries as well as related issues concerning ways to prepare for ethical and supervisory challenges that you and your colleagues may experience.

COMMON CONCERNS OF BEGINNING HELPERS

In the first section of this chapter, we discuss common concerns of beginning helpers. These include managing stress and personal issues; managing anxiety in all shapes and forms; and managing the inevitable gulf between theory and practice. We also present some of the distorted cognitions that underlie these common concerns.

---

*Parts of the original chapter were written by Janine Bernard, Ph.D., and T. Anne Hawkins, Ph.D.

Managing Stress and Personal Issues

For many students in the helping professions, learning how to manage stress is key to their ongoing personal and professional development. How you manage stress today may predict how you manage it (or let it manage you) in your future. Obvious stressors for students in the helping professions include establishing a professional identity; managing the logistics of training programs (finances, accessing resources, and navigating numerous policies, procedures, and deadlines); juggling family and relationship responsibilities; managing and responding to competitiveness; meeting expectations of faculty, advisors, and supervisors; and meeting mounting academic and employment responsibilities.

Less obvious are stressors that relate to establishing personal competency and identity. Hazler and Kottler (2005) have suggested that training for the helping professions by its nature can be destabilizing. It requires changes in how you view yourself, others, and your world. For example, you may become challenged to consider the value of process rather than content and meaning rather than events. As you navigate your training in the helping professions, questions about the meaning of life and your role in the world may surface. Relationships with significant others, friends, and family may look and be experienced very differently as you proceed through your training program. You may find that as you examine and change your values and priorities that your expectations for intimacy in these relationships increase. These changes can feel unsettling and can initially create conflict and stress.

Stress and conflict are also increased as core interpersonal issues are inevitably triggered by course and clinical work. Unresolved interpersonal issues (that is, struggles with trust and emotional intimacy, competency, perfectionism, low self-esteem, and so on) can create seemingly insurmountable barriers as you navigate coursework, as you confront potential power struggles in departments and agencies, and especially as you work with clients. For example, if you experience a high need for approval, you may struggle to please family and friends, faculty, advisors, peers, site supervisors, faculty supervisors, site colleagues, clients, clients' families, and clients' referral sources (this is a long list of people to please) .

These and other unresolved interpersonal issues may adversely impact your development as a counselor and your work with clients. Hazler and Kottler (2005) provided the following list of common unresolved issues that many helpers experience:

- Being adult children of alcoholics
- Being victims of childhood sexual/physical/verbal abuse
- Undergoing a separation, divorce, or another family problem
- Living through an age-related developmental transition
- Being substance abusers or having other addictions
- Living through culture-, race-, or gender-related developmental transitions
- Lacking self-esteem/self-confidence
- Dealing with dependence/independence issues with a significant other (pp. 98–99)

More enduring problematic personality traits may affect your ability to manage stress and to navigate relationships with peers, faculty, supervisors, and clients. Helpers who are rigid, dogmatic, easily threatened by others, controlling, extremely vulnerable, or narcissistic may experience difficulties as they attempt to make sense of peer and supervisor relationships and especially as they develop relationships with clients.

As a result of these and similar issues, many students seek counseling for themselves. Not only can the process of self-exploration be healing, but it can also provide beginning helpers with valuable information about the vulnerable experience of being a client. Despite the value of this experience, many students struggle with the stigma they associate with seeking psychological help. However, a great many students and helpers do seek help for themselves, and the most common reasons reported for seeking helping services include:

- Depression/general unhappiness
- Marriage/divorce issues
- Relationship issues
- Self-esteem and confidence issues
- Anxiety
- Family of origin concerns

Although it may seem convenient to seek help from a faculty member in your department, this option raises privacy and ethical issues surrounding conflict of interest, confidentiality, evaluation, and multiple-role relationships. We discuss multiple relationships in greater detail in a later section of this chapter. Alternatively, counseling may be available at no cost or for a nominal fee at many college and university counseling centers. Those who have completed their professional training may seek counseling from community agencies or from practitioners in private practice settings.

Anxiety: All Combinations and Flavors

Exams, research papers, audio or video counseling tapes, clients who do not show up, clients who keep showing up, clients who adore and/or despise you, progress notes, confusing treatment plans, complicated individualized educational plans, and faculty and supervisors who magically know the "right" words for every situation—it is a wonder that beginning helpers ever wade through all of their hurdles! Somehow, though, you manage the anxiety that these situations and responsibilities provoke, and you graduate, pass licensing and certification exams, and become a professional helper, ultimately assisting clients in managing change and finding meaning and support.

This process is not without its challenges, particularly early in the journey. Typically, beginning helpers struggle with anxiety about competency and evaluation. Given the great responsibility of the work that you have chosen, the secrets you cradle, and the sometimes fragile helping relationships in which you find yourself, some anxiety is certainly warranted. In fact, low degrees of anxiety may drive beginning helpers to excel, but higher levels can create "analysis paralysis"—a state that makes it difficult for beginning helpers to retrieve and articulate words, to conceptualize and track client issues, to recall session content, and, most significantly, to attend to and be present for clients (Baird, 2008). The ambiguity that often characterizes the helping process can compound this anxiety, particularly for students who take comfort in order, structure, and predictability. Unresolved interpersonal issues regarding personal and professional competency, pleasing others, establishing and maintaining boundaries, and inaccurate self-evaluation can inadvertently shift the focus of helping sessions from the client to the clinician. Beginning helpers may find themselves caught up in a new but strangely familiar quest for the perfect theory, intervention, or interpretation. For example, you may become so immersed in a theory that you apply it indiscriminately in every helping relationship (and social situation). You may also become so focused on achieving competence that you confuse it with perfection. With so much riding on your performance, the focus may shift from the needs of the client to "What am I going to say next and how will I say it?" and, perhaps most familiar, "Will I be good enough?" You may lose sight of the fact that you are expected to be a beginner, not an immediate expert. You may measure your competency against that of senior faculty members and/or seasoned professionals at your field placement sites.

This need to be the "all-knowing" or "perfect" practitioner can significantly impede the helping process (Baird, 2008). Ironically, it may create distance between helpers and clients, decreasing feelings of empathy, approachability, and shared worldview. Beginning helpers who struggle with this need to be perfect may also experience the impostor phenomenon known as the overshadowing sense of fraudulence and incompetence that exists despite disconfirming data. Beginning helpers who experience this phenomenon may find themselves focusing on their mistake or missteps, searching endlessly for evidence of their incompetence, exaggerating both the frequency and the magnitude of their mistakes, and, ultimately, losing sight of the reality that all helpers make mistakes. They may be unaware of or resistant to the reality that mistakes can encourage increased self-awareness, genuineness, and flexibility on the part of helpers.

Many beginning helpers also experience varying degrees of evaluation anxiety. Making audiotapes and videotapes for a class requirement can feel like a daunting, overwhelming assignment. Developing and presenting a case presentation can trigger old, unresolved perfectionism and competency issues. Meeting a client or a supervisor for the first time also can evoke many similar anxieties and concerns. Clients with difficult relational styles or particularly defensive coping responses can strike anxiety and fear in even the most experienced helpers. It may help you to know that many of your colleagues may also be experiencing similar feelings and thoughts. Students in the helping professions commonly find themselves struggling with a variety of distorted cognitions, which can impact their feelings and behaviors as they work with clients. Following is a list of some of these distorted cognitions (some may sound familiar to you). We also list alternative cognitions for you to contemplate when finding yourself in the midst of such "cognitive pollution."

Distorted Cognitions
- "If I have any problems or unresolved issues in my life, I can't be an effective helper."
- "If my clients don't get better, it's my fault and/or I'm a terrible helper."
- "If my clients don't come back, I'm a lousy helper."
- "I'm the helper now; I have to know everything."

Alternative Cognitions
- "Every helper has problems and unresolved issues. If I work on issues, I'll be a better helper."
- "Clients are responsible for their own change process. I can help, but ultimately, it's their responsibility."
- "Clients don't come back for a variety of reasons. I need more information before I draw a conclusion."
- "I don't have to know everything. I'm a beginning helper; I'm still learning."

Managing the Theory and Practice Gulf

Bridging the gulf between theory and practice can be difficult for even the most competent and committed student. For example, you may have read about—and read about—and even practiced progressive relaxation with a colleague but have never applied the intervention in a session with a "real client" when, unexpectedly, the opportunity presents itself. This learning edge—or zone of proximal development, as described by Baird (2008)—depicts the point just beyond your current

APPLICATION EXERCISE 10.1

Exploring Common Concerns of Beginning Helpers

In this activity—which you can complete on your own, with a partner, or in a small group—explore the following open-ended questions about your concerns regarding the helping process and being a helper.

- The best approach with clients is . . .
- The most annoying thing about being a helper is . . .
- Helpers are . . .
- I want to be a helper because . . .
- The best way to get a client to change is . . .
- The most important thing to remember about the helping process is . . .
- The hardest thing about the helping process is . . .
- When I'm counseling a client, I feel . . .
- When I'm counseling a client, I get nervous when . . .
- When I'm counseling a client, I get distracted when . . .
- As a helping professional, I wish I could . . .
- As a helper, I think I'm at my best when . . .
- Helpers get burned out because . . .
- I want my clients to think that I'm . . .
- One thing I do that might get in the way with my clients is . . .
- The most valuable thing I have learned in my counseling class is . . .

level of knowledge or skill. When you are in this zone, you may experience anxiety, confusion, dissonance, discomfort, and sometimes excitement. Often, these unsettling feelings propel forward movement, urging you to take learning risks, to extend yourself, and to try out new skills in a session with a client. In this moment, you are in the "zone" and are faced with the challenge of trying out a new skill or resorting to an intervention with which you are more familiar. What choice will you make? What skills or interventions will you use? Whose needs will be served by your choices? We discuss this further in the next section of this chapter, "Preparing for Ethical Challenges."

PREPARING FOR ETHICAL CHALLENGES

Corey, Corey, and Callanan (2010) defined *ethics* as "moral principles adopted by an individual or a group to provide rules for right conduct" (p. 14). Ethical codes represent "aspirational goals, or the maximum or ideal standards set by the profession, and they are enforced by professional associations, national certification boards, and government boards that regulate professions" (p. 14). Recall that we earlier discussed the major professional organizations for helpers and their related codes of ethics. (Refer to Appendix A for this list.)

It is important for all helpers to become familiar with the ethical code for their professional group because these codes serve several useful functions. First, they give you knowledge about ethical behavior on your part with your clients. As Corey et al. (2010) noted, "[T]he primary purpose of a code of ethics is to safeguard the welfare of clients by providing what is in their best interest" (p. 9). Another purpose of ethical codes is to provide accountability—to help ensure that all helping professionals practice within the scope of the ethical guidelines for their profession. As a result, these codes not only govern your behavior but also the behavior of those colleagues with whom you work. Violations of ethical codes can result in sanctions against the practitioner who has violated the codes.

Often, after reviewing your ethical code, you might feel frustrated because the codes provide general, broad guidelines for ethical conduct rather than specific cookbook-like recipes for knowing exactly what to do in every ethical dilemma you face. Although we review some of the major guidelines for ethical conduct in this section of the chapter and also in other chapters of this book, neither our discussion nor the ethical codes are going to be enough to ensure that you behave in an ethical and responsible way with clients (Corey et al., 2010). Corey et al. elaborated on this when they stated that "codes are not intended to be blueprints for resolving every ethical dilemma nor do they remove all need for judgment and ethical reasoning . . . as each client's situation is unique and calls for a different solution" (p. 8). Indeed the most difficult part of being an ethical practitioner is making these difficult decisions and then assuming personal responsibility for the consequences (Kottler, 2010). This process needs time to be done well, and it should include consultation and documentation. For these reasons, we will also introduce you to an ethical decision-making model in this section of the chapter.

Confidentiality, Informed Consent, and Privacy

The concepts of confidentiality and privacy were introduced to you in Chapter 5. Confidentiality means that helpers do not share information about clients without their consent. However, suffice it to say that violations of confidentiality are a major reason why helpers are sued by clients for malpractice. Practitioners have indicated that confidentiality is the most frequent ethical dilemma they face. In Chapter 1, we discussed *virtue* as an important characteristic of helpers. Virtue comes into play when helpers are confronted with confidentiality dilemmas. As Welfel (2010) noted, "[F]rom a virtues perspective, when professionals honor confidentiality they are demonstrating the virtues of integrity, trustworthiness, and respectfulness" (p. 110).

All major professional associations for helpers stipulate that clients have the right to have their confidentiality safeguarded by their helper, with limitations in some situations. This safeguarding pertains not only to face-to-face interactions but also to electronic communication and transmission of information. Furthermore, safeguarding communication even extends to clients after they are deceased. Because confidentiality belongs to the client, it is generally not an issue when the client provides a written authorization to allow the counselor to release information. But as Glosoff, Herlihy, and Spence (2000) observed, the ethical dilemma is posed when there is a demand or state law that suggests a helping professional should release information the client does not want released. For example, all states have laws requiring helpers to disclose child abuse and neglect, and most state statutes also include elder abuse. (Since the wording of state laws varies, it is wise to become very familiar with these specific statutes in the state in which you practice.) Yet, in some circumstances, a child or an elderly person may not want the helper to notify the appropriate authorities of the abuse. It is important to note that one way to protect both the client and yourself is to inform clients at the outset of any limitations to confidentiality based on your state laws and your professional code of ethics. This is referred to as *informed consent.*

Informed consent is a way to give clients an active role in the helping process and to protect their rights by providing information to them about the helping process. Ethical codes stipulate that helping professionals are expected to discuss any and all aspects of counseling and treatment that impact clients, such as the right to confidentiality, including all the exceptions to it; the nature of the therapeutic relationship; the nature of helping and of the change process; the type of records kept; information about fees and insurance reimbursement; and rationale, benefits, and risks of any treatment strategies used. Informed consent statements should specifically address any limits to confidentiality. Welfel (2010, pp. 118–137) described these nine major types of exceptions to confidentiality as follows:

1. When the client requests a release of information
2. When a court of law orders release of information
3. When a client files an ethical complaint or a lawsuit against the mental health professional
4. When a client initiates civil legal action against another person that includes claims of psychological distress and refers to counseling services used to alleviate such distress
5. When state and/or federal statutes mandate disclosure, such as in instances of elder or child abuse
6. When the client poses an immediate threat or danger to self or others, such as suicide or homicide—although these issues are very complex and do not always require disclosure, "clearly, however, communications from clients who are dangerous to themselves or other people are not always protected by the same level of confidentiality as other material" (Welfel, 2010, p. 126). These instances require a risk assessment and careful consultation and supervision before proceeding! While most ethical codes permit disclosure when clients pose a danger to themselves or others, the legal statues vary and are somewhat complicated. Generally speaking, there is a legal duty to *protect* the victim, and while this may mean disclosure, this can sometimes also be accomplished by an increased frequency of sessions and/or hospitalization of the client.
7. When the client discloses he or she is planning criminal action in the future (note that this disclosure is required in some states—but not all—and even then in limited situations)
8. When, in *some* situations, a client discloses that an identifiable third party is at high risk of contracting the client's communicable and fatal disease (for example, HIV). This is still somewhat of a complicated and "gray" area, and practitioners should not disclose without careful consultation and consensus.
9. When, in an end-of-life issue, the client wishes to hasten death and seems to be either too depressed or incompetent to consent due to a compromised medical and/or health condition. Generally, in this situation, currently no helping professional is mandated to breach confidentiality, although state statutes and case law are rapidly changing in this debate (Welfel, 2010).

Informed consent begins in the initial interview and continues throughout the remainder of the helping process (Welfel, 2010). If the client is a minor or is deemed not competent to give consent, a parent or a legal guardian then provides the consent. In these situations, the helper must discuss both confidentiality and privacy with the client who cannot give informed consent to help these clients understand how information will be shared and used by others. Regulatory boards in many states now require practitioners to provide informed consent via a written disclosure statement in addition to a verbal discussion of such issues. As Welfel (2010) asserts, "[A]ny method of developing informed consent requires a professional who can communicate a lot of information in an efficient and interesting way so that the process doesn't become tedious and overwhelming" (p. 168).

An important part of informed consent and a disclosure statement is the client's right to privacy. This involves a requirement to provide clients with information about the federal privacy act, although "compliance with HIPAA is not in itself sufficient to meet most of the ethical standards for informed consent" (Welfel, 2010, p. 165). Chapter 5 discussed the role of the Health Insurance Portability and Accountability Act (HIPAA) federal regulations as well as some state laws governing the privacy of individual clients and their health records. Corey et al. (2010) stated that privacy is a constitutional right of every individual to "control their personal information (p. 215). Before HIPAA, privacy was protected by the client's signed informed consent statement. Following HIPAA, practitioners are now required to give each client a Notice of Privacy Practices (NPP), which spells out what your agency's privacy policies are and what protected health-related information can be released to a "covered entity" (that is, another person or persons) without client consent or authorization. This NPP must be given to clients in the initial interview. Now, under HIPAA, consent "is no longer required and is now only an acknowledgment of being notified of one's rights. The 'consent' is blanket, required for receiving treatment, not time limited, and is not in any sense informed. It allows disclosure much more freely . . .. This is a very low floor of privacy" (Zuckerman, 2003, p. 20). However, disclosure is limited to diagnosis, treatment plans, appointment times, and symptoms as well as routine treatment, payment, and health care operations. For nonroutine disclosures or for disclosure of any other information, such as private psychotherapy notes, a specific written client authorization is required. For further detailed information on HIPAA and mental health, we recommend you consult the websites of various professional organizations listed in Appendix A and at the federal HIPAA website at http://www.hhs.gov/hipaafaq.

Freeny (2003) observed that the effects of the HIPAA regulations on mental health therapeutic relationships are largely unknown at this point. One potentially useful part of the HIPAA regulations is that practitioners are also required to conduct privacy and security overviews of office procedures, recordkeeping procedures, and the transmission of clinical information in and out of the office. Welfel (2010, p. 165) adds to this discussion in noting that while "technically, HIPAA requirements apply narrowly to electronic communication of personal client/patient information, the wording in the legislation makes its provisions applicable to any professional who uses a fax or an email for any client." HIPAA raises privacy questions such as the following ones: Are telephone conversations private? Who can view computer screens? Who else has access to client information? How is your client-related information on your computer secured and backed up? Is a fax machine used to transmit client information? How is client e-mail handled? As Corey et al. (2010) noted, the use of various telecommunication devices can pose a number of potential ethical issues in terms of safeguarding the client's right to privacy. The American Psychiatric Association (2002) concluded that "no existing security system absolutely protects electronic records in data banks from human error or malice" (p. 2). For example, computerized records that may be stored on a CD or a laptop could be lost or stolen. Cooper (2003) recommended that because of the potential privacy risks to certain telecommunication devices such as faxes and e-mail, helpers should either avoid using them or should obtain client informed consent first, noting to clients the potential risks to privacy and confidentiality. In addition, professionals need to add safeguards in these cases for protecting client confidentiality, such as adding a telephone contact before and after a fax is sent and avoiding facsimile transmissions with very sensitive client records (Welfel, 2010, p. 147). Pope and Vasquez (2007) assert that professionals who use computers to create and store client records should use computers *without* an Internet connection to avoid all opportunities for electronic leaks.

Most professional codes of ethics address the provision of web counseling (technology-assisted distance counseling) and stipulate that helpers who provide these services must determine if the client they are serving is capable of using the required applications and whether this form of helping appropriately meets the client's needs. For example, accessibility to computers may be a greater issue for economically challenged clients as well as some clients with certain disabilities. Also, web counseling poses additional potential risks to client confidentiality, as virtually no encryption method is totally guaranteed from hackers, although using an encryption method is certainly recommended compared to nothing at all. Password protection should be coupled with encryption for added security. Avoiding the storage of client data on mobile devices is also another important security step in protecting client privacy. It is important in cyber counseling that the helper is able to verify the identity of the cyber client to ensure that the person at the other end is in fact the client and not a hacker or relative or friend. Heinlen, Welfel, Richmond, and Rak (2003) have recommended that any and all web counseling be conducted according to a set of professional standards for the ethical practice of web counseling, such as the ones provided by the International Society of Mental Health Online (ISMHO), which is available at http://www.ismho.org. (See also Appendix A.) Welfel (2010) concluded that "in light of the risks to confidentiality and the experimental nature of the medium, professionals entertaining the use of the Web as a means of clinical service need to be cautious about this venture. Not only is careful attention to compliance with all ethics codes crucial, but consultation with an attorney about the legal risks of Internet counseling is also essential if clients are dissatisfied with services, are harmed by them, or their confidentiality is violated" (p. 149).

An emerging issue for helpers has to do with participation in social networking and online communities, such as Facebook, MySpace, Twitter, and YouTube. Jencius and Finnerty (2009) point out that the challenge for helpers represented by these sites involves how to use the sites ethically and wisely. For example, many professional organizations in the helping professions have a presence on social networking sites, such as a Facebook page. But the challenges for individual helpers who post on these sites can be daunting. Some personal information of helping professionals shared on Facebook has ended up as video material published on YouTube—information that would be unprofessional to share with clients. Blogging among helping professionals may compromise client confidentiality. Sometimes, job applicants have been denied employment when potential employers have found information about them through Internet sources. Students have been disciplined or dismissed from sites due to inappropriate or unprofessional content on such sites or due to having clients as "friends" on these sites. As a helper, if you decide to participate in a social networking site, be sure to make it private. On Facebook in particular, helpers need to be attentive to how the site manages advertisement tools known as *apps*, "as once a user initiates an app, it will allow other users and advertisers to access the user's profile even if the security settings are set to hide profiles" (Jencius & Finnerty, 2009, p. 27). Thompson (2008) points out that online communities can potentially blur professional boundaries, and this topic needs to be broached as part of the informed consent process. We further discuss boundary blurring in the following section.

Multiple Nonprofessional Relationships and Boundary Issues

Boundary issues involve some form of limit setting. In ethical conduct, this sort of limit setting occurs in several areas. One area has to do with training, education, and competence. It is important to practice within the areas that you have received training and/or certification. For example, it would be considered unethical to do a vocational assessment unless you have been trained in that area, have a degree in rehabilitation counseling, or are a certified rehabilitation counselor. Generally, the most ethical course of action involves using interventions in which you have received some training and experience. For example, if you have never been exposed to gestalt therapy except in a textbook, it is prudent to seek supervision and training before trying a gestalt intervention on your own with a client.

It is also important to consider what your competence is with age groups, populations, and cultural groups. As Welfel (2010) suggested, "The boundaries of competence extend not just to intervention strategies . . . but also to new populations and age groups" (p. 92). For example, you may be trained to deal with depression in European-American adult clients, but dealing with depression in a child or adolescent or in a refugee from another country (where depression may present very differently) may require different interventions.

Welfel (2010) asserted that helpers have a duty to recognize the "unique parameters" of a case (p. 92). In instances where you are not competent to provide the necessary services, you should either seek additional training or consultation or refer the client to another helping professional who is deemed competent to work with these issues (p. 92). This can be especially challenging when helpers work in rural areas and do not have many referral sources or consultation sources. The ethical challenge for rural helpers "is to provide competent service across a wide range of issues, age groups, and populations, while acknowledging that they are not omnipotent" (Welfel, 2010, p. 93). In these situations, Welfel suggested that if the risk of harm is high and the chance to help is less high, the helper should not intervene. However, if the risk of harm is low and the chance to do well is high, then the intervention is more warranted (p. 94).

In a similar vein, it is risky to use interventions or treatments with clients that fall outside what would be considered the common or typical standards for practice by most helping professionals. According to Corey et al. (2010), if your procedures represent an "unjustified departure from usual practice," you are more vulnerable to a malpractice action (p. 195). Honoring the usual standards of practice has become even more important in recent years because there are now empirically developed guidelines for practice for various kinds of psychological and emotional disorders. For example, with depression, interventions based on either cognitive therapy or interpersonal therapies have been found through research studies to be superior to or more efficacious than other kinds of interventions (Nathan & Gorman, 2007). One cautionary note involving these practice guidelines (often referred to as evidence-based treatments) is that they have not been validated on diverse groups of clients, so their applicability with diverse clients is less clear (Quintana & Atkinson, 2002). (For information about evidence-based treatments, see Gibbs, 2003; Goodheart, Kazdin & Sternberg, 2006; Nathan & Gorman, 2007; Wampold, Lichtenberg & Waehler, 2002). All these challenges to competence require limit-setting or boundary management on your part as the practitioner.

Another very important kind of boundary management has to do with the relationship you develop with clients—specifically, with the kinds of roles reflected by your behavior. When helpers have "connections with a client in addition to the therapist-client relationship, a secondary relationship exists" (Welfel, 2010, p. 217). These kinds of overlapping relationships, formerly referred to as dual relationships, are now called *nonprofessional relationships* or *multiple relationships*. In these situations the ethical challenge is to honor a division or a boundary between "the professional and personal lives of professional and client," as boundaries provide "structure for the process, safety for the client, and the required emotional distance for effective therapeutic work" (Welfel, 2010, p. 218).

The practice of establishing multiple relationships with clients is addressed by the ethical codes of all the helping profession associations. None of these ethical codes refer to *nonsexual* multiple relationships as unethical although, most warn against them. Many of the more recent revisions of ethical codes suggest that some *boundary crossings*—defined by Welfel (2010, p. 218) as "a departure from common practice with the intent to help a client and with some credible evidence that benefit is likely to result"— are unavoidable. For example, there could be potential benefits for clients with a multiple nonsexual relationship if the helper attends the client's graduation or the funeral of the client's family member. Also, clients from some cultural backgrounds may view very rigid boundaries as puzzling and offensive. Anderson and Freeman (2006) referred to these changes as a "paradigm shift" in how the helping professions view multiple relationships with clients because helpers were historically required to make every effort to avoid nonprofessional or multiple relationships (p. 231). Despite these changes, entering into multiple nonsexual relationships with clients should not be undertaken without considerable caution, forethought, and consultation with peers and/or supervisors. In addition, discussions and consultations about potential benefits and harm that could occur from a nonprofessional relationship should be entered into the helper's records. In contrast to *boundary crossings, boundary violations* represent a "departure from accepted practice that causes the client harm—or is likely to cause harm—and are never ethical" (Welfel, 2010, p. 218). A primary example of a boundary violation would be having a s*exual* multiple relationship with a client.

All ethical codes in the helping professions prohibit sexual intimacy of any kind in the helper-client relationship. Most of the codes also state that if a helper has had a previous sexual relationship with a person, that person should never become the helper's client. According to Corey et al. (2010), "It is clear from the statements of the major mental health organizations that these principles go beyond merely condemning sexual relationships with clients. The existing codes are explicit with respect to sexual harassment and sexual relationships with clients, students, and supervisees" (p. 307). A sexual relationship with a client is perhaps the most serious ethical violation that exists and is also one of the most common reasons for a malpractice suit. Helpers can face both civil and criminal charges for sexual boundary violations with clients as well as other serious consequences, such as the loss of licensure. A sexual relationship with a client is the most damaging kind of boundary violation that exists and is often preceded in the helping relationship by much more subtle behaviors, such as excessive self-disclosure by the helper (Smith & Fitzpatrick, 1995). In the earlier section, we discussed the unintended self-disclosure that may occur through social networking sites and how this may also compromise the helping relationship.

It is important to note the distinction between sexual feelings about a client and sexual behavior with a client. A general guideline is that a sexual feeling toward a client is not an unusual occurrence, but acting on these feelings is always harmful and in violation of the ethical codes. This is a good example of a situation in which it is simply imperative to seek consultation with an instructor or a supervisor. The ethical codes also stipulate that sexual relationships with former clients or their families and partners should be avoided. There now appears to be a trend in ethical code revisions toward severely limiting the circumstances under which any post-termination sexual relationship with former clients can occur. This trend may be due to an increased recognition of possible exploitation factors, continued imbalance of power within the counseling dyad, and the lack of clarity about when and whether the professional relationship actually terminated (Corey et al., 2010).

Ethics and Multicultural Issues

All the major helping profession ethical codes mandate that helpers possess an awareness and a knowledge of cultural issues in order to work with clients from diverse cultures and backgrounds in a competent and respectful manner. This mandate is underscored by virtually all codes of ethics that incorporate multicultural and diversity issues into key areas of the code, and more recent revisions of ethical codes show much greater attention to this topic. For example, one way that ethical codes address multicultural and diversity issues relates to broadening of the definition and concept of family to include other individuals who may play critical roles in the lives of our clients (i.e., friends, ministers, etc.). Another ethical issue in the multicultural arena reflects a more thoughtful consideration of the impact that diagnosis can have on marginalized groups when cultural factors are not considered. Finally, helpers need to understand the cultural issues involved in the giving of small gifts and in the cultural meanings of confidentiality and privacy. Houser, Wilczenski, and Ham (2006) note that the values underlying most helping professions' codes of ethics are based on Western principles and values and may not be culturally relevant for clients from different cultural backgrounds with different values and worldviews. These authors have formulated an ethical decision-making model that includes a contextual component, and we include it in the subsequent discussion on ethical decision-making.

Ethical Decision-Making

Given the complexity of the various ethical codes and the complexity of client issues, it is useful to develop a way to make decisions about ethical dilemmas. Recall that the ethical codes are not cookbook-like recipes. They do contain guidelines, which in some cases—such as prohibiting sexual relationships with clients—are very explicit. In other situations, the guidelines are less clear and require that challenging decisions be made by the helper. In this section, we present a generic ethical decision-making model to help you sift through and think critically about the application of ethical codes to various ethical dilemmas that will arise during practice. We draw on this model from a number of sources: Corey et al., 2010; Ford, 2006: Haas & Malouf, 2005; Houser et al., 2006; Welfel, 2010). In general, there are two important guidelines to follow in making decisions about ethical dilemmas: *consultation* and *documentation.* We advise that whenever you are faced with an ethical dilemma, immediately consult with your supervisor(s), as facing ethical conflicts can be stressful for helpers. Second, be sure to document in some written fashion the consultations in which you participate.

The steps associated with ethical decision-making involve the following:

1. Identify the problem, dilemma, or conflict. Most ethical dilemmas and conflicts have some degree of ambiguity about them, which is what makes them dilemmas. In a nutshell, identify what is the core or the heart of the dilemma. Describe how your client is potentially impacted by the dilemma and also how your values and the client's values are impacted by the dilemma. Welfel (2010) notes that part of this identification process includes organization of all relevant case information, including the sociocultural context of the case (p. 33).

2. Identify the ethical dimensions of the dilemma or the conflict and the potential issues involved. What are the most important issues reflected by the dilemma? Who is impacted in this conflict and how? How does the dilemma create risk and for whom? Be sure you are also sensitive to possible cultural issues. As Houser et al. (2006) point out, these issues involved in the dilemma also include such cultural variables as the client, helper, and supervisor's race, gender, personal history as well as agency policies and geographical region.

3. Consider the relevant ethical codes. What do the ethical codes say about this dilemma? How do you feel about the position of the ethical codes? If the codes are ambiguous, consider consulting with the ethical board or committee of your professional organization or the state in which you are working or a seasoned supervisor or colleague who has dealt with such ethical practice issues before. Consult related professional literature.

4. Review relevant laws and regulations. In many ethical dilemmas, there are both state and federal statutes and regulations that impact ethical and legal practices. Consider whether any of these affect your particular dilemma. For example, what does your state say, if anything, about breaking confidentiality if the client is considered to be a danger to self? Does the place where you work have any regulatory guidelines or policies that also affect your decision? Houser et al. (2006) provide a comprehensive list of federal and state statute websites impacting the helping process in an appendix of their book.

5. Generate possible and probable courses of action. At this stage of ethical decision-making, you are basically engaging in a brainstorming process. In brainstorming, your initial task is to identify any and all solutions rather than judging or evaluating the effectiveness of each solution at this point in the process (evaluation of each option is the next step). Often, it is useful to include the client in this brainstorming process too.

6. Estimate the possible consequences of the various options you identified using any evidence available to support each option. After identifying potential solutions through brainstorming, start to scrutinize each solution very carefully. Weigh the advantages and disadvantages of each solution for all those impacted by your decision. Again, it is often useful to assess the potential consequences with your client. Usually, you will end up discarding options that are inconsistent with your values, the client's values, relevant guidelines, and for which there is no support or resources. One of the benefits of this step is to avoid acting impulsively (Ford, 2006).

7. Choose and commit to what seems the best possible course of action. After gathering all your information and seeking consultation, you can at this point decide on the best course of action—the one with the most benefits and the least costs and the one that puts the client's well-being at the top of the list without violation of ethical and/or legal codes and statutes. It is still wise to decide on the course of action with consultation, often involving the client and always involving your supervisor. Now you are ready to implement your decision. Remember to document every step of this process and the actions taken as well as your rationale for such actions.

PREPARING FOR SUPERVISION CHALLENGES

In a nutshell, supervision can be defined as "overseeing," although we provide a more sophisticated definition in the next section, "The Parameters of Supervision." From the time you begin a professional preparation program, such as the one we described in Chapter 1, throughout your field placements and even after you obtain your degree(s) and begin employment, you will be supervised or "overseen" by someone. This is usually a novel experience for most people. Because supervision seems to make individuals feel scrutinized, especially initially, we end this chapter with a section on what supervision is and how you can best prepare for it and use it for your own professional growth and development.

The Parameters of Supervision

In order to understand supervision, one must consider what happens in supervision, who provides the supervision, and in what context supervision occurs. It makes sense to start with a definition. *Clinical supervision* is

> an intervention provided by a more senior member of a profession to a more junior member or members of that same profession. This relationship is evaluative and hierarchical, extends over time, and has the simultaneous purposes of enhancing the professional functioning of the more junior person(s); monitoring the quality of professional services offered to the clients she, he, or they see(s); and serving as a gatekeeper for those who are to enter the particular profession. (Bernard & Goodyear, 2009, p. 7)

APPLICATION EXERCISE 10.2

Preparing for Ethical Challenges

In this activity, we describe two case vignettes. Read each case carefully. Then, apply the ethical decision-making model to identify potential dilemmas, to identify the scope and context of and issues in the dilemma, to review relevant ethical codes and laws, and to brainstorm and evaluate the best course of action for resolving the dilemmas. You may wish to complete the activity on your own at first and then discuss your findings and ethical decision-making process with a group.

A. CASE 1

You are a licensed professional counselor working in a small rural area. You have been seeing a woman for several months. She is financially challenged. At the outset, there was an agreement to see her for a reduced fee. She is a single mom supporting three children. At your next session, she tells you about a family medical emergency. She has no health care insurance and does not have resources to pay for the emergency. She indicates that she will not be able to afford any additional counseling sessions at this time but does not wish to terminate with you since her stress level is so high. She suggests that the two of you trade services to cover the cost of future sessions with you. What do you believe is the best ethical action to take and why? How have you considered contextual variables and ethical codes in your decision-making process?

B. CASE 2

You are working in a local high school. One evening, one of your clients obtains your home telephone number and calls you in a very distraught state. She indicates that she was pregnant and had an abortion several months ago (before she started seeing you for counseling). Now she is having severe misgivings about her decision and is feeling very guilty. She has not told anyone about this, including her boyfriend or her parents—only now is she telling a soul, and that is you. She begs you not to tell anyone. What do you believe is the best ethical action to take in this situation and why? How have you considered contextual variables and ethical codes in your decision-making process?

We will now examine this definition more closely by looking at its parts:

1. Supervision is an intervention. Clinical supervision is different from counseling and teaching, although it is related to both. There are competencies and skills involved in supervision that allow the supervisor to help the supervisees gain competence and insight into the dynamics of counseling. Supervision does not just happen—it is planned.

2. Supervision is provided by a more advanced practitioner and involves evaluation. A clinical supervisor is more advanced than the supervisee, at least on some important variables. Supervision also has an evaluative aspect. It is conducted in part to evaluate the helper. This summative evaluation will occur after there has been enough supervision to expect a certain degree of competence. However, throughout the supervision experience, there is an evaluative component. When the supervisor suggests that the helper should move in a different direction with a client, that supervisor is making a judgment regarding what has transpired during the helping process up to this point.

3. Supervision extends over time. An important aspect of supervision is establishing some clarity regarding the supervision contract. In other words, the relationship between helper and supervisor will be different depending on how long the two will be working together and under what conditions. However, an assumption of supervision is that the supervision relationship will last long enough to allow for some developmental progress for the supervisee.

4. The supervisor monitors and serves as a gatekeeper. While conducting supervision, the supervisor is always aware that the supervisee represents only one level of the supervisor's responsibility. Ethically and legally, the supervisor must also monitor the quality of the services that are being delivered to the supervisee's clients.

Responsibilities of Supervisors and Supervisees

You and your supervisor have certain responsibilities to each other. These responsibilities include having formally scheduled contacts with one another on a regular basis as well as access to supervision on an as-needed basis for crises or emergencies. Another responsibility involves providing each other with information about your cases, especially the management of difficult and problematic cases. You and your supervisor are ethically obligated to safeguard the communication of your clients in a confidential manner within the limits that we discussed earlier in this chapter. Additionally, your supervisor is required to track your work with clients, monitor the quality of it, and provide you with regular and periodic feedback, including suggestions for improvement. The issues surrounding a multiple nonprofessional relationship with your supervisor parallel the issues we discussed previously about multiple relationships between helpers and clients. Bernard and Goodyear (2009) acknowledge there may be instances in supervision in which a structured multiple relationship between supervisor and supervisee can be one that occurs "within the positive context of a maturing professional relationship" (p. 62). However, if a supervisor is also your relative or close friend, employee or business partner, or therapist or confidante, this is considered a potential conflict of interest that may compromise the supervisory relationship. Ethical codes also prohibit supervisors from having a sexual or romantic relationship with supervisees and from condoning or subjecting supervisees to any form or type of sexual harassment.

Another important distinction is that of *clinical supervision* and *administrative supervision*. For example, your employer in a mental health center is your administrative supervisor because this person has the power to hire and/or fire you, to increase your salary, to determine your job description, and so forth. However, this person is not automatically your clinical supervisor. A clinical supervisor must be working with you in some manner to improve your helping abilities. In a situation where supervisors wear both administrative and clinical "hats" simultaneously, they must minimize potential role conflicts and explain clearly to supervisees the expectations and responsibilities associated with each of these supervisory roles.

Finally, supervisors need to be responsive and respectful of contextual differences in supervision. *Context* refers to more than the work or training setting in which supervision occurs; it also refers to larger social and political contexts. Your supervisor must share some values with you in order to be an effective supervisor. He or she must also help you appreciate that both counseling and supervision relationships are determined in part by the parameters reflected in a diverse society.

The Focus of Supervision

What is your supervisor looking for? For beginning helpers or helpers who are working with a new supervisor, this is a common and legitimate question. In fact, role ambiguity (i.e., not knowing what is expected of you) is considered a common issue for novice helpers. Here are some of the areas that most supervisors use to assess and evaluate supervisees:

- Intervention knowledge and skills
- Assessment knowledge and skills
- Relationships with staff and clients
- Responsiveness to supervision
- Awareness of limitations
- Knowing when to seek help
- Communication skills
- Ethical and legal practice
- Multicultural competence
- Judgment and maturity
- Openness to personal development
- Compliance with field placement policies and procedures (Corey, Haynes, Moulton, & Muratori, 2010)

Styles and Roles of Supervisors

Now that you have a better idea of what supervisors look for in training and supervising helpers, we will discuss the choices supervisors make about their own behavior. As you will soon discover—if you have not already—different supervisors have different styles.

APPLICATION EXERCISE 10.3

The Focus of Supervision

For your own part, you can begin to determine the focus of your helping sessions by asking five simple questions:

1. Did I know what to do in the session?
2. Did I know what I wanted to do?
3. Was I comfortable at that point?
4. Was my performance that of a professional helper?
5. What issues came up for me in the session(s) regarding any of the following:
   - Interventions
   - Assessment
   - Relationships
   - Ethics
   - Multiculturalism
   - My own limitations

You can do this with role-plays or tapes of sessions.

Sometimes, their style makes you feel confident and supported, and sometimes, their style has a less positive effect on you. At least some of this has to do with the role they choose as they work with you.

THE ROLE OF TEACHER.   The most common role for supervisors during the initial training of helpers is the teacher role. When in the teacher role, the supervisor takes responsibility for knowing what the helper needs to do or learn. Therefore, the supervisor might instruct the helper about a new technique, model a new intervention, or make other direct suggestions regarding the helper's work. When the supervisor acknowledges the advantages or limitations of a particular helping strategy or the timing of a particular helping strategy, the teacher role is being used. When a supervisor is in the teacher role, there is no question who is in charge.

THE ROLE OF COUNSELOR.   When supervisors focus on the interpersonal or intrapersonal dynamics of their helpers or trainees, they are most likely in the counselor role. The goal of the supervisor in this role is most often the personal growth of the helper. Historically, this role has been widely used by supervisors, based on the assumption that the most legitimate way for helpers to grow professionally is to grow personally. Although the last two decades have offered differing opinions of this premise, there are times when the counselor role is the necessary and most desirable option for the supervisor to use. Furthermore, later in your career, supervisors are more likely to rely on the counselor role to stimulate your growth (Ronnestad & Skovholt, 2003). (However, it is important for the supervisor to be careful to avoid a multiple relationship and to suggest a referral to someone else if extensive counseling for personal issues is needed.)

THE ROLE OF CONSULTANT.   When the goal of the supervisor is to encourage trainees to think on their own and to trust their own insights, the consultant role is most appropriate. When in this role, supervisors limit themselves to being a resource for their supervisees. The authority for what will transpire in the supervisee's counseling is more equally shared. As a result, the consultant role conveys a degree of mutual trust and professional respect not necessarily found in the other two roles. On the other hand, respect is based on the expectation that the helper can and will put forth the effort to use this role suitably.

THE NEED FOR DIFFERENT ROLES.   One well-documented model of supervision is the developmental model, which describes growth as a helper as advancing through sequential skill levels (Stoltenberg & McNeil, 2010). Depending on the developmental level of the helper, different supervisor roles may be warranted.

Research indicates that trainees prefer their supervisors to be in the teacher role initially (Bernard & Goodyear, 2009). This is because novice helpers tend to be unsure of themselves, and the teacher role gives the structure and sense of security that they need at first. After they have received considerable training, they are more likely to prefer a consultant approach. When the supervisor is in this role, it allows the helpers to stretch their wings and use their supervisor primarily as a resource. Throughout training and beyond, the counselor role may be needed (if not welcome) because trainees occasionally hit personal snags that block their therapeutic efforts. You might be asking, "What if I don't like my supervisor's style? What can I do about it?" First of all, you might determine if you encourage a certain role behavior. For example, if you approach supervision by asking a lot of questions, you are inviting your supervisor to assume the teacher role. If you try to convince your supervisor that you felt very emotional about your last session, you are (perhaps inadvertently) requesting the counselor role. When you make definitive statements about your work, you are encouraging a consultant role from your supervisor.

Second, if you believe that the problem is not in your approach but due to your supervisor's preference, you can ask if another role might be tried for a while. Again, knowing about the supervision process allows you to influence it. You might want to have your supervisor in the consultant role rather than in the teacher or counselor role. One supervisee approached her supervisor with this request. Her supervisor's reaction was: "I think that's a good idea. I agree that I've been too active in supervision. On the other hand, if it's going to work, I think you need to come to supervision more prepared. Perhaps you could review your tapes ahead of time and be prepared to identify segments that gave you difficulty and give your opinion of what felt challenging for you and why."

As a final note, we would like to mention that many—if not most—supervisors use all three styles in their work. It is not necessary that you be able to track your supervisor's style at all times. Rather, the issue of supervision role becomes relevant when you are trying to pinpoint why you are feeling stressed under supervision or why you do not think you are progressing as quickly as you would like. The supervisor's role may or may not be the problem, but it is one more important piece of the puzzle for you to consider. Ultimately, it is important for both you and your supervisor to work through any difficulties that arise in your supervision relationship. Your supervisor is ethically bound to refer you to another supervisor if legitimate difficulties between the two of you cannot be resolved. Occasionally, difficulties in supervision arise from supervisee avoidance of supervision rather than from problematic supervisory styles. We address supervisee avoidance in the following section.

Avoiding Supervision: Anxiety and Shame

As we stated elsewhere, supervision is evaluative in nature. Helping clients is a very personal activity, and feedback about your helping style and behaviors can be taken very personally, leaving you feeling highly anxious and threatened by the prospect of receiving supervision. It can be difficult to separate your value as a person from your success as a helper when your motivation to help is strong. Therefore, we will address the issue of avoiding supervision. Most helpers who avoid supervision do so psychologically, not physically, although there are helpers who do avoid actual supervision by missing or coming late to their supervision sessions.

Liddle (1986) has asserted that supervisees' resistance represents self-protective behavior stemming from a perceived threat. She has listed five possible sources of threat in supervision: (1) evaluation anxiety; (2) performance anxiety (living up to one's own standards of performance); (3) personal issues within the supervisee (such as having unresolved feelings about death when counseling a client who is mourning the loss of a loved one); (4) deficits in the supervisory relationship; and (5) anticipated consequences (resisting learning how to confront from fear of client anger). Does knowing about potential threats help to avoid them? How do you overcome those things that threaten you in supervision? First of all, it is essential that you realize and accept that some anxiety in supervision is unavoidable. It could even be said that feeling no anxiety is in itself a form of avoidance. Second, you must try to identify the sources of your anxiety if you are to resolve them. If you feel yourself avoiding supervision, you might discuss this with your supervisor. If that seems too threatening, you could find a peer or alternate supervisor you trust to help you uncover the motives or fears underlying your self-protective behavior. Recognizing that some amount of anxiety is typical for beginning helpers may also be useful.

Shame is another emotion that can get activated in the supervision experience, particularly because of the evaluative nature of the supervision process. Often, the "exposure" that goes along with having one's work scrutinized and assessed provokes shame in the supervisee. And when shame is provoked, your response may be to withdraw or forget, to avoid or withhold information, or to be overly critical of yourself or of your supervisor (Bernard & Goodyear, 2009). What underlies a feeling of shame in supervision is the feeling that you are somehow flawed as a helper. Like anxiety, shame can be better managed when identified, recognized for what it is, and discussed with your supervisor or a trusted colleague. If either anxiety or shame persists throughout your development as a helper and throughout your supervisory experiences, these may represent issues that warrant some professional counseling for yourself, as these emotions often have their beginnings in long-standing family of origin issues.

Putting Your Development as a Helper in Perspective

Although most helpers manage to resist the urge to sabotage their supervisors, why is supervisee self-protective behavior so common, especially early in training? Why are fears so poignant at this juncture? At least one answer lies in understanding the development of the helping professional. A common frustration among novice supervisees is that they feel they are getting worse, not better, during the initial phases of training. What once came naturally to them (i.e., being helpful to others) now seems a monumental challenge that causes humiliation and even shame. It can be very helpful to understand the development of expertise from novice to senior practitioners to assuage some of this frustration.

Ronnestad and Skovholt (2003) described six stages of professional development for helpers from pretraining to retirement. These stages include (1) the lay helper phase, (2) the beginning student phase, (3) the advanced student phase, (4) the novice professional phase, (5) the experienced professional phase, and (6) the senior professional phase. The transition from stage one to stage two is most relevant to our discussion here. In stage one, the future helper is in the lay helper stage—that of being a natural helper in his or her world. It is in this stage that you determine—from a combination of self-evaluation and feedback from friends and family—that becoming a helper might be a good profession for you. The next stage—the transition to professional training or the beginning student phase—upsets the balance that you had as a natural helper. You once had confidence that you had some innate ability to be of help to others; you now feel enthused but insecure. You once relied on what you already knew and your common sense; you are now overwhelmed with new concepts that seem to be coming from several different sources. Feeling overwhelmed is noted by Ronnestad and Skovholt as one of the major reactions to this stage. There are four more stages to follow, none as fraught with insecurity as this one. That is the good news. The more challenging news is that there is no way to get to these more advanced stages without working through this stage and its challenges. The point is that your first supervisory experiences may feel the most uncomfortable for developmental reasons alone. Once you have some experience (and some success) under your belt, supervision should become safer and more rewarding.

Preparing for and Using Supervision

All things being equal, supervision is a shared responsibility between the supervisor and the supervisee. That is, the supervisor needs to conduct the session so it is clear how you are to implement his or her suggestions. However, if this is not clear, you should ask for clarification before you are expected to perform again. This will avoid a common complaint made by supervisors that certain trainees are enjoyable to work with but they do not seem to follow through on supervisory suggestions.

Even if it is clear how you are to use a supervisory suggestion, it is wise to give yourself some time to review what was gleaned from supervision before your next helping session. What seems perfectly clear in a discussion with your supervisor may become muddled or somehow out of reach during the counseling session if you have not integrated the concepts into your own frame of reference prior to the session. This failure to integrate is a common mistake made by supervisees—one that causes them unnecessary feelings of discouragement and embarrassment. The key to maximizing supervision is to invest additional energy between supervision and subsequent sessions with your clients. This will help you avoid having to expend energy after the session to recover from disappointment of lack of success.

Hess and Hess (2008) co-authored a very useful chapter entitled "On Being Supervised." Drawing from the experiences of both a novice supervisee and a senior supervisor, they have recommended a variety of ways that supervisees can prepare for and best utilize supervision. Among these are the following:

- Take an active role in supervision
- Seek to learn what your particular supervisor can offer
- Learn about record-keeping, fee collection, and other agency administrative requirements and then meet these promptly
- Read the pertinent literature
- Avoid the temptation to be evasive in supervisory sessions
- Be respectful of the supervisor's time and of the supervisory "hour"
- Remember that supervision is interpersonal and can feel personal to you (pp. 56–57)

APPLICATION EXERCISE 10.4

Reflective Journaling

Keeping a journal enhances your ability to be reflective and to explore your actions, thoughts, and feelings about aspects of your professional practice. "Reflective journals allow students to raise important questions, reflect on activities and progress, and consider new approaches and resources" (Morrissette, 2001, p. 75). Morrissette (p. 75) suggested the following steps in keeping a reflective journal about your professional helping activities:

1. Your first journal entry should be a short narrative reflecting on the persons, circumstances, situations, and values that drew you to the helping profession.
2. Subsequent entries can focus on your educational experiences and/or your field placement experiences, noting the following:
   - What was the most significant experience I had this week?
   - What questions did the experience raise for me personally? Professionally?
   - How can I use what I learned from this experience in my development as a professional helper?

Summary

In this chapter, we considered the transition that occurs from student to professional. Specifically, we addressed some common concerns that face helpers as they begin seeing actual clients. These include managing stresses induced by the training program and evaluation of one's work, challenges to one's competency and identity, and potential conflict in interpersonal relationships. Many students seek personal counseling for themselves to deal with these and other such challenges, such as anxiety, shame, and the impostor phenomenon. Students also have to bridge the gap between theory and practice.

We described a number of ethical challenges that face helpers, such as confidentiality and its limits, informed consent, and privacy. We pointed out the risks to confidentiality in using telecommunication. We also discussed boundary issues and nonprofessional and multiple relationships, noting that although these are generally to be avoided, exceptions are sometimes made when working in rural areas or when such connections are of clear benefit to clients. Clearly, a sexual relationship with a client is always unethical and must always be avoided. We commented on the need to be familiar with and adhere to ethical codes such as those listed on professional organizations' websites in Appendix A. We also noted changes associated with more recent ethical code revisions, such as the broadening of the concept

of family to include support networks and the role of the counselor in addressing multicultural issues, such as giving gifts. Given the complexity of the various helping ethical codes and the complexity of client issues, we described a model for making ethical decisions that incorporates contextual variables into the decision-making process.

We also explored some components of clinical supervision, such as the parameters and focus of supervision and the style and role of supervisors. Clinical supervision exists only when all these segments operate in union. Regardless of focus, role, or style, supervision is most often described as the most rewarding part of a professional helper's training. Likewise, supervisors report a high degree of satisfaction in their work with supervisees. Both parties are reflecting the distinct pleasure of passing on and safeguarding their profession.

Reflective Questions

1. Reflect on and discuss the primary stresses that face you at this stage of your life. What strategies do you have for managing stress?
2. What do you see as some benefits for getting personal counseling for yourself? What obstacles might stand in the way of this?
3. Describe what your concerns are at this stage of your training and education.
4. Has our discussion about confidentiality changed your views in any way? What do you see as the advantages and the pitfalls of providing disclosure to clients about the limits of confidentiality in an initial session?
5. Discuss some ways to maintain a client's privacy. How might a practitioner unintentionally violate a client's privacy?

6. Identify potential situations in which it might be easier for you to relax boundaries with a client and establish another relationship in addition to the counseling one. In these situations, what steps would you take to safeguard the client?
7. What do you think are the ethical risks in using electronic communication with clients? What about social networking sites?
8. Everyone approaches a new experience with certain expectations. List three things you hope to receive from supervision. List three things you know that you do not want from supervision. Discuss.
9. Knowing yourself as you do, what issues should be a focus during one of your initial sessions with your supervisor?

My Helping Lab

For each exercise, log on to MyHelpingLab at http://www.myhelpinglab.com and then click the Topics tab.

1. Click the Ethical, Legal, and Professional Issues in Counseling tab to locate the Competence and

Malpractice tab. Choose the Video Lab and watch the following selections: Slippery Slope and Response to Slippery Slope. What ethical dilemmas were represented by this helper's behavior?

Did she appear to have a clinical rationale for such behaviors? How could she potentially have avoided being sued for this slippery slope of boundary crossings?

2. Continuing with the Ethical, Legal, and Professional Issues in Counseling tab, locate the Boundary Issues tab. Select the Video Lab and then watch the following selections:
   - An Ethical Decision
   - Response to an Ethical Decision
   - A Sexual Attraction
   - Response to a Sexual Attraction
   - A Wedding Invitation
   - A Response to a Wedding Invitation

   How would you have handled these situations if you had been the helper? You may discuss this, identify this in writing, or even work this out in role-play situations.

3. Continuing with the Ethical, Legal, and Professional Issues in Counseling tab and also continuing with the Boundary Issues tab, select the Case Archive for A Mother's Concern about her Son and a Teacher's Intervention. Read the case and respond to the questions following the case.

4. Continuing with the Ethical, Legal, and Professional Issues in Counseling tab, click the Ethical and Legal Issues in School Counseling tab and then select the Video Lab to watch the following two selections: A Teacher Asks a Student Counselor for Help and Response to a Teacher Asks a Student Counselor for Help. Identify any challenges both to confidentiality and to the working relationship between the counselor and the teacher in this scenario. You may want to role-play this situation to see how you might handle a situation like this in actual practice.

5. Again, continuing with the Ethical, Legal, and Professional Issues in Counseling tab, click the Issues in Counselor Education tab. Choose the Video Lab to watch the following two selections: A Student Faces an Ethical Challenge and Response to a Student Faces an Ethical Challenge. What can you conclude about the ethical challenges in this situation? Can the ethical decision-making model in this chapter help you identify what potential responses could be?

Recommended Readings

Baird, B. (2008). *The internship practicum and field placement handbook, 5th edition*. Upper Saddle River, NJ: Prentice-Hall.

Barnett, J. & Johnson, W. (2010). *Ethics desk reference for counselors*. Washington DC: American Counseling Association.

Bernard, J. M. & Goodyear, R. K. (2009). *Fundamentals of clinical supervision, 4th edition*. Upper Saddle River, NJ: Prentice-Hall.

Corey, G., Corey, M. S., & Callanan, P. (2010). *Issues and ethics in the helping professions, 8th edition*. Belmont, CA: Brooks/Cole, Cengage.

Corey, M. S. & Corey, G. (2011). *Becoming a helper, 6th edition*. Belmont, CA: Brooks/Cole, Cengage.

Heinlen, K. T., Welfel, E. R., Richmond, E. N., & Rak, C. F. (2003). The scope of webcounseling: A survey of services and compliance with NBCC Standards for the Ethical Practice of WebCounseling. *Journal of Counseling and Development, 81*, 61–69.

Houser, R., Wilczenski, F., & Ham, M. (2006). *Culturally relevant ethical decision-making in counseling*. Thousand Oaks, CA; Sage.

Jencius, M. & Finnerty, P. (2009, August). Counselors and social networking. *Counseling Today*, 26–27.

Stoltenberg, C. D. & McNeil, B. W. (2010). *IDM Supervision: An integrative developmental model for supervising counselors and therapists, 3rd edition*. NY: Taylor and Francis.

Thomas, J. T. (2010). *The ethics of supervision and consultation*. Washington, DC: American Psychological Association.

Thompson, A. (2008, August). Counselors' right to privacy: Potential boundary crossings through membership in online communities. *Counseling Today*, 44–45.

Welfel, E. R. (2010). *Ethics in counseling and psychotherapy, 4th edition*. Belmont, CA: Brooks/Cole, Cengage.

APPENDIX A

Websites for Ethical Codes and Related Standards of Professional Organizations

American Association of Marriage and Family Therapy:
http://www.aamft.org

American Association of Pastoral Counselors:
http://www.aapc.org

American Counseling Association:
http://www.counseling.org

American Mental Health Counselors Association:
http://www.amhca.org

American Psychological Association:
http://www.apa.org

American School Counselor Association:
http://www.schoolcounselor.org

Association for Multicultural Counseling and Development:
http://www.amcdaca.org/amcd/default.cfm

Canadian Psychological Association:
http://www.cpa.ca

Code of Professional Ethics for Rehabilitation Counselors:
http://www.crccertification.com

International Association of Marriage and Family Counselors:
http://www.iamfc.com

International Society for Mental Health Online:
http://www.ismho.org

National Association of Social Workers:
http://www.naswdc.org

National Board for Certified Counselors:
http://www.nbcc.org

National Organization for Human Services:
http://www.nationalhumanservices.org

APPENDIX B

Counseling Strategies Checklist

Most trainees view the opportunity for supervision as a mixed blessing. They know that their performance has weaknesses that are more easily identified by an observer. On the other hand, they feel vulnerable at the prospect of having someone view and assess their interview behavior, particularly when they cannot see that person. There are no easy solutions to this problem. Learning to feel comfortable is uniquely a function of your own goals and the observer's awareness of your discomfort. Therefore, you must identify the implications of your helping goals in terms of your own risk-taking, and you must be prepared to communicate your fears.

The Counseling Strategies Checklist (CSC) is suggested as one means of assessing your performance. It is divided into categories that conform to the skills chapters in this text. The instructor or supervisor may want to use parts of the checklist for each interview rather than attempt to complete the total checklist each time you are observed. The checklist provides a point of departure for you and your supervisor to discuss the progress of the interview as well as your input and its effect on your client.

HOW TO USE THE COUNSELING STRATEGIES CHECKLIST (CSC)

Each item in the CSC is scored by circling the most appropriate response. The items are worded so that desirable responses are "Yes." "No" is an undesirable response. Following each section of the CSC, there is space for observer comments. You can use this to record general impressions and specific observations. One way we like to use the CSC is to note to what degree the helper's responses are culturally appropriate for each client. Specific assessment of multicultural competencies can be found in Part VII of the checklist.

After the instructor or supervisor has observed and rated the interview, the two of you can plan to sit down and review the ratings. Where noticeable limitations exist, you and the supervisor can identify a goal or goals that will remedy the problem. Beyond this, you should list two or three action steps that permit you to achieve the goal. After three or four more interviews, have the observer evaluate you again and then compare the two sets of ratings to determine whether progress was evident.

Part I: Counselor Attending Behavior (Nonverbal)

1.	The counselor maintained eye contact with the client.	Yes	No
2.	The counselor displayed several different facial expressions during the interview.	Yes	No
3.	The counselor's facial expressions reflected the mood of the client.	Yes	No
4.	The counselor often responded to the client with facial animation and alertness.	Yes	No
5.	The counselor displayed intermittent head movements (up and down; side to side).	Yes	No
6.	The counselor refrained from head nodding when the client did not pursue goal-directed topics.	Yes	No

7. The counselor demonstrated a relaxed body position.	Yes	No
8. The counselor leaned forward as a means of encouraging the client to engage in some goal-directed behavior.	Yes	No
9. The counselor demonstrated some variation in voice pitch when talking.	Yes	No
10. The counselor's voice was easily heard by the client.	Yes	No
11. The counselor used intermittent one-word vocalizations ("mm-hmm") to reinforce the client's demonstration of goal-directed topics or behaviors.	Yes	No

Counselor Attending Behavior (Verbal)

12. The counselor usually spoke slowly enough so that each word was easily understood.	Yes	No
13. A majority (60 percent or more) of the counselor's responses could be categorized as complete sentences rather than monosyllabic phrases.	Yes	No
14. The counselor's verbal statements were concise and to the point.	Yes	No
15. The counselor refrained from repetition in verbal statements.	Yes	No
16. The counselor made verbal comments that pursued the topic introduced by the client.	Yes	No
17. The subject of the counselor's verbal statements usually referred to the client, either by name or the second-person pronoun *you*.	Yes	No
18. A clear and sensible progression of topics was evident in the counselor's verbal behavior; the counselor avoided rambling.	Yes	No

Comments: _____

Part II: Opening the Interview

1. In the first part of the interview, the counselor used several different nonverbal gestures (smiling, head nodding, hand movement, etc.) to help put the client at ease.	Yes	No
2. In starting the interview, the counselor remained silent or invited the client to talk about whatever he or she wanted, thus leaving the selection of an initial topic up to the client.	Yes	No
3. After the first five minutes of the interview, the counselor refrained from encouraging social conversation.	Yes	No
4. After the first topic of discussion was exhausted, the counselor remained silent until the client identified a new topic.	Yes	No
5. The counselor provided structure (information about nature, purposes of counseling, time limits, etc.) when the client indicated uncertainty about the interview.	Yes	No

6. In beginning the *initial* interview, the counselor used at least one of the following structuring procedures:

a. Provided information about taping and/or observation	Yes	No
b. Commented on confidentiality and privacy; stated limits of confidentiality	Yes	No
c. Made remarks about the counselor's role and purpose of the interview	Yes	No
d. Discussed with the client his or her expectations about counseling	Yes	No

Comments: _____

_____

Part III: Termination of the Interview

1. The counselor informed the client before terminating that the interview was almost over.	Yes	No
2. The counselor refrained from introducing new material (a different topic) at the termination phase of the interview.	Yes	No
3. The counselor discouraged the client from pursuing new topics within the last five minutes of the interview by avoiding asking for further information about it.	Yes	No
4. Only one attempt to terminate the interview was required before the termination was actually completed.	Yes	No
5. The counselor initiated the termination of the interview through use of some closing strategy, such as an acknowledgment of time limits and/or summarization (by self or client).	Yes	No
6. At the end of the interview, the counselor offered the client an opportunity to return for another interview.	Yes	No

Comments: _____

_____

Part IV: Goal Setting

1. The counselor asked the client to identify some of the conditions surrounding the occurrence of the client's problem ("When do you feel _____?").	Yes	No
2. The counselor asked the client to identify some of the consequences resulting from the client's behavior ("What happens when you _____?").	Yes	No
3. The counselor asked the client to state how he or she would like to change his or her behavior ("How would you like for things to be different?").	Yes	No

4. The counselor and client decided *together* on counseling goals.	Yes	No
5. The goals set in the interview were specific and observable.	Yes	No
6. The counselor asked the client to orally state a commitment to work for goal achievement.	Yes	No
7. If the client appeared resistant or unconcerned about achieving change, the counselor discussed this with the client.	Yes	No
8. The counselor asked the client to specify at least one action step he or she might take toward his or her goal.	Yes	No
9. The counselor suggested alternatives available to the client.	Yes	No
10. The counselor helped the client to develop action steps for goal attainment.	Yes	No
11. Action steps designated by counselor and client were specific and realistic in scope.	Yes	No
12. The counselor provided an opportunity within the interview for the client to practice or rehearse the action step.	Yes	No
13. The counselor provided feedback to the client concerning the execution of the action step.	Yes	No
14. The counselor encouraged the client to observe and evaluate the progress and outcomes of action steps taken outside the interview.	Yes	No

Comments: _____

_____

Part V: Counselor Differentiation

1. The counselor's responses were usually directed toward the most important component of *each* of the client's communications.	Yes	No
2. The counselor followed client topic changes by responding to the primary idea communicated by the client.	Yes	No
3. The counselor usually identified and responded to the feelings of the client.	Yes	No
4. The counselor usually identified and responded to the behaviors of the client.	Yes	No
5. The counselor verbally acknowledged several (at least two) nonverbal affect cues.	Yes	No
6. The counselor encouraged the client to talk about his or her feelings.	Yes	No
7. The counselor encouraged the client to identify and evaluate his or her actions.	Yes	No
8. The counselor asked questions that the client could not answer in a yes or no fashion (typically beginning with words such as *how*, *what*, *when*, *where*, *who*, etc.).	Yes	No

9. Several times (at least two) the counselor used responses that supported or reinforced something the client said or did.	Yes	No
10. The counselor sometimes restated or clarified the client's previous communication.	Yes	No
11. The counselor used several (at least two) responses that summarized ambivalent and conflicting feelings of the client.	Yes	No
12. The counselor encouraged discussion of negative feelings (anger, fear) expressed by the client.	Yes	No

Comments: _____

_____

Part VI: The Process of Relating

1. The counselor made statements that reflected the client's feelings.	Yes	No
2. The counselor responded to the core of a long and ambivalent client statement.	Yes	No
3. The counselor verbally stated his or her desire and/or intent to understand.	Yes	No
4. The counselor made verbal statements that the client reaffirmed without qualifying or changing the counselor's previous response.	Yes	No
5. The counselor made attempts to verbally communicate his or her understanding of the client that elicited an affirmative client response ("Yes, that's exactly right," and so forth).	Yes	No
6. The counselor reflected the client's feelings at the same or at a greater level of intensity than originally expressed by the client.	Yes	No
7. In communicating understanding of the client's feelings, the counselor verbalized the anticipation present in the client's communication (i.e., what the client would like to do or how the client would like to be).	Yes	No
8. When the counselor's nonverbal behavior suggested that he or she was uncertain or disagreeing, the counselor verbally acknowledged this to the client.	Yes	No
9. The counselor answered directly when the client asked about his or her opinion or reaction.	Yes	No
10. The counselor encouraged discussion of statements made by the client that challenged the *counselor's* knowledge and beliefs.	Yes	No
11. Several times (at least two) the counselor shared his or her own feelings with the client.	Yes	No
12. The counselor encouraged the client to identify and discuss his or her feelings concerning the counselor and the interview.	Yes	No
13. The counselor voluntarily shared his or her feelings about the client and the counseling relationship.	Yes	No

14. The counselor expressed reactions about the client's strengths and/or potential. Yes   No

15. The counselor made responses that reflected his or her liking. Yes   No

Comments: _____

Part VII: **Multicultural Competencies***

1. The counselor displayed an awareness of his or her own racial and cultural identity development and its impact on the counseling process. Yes   No

2. The counselor was aware of his or her own values and biases about other racial and cultural groups and did not let these biases and assumptions impede the counseling process. Yes   No

3. The counselor exhibited a respect for cultural differences among clients. Yes   No

4. The counselor was sensitive to nonverbal and paralanguage cross-cultural communication clues. Yes   No

5. The counselor demonstrated the ability to assess the client's level of acculturation and to use this information in working with the client to implement culturally sensitive counseling. Yes   No

6. The counselor displayed an understanding of how race, ethnicity, and culture influence the treatment, status, and life chances of clients. Yes   No

7. The counselor was able to demonstrate awareness of the client's worldview. Yes   No

8. The counselor was able to recognize and work with the client dealing with multiple oppressions. Yes   No

9. The counselor and client *worked together* to determine mutually acceptable and culturally sensitive goals. Yes   No

10. The counselor was able to identify and utilize culturally appropriate intervention strategies. Yes   No

Comments: _____

*Adapted from Robinson and Howard-Hamilton, 2000; Sue and Sue, 2008; and Wehrly, 1995

REFERENCES

Adler, A. (1958). *What life should mean to you.* New York: Capricorn.

Alvord, L. A. & Van Pelt, E. C. (1999). *The scalpel and the silver bear.* New York: Bantam.

American Association for Marriage and Family Therapy. (2001). *Code of ethical principles for marriage and family therapists.* Washington, DC: Author.

American Counseling Association. (1997). Governing council minutes of the September 1997 governing council meeting. Alexandria, VA: Author.

American Counseling Association. (2005). *Code of ethics.* Alexandria, VA: Author.

American Psychiatric Association. (2002). Documentation of psychotherapy by psychiatrists, 2002 (data file). Available from the American Psychiatric Association website: http://www.psych.org.

American Psychological Association. (2003). *Ethical principles of psychologists, revised edition.* Washington, DC: Author.

American School Counselor Association. (2005). *The ASCA National Model: A framework for school counseling programs, 2nd edition.* Alexandria, VA: American Counseling Association.

Americans with Disabilities Act of 1990, Pub. L., No. 101-336 & 2, 104 Stat.328 (1991).

Anderson, D. & Freeman, L. (2006). Report of the ACA Ethics Committee: 2004–2005. *Journal of Counseling and Development, 84,* 225–254.

Arredondo, P. & Perez, P. (2006). Historical perspectives on multicultural guidelines and contemporary applications. *Journal of Counseling Psychology, 37,* 1–5.

Atkinson, D. R. & Hackett, G. (2004). *Counseling diverse populations, 3rd edition.* New York: McGraw-Hill.

Atkinson, D. R., Thompson, C. E. & Grant, S. K. (1993). A three dimensional model for counseling racial/ethnic minorities. *The Counseling Psychologist, 21,* 257–277.

Baird, B. (2008). *The internship, practicum and field placement handbook, 5th edition.* Upper Saddle River, NJ: Prentice Hall.

Baker, S. B. (2000). *School counseling for the twenty-first century.* Upper Saddle River, NJ: Prentice Hall.

Bandura, A. (1969). *Principles of behavior modification.* New York: Holt, Rinehart & Winston.

Bandura, A. (1997). *Self-efficacy: The exercise of self-control.* New York: Freeman.

Banikiotes, P. G., Kubinski, J. A. & Pursell, S. A. (1981). Sex role orientation, self-disclosure, and gender-related perceptions. *Journal of Counseling Psychology, 28,* 140–146.

Bartholomew, C. G. (2003). *Gender-sensitive therapy: Principles and practices.* Prospect Heights, IL: Waveland Press.

Beck, A. T. (1976). *Cognitive therapy and the emotional disorders.* New York: International Universities Press.

Beck, A. T. (2005). The current state of cognitive therapy: A 40-year retrospective. *Archives of General Psychiatry, 62,* 953–959.

Beck, J. S. (1995). *Cognitive therapy.* New York: Guilford.

Beck, A. T. & Alford, B. A. (2009). *Depression: Causes and treatment, 4th edition.* Philadelphia: University of Pennsylvania Press.

Bedi, R. P., Davis, M. & Williams, M. (2005). Critical incidents in the formation of the therapeutic alliance from the client's perspective. *Psychotherapy: Theory, Research, Practice, Training, 42,* 311–323.

Bemak, F. & Chung, R. C.-Y. (2008). New professional roles and advocacy strategies for school counselors: A multicultural/social justice perspective to move beyond the nice counselor syndrome. *Journal of Counseling and Development, 86,* 372–381.

Bernard, J. M. & Goodyear, R. K. (2009). *Fundamentals of clinical supervision, 4th edition.* Upper Saddle River, NJ: Pearson.

Bitter, J. (2009). *Theory and practice of family therapy and counseling.* Belmont, CA: Brooks/Cole, Cengage.

Bohart, A. C., Elliott, R., Greenberg, L. & Watson, J. C. (2002). Empathy. In J. C. Norcross (Ed.), *Psychotherapy relationships that work* (pp. 89–108). New York: Oxford University Press.

Bohart, A. & Greenberg, L. (1997a). Empathy and psychotherapy: An introductory overview. In A. Bohart & L. Greenberg (Eds.), *Empathy reconsidered* (pp. 3–32). Washington, DC: American Psychological Association.

Bohart, A. & Greenberg, L. (Eds.). (1997b). *Empathy reconsidered.* Washington, DC: American Psychological Association.

Boyd, V., Hattauer, E., Spivack, J., Deakin, S., Hurley, G., Buckles, N., Erskine, C., Piorkowski, G., Brandel, I., Simono, R. B., Locher, L., Steel, C., Davidshofer, C. (2003). Accreditation standards for university and college counseling centers. *Journal of Counseling and Development, 81,* 168–177.

Bozarth, J. (1997). Empathy from the framework of client-centered theory and the Rogerian hypothesis. In A. Bohart & L. Greenberg (Eds.), *Empathy reconsidered* (pp. 81–102). Washington, DC: American Psychological Association.

Bradley, L., Sexton, T. & Smith, H. (2005). The American Counseling Association Practice Research Network (ACA_PRN): A new research tool. *Journal of Counseling and Development, 83,* 488–491.

Brammer, L. M., Abrego, P. J. & Shostrom, E. L. (1993). *Therapeutic counseling and psychotherapy: Fundamentals of counseling and psychotherapy, 6th edition.* Englewood Cliffs, NJ: Prentice Hall.

Branden, N. (1971). *The disowned self.* Los Angeles: Nash.

Brooks-Harris, J. (2008). *Integrative multitheoretical psychotherapy.* Boston: Houghton Mifflin, Lahaska Press.

Brown, L. (1994). *Subversive dialogues: Theory in feminist therapy.* New York: Basic Books.

Brown, L. S. & Ballou, M. (1992). *Personality and psychopathology: Feminist reappraisals.* New York: Guilford.

Buie, D. (1981). Empathy: Its nature and limitations. *Journal of the American Psychoanalytic Association, 29,* 281–307.

Casas, J. M. (2005). Race and racism: The efforts of counseling psychology to understand and address these terms. *The Counseling Psychologist, 33,* 501–512.

Castillo, R. J. (1997). *Culture and mental illness.* Pacific Grove, CA: Brooks/Cole.

Chung, R. C.-Y. & Bemak, F. C. (2002). The relationship of culture and empathy in cross-cultural counseling. *Journal of Counseling and Development, 80,* 154–159.

Claiborn, C. D., Goodyear, R. K. & Horner, P. A. (2002). Feedback. In J. C. Norcross (Ed.), *Psychotherapy relationships that work* (pp. 217–234). New York: Oxford University Press.

Clark, A. J. (2007). *Empathy in counseling and psychotherapy.* New York: Erlbaum.

Clark, D. A. & Beck, A. T. (2010). *Cognitive therapy of anxiety disorders.* New York: Guilford.

Clark, M. A. & Breman, J. C. (2009). School counselor inclusion: A collaborative model to provide academic and social-emotional support in the classroom setting. *Journal of Counseling and Development, 87,* 6–11.

Colbert, R. D., Vernon-Jones, R. & Pransky, K. (2006). The school change feedback process: Creating a new role for counselors in education reform. *Journal of Counseling and Development, 84,* 72–82.

Constantine, M. G., Smith, L., Redington, R. M. & Owens, D. (2008). Racial microaggressions against black counseling and counseling psychology faculty: A central challenge in the multicultural counseling movement. *Journal of Counseling and Development, 86,* 348–355.

Cooper, G. (2003, March–April). Clinician's digest. *Psychotherapy Networker,* 15–18.

Corey, G. (2009). *Theory and practice of counseling and psychotherapy, 8th edition.* Belmont, CA: Brooks/Cole, Cengage.

Corey, G., Corey, M. S. & Callanan, P. (2010). *Issues and ethics in the helping professions, 8th edition.* Belmont, CA: Brooks/Cole, Cengage.

Corey, G., Haynes, R., Moulton, P., & Muratori, M. (2010). *Clinical supervision in the helping professions: A practical guide, 2nd edition.* Washington D.C.: American Counseling Association.

Cormier, S., Nurius, P. S. & Osborn, C. J. (2009). *Interviewing and change strategies for helpers: Fundamental skills and cognitive behavioral interventions, 6th edition.* Belmont, CA: Brooks/Cole, Cengage.

Corsini, R. & Wedding, D. (Eds.). (2010). *Current psychotherapies, 8th edition.* Belmont, CA: Brooks/Cole, Cengage.

Costantino, G., Malgady, R. G. & Rogler, L. H. (1994). Storytelling through pictures: Culturally sensitive psychotherapy for Hispanic children and adolescents. *Journal of Clinical Child Psychology, 23,* 13–20.

Cournoyer, B. (2011). *The social work skills workbook, 6th edition.* Belmont, CA: Brooks/Cole, Cengage.

Crethar, H. C., Rivera, E. T. & Nash, S. (2008). In search of common threads: Linking multicultural, feminist, and social justice counseling paradigms.

Journal of Counseling and Development, 86, 269–278.

Daughtry, D., Abels, A. & Gibson, J. (2009). Mentoring students and professionals with disabilities. *Professional Psychology, 40,* 201–205.

Daw, J. (1997). Cultural competency: What does it mean? *Family Therapy News, 28,* 8–9, 27.

Day-Vines, N. L., Wood, S. M., Grothaus, T., Craigen, L., Holman, A., Dotson-Blake, K. & Douglas, M. J. (2007). Broaching the subjects of race, ethnicity, and culture during the counseling process. *Journal of Counseling and Development, 85,* 401–409.

De Jong, P. & Berg, I. K. (2008). *Interviewing for solutions, 3rd edition.* Belmont, CA: Brooks/Cole, Cengage.

Dobson, K. S. (Ed.). (2010). *Handbook of cognitive-behavioral therapies, 3rd edition.* New York: Guilford.

Dryden, W. (2009). *Skills in rational emotive behaviour counselling and psychotherapy.* Thousand Oaks, CA: Sage.

Edwards, C. & Murdock, N. (1994). Characteristics of therapist self-disclosure in the counseling process. *Journal of Counseling and Development, 72,* 384–389.

Efthim, P. W., Kenny, M. E. & Mahalik, J. R. (2001). Gender role stress in relation to shame, guilt, and externalization. *Journal of Counseling and Development, 79,* 430–437.

Egan, G. (2010). *The skilled helper: A problem-management and opportunity-development approach to helping, 9th edition.* Belmont, CA: Brooks/Cole, Cengage.

Ekman, P. & Friesen, W. V. (1967). Head and body cues in the judgment of emotion: A reformulation. *Perceptual and Motor Skills, 24,* 711–724.

Ekman, P. & Friesen, W. V. (1969). Non-verbal leakage and clues to deception. *Psychiatry, 32,* 88–105.

Enns, C. B. (1993). Twenty years of feminist counseling and therapy: From naming biases to implementing multifaceted practice. *The Counseling Psychologist, 21,* 33–87.

Enns, C. (2000). Gender issues in counseling. In S. D. Brown & R. W. Lent (Eds.), *Handbook of counseling psychology* (pp. 601–638). New York: John Wiley & Sons.

Faqrrell, E. F. (2005, December 16). Need therapy? Check your in box. *The Chronicle of Higher Education, 52,* 17.

Farber, B. A. & Lane, J. S. (2002). Positive regard. In J. C. Norcross (Ed.), *Psychotherapy relationships that work* (pp. 175–194). New York: Oxford University Press.

Foa, E. B., Keane, T. M. & Friedman, M. J. (Eds.). (2009). *Effective treatment for PTSD: Practice guidelines from the International Society for Traumatic Stress Studies, 2nd edition.* New York: Guilford.

Ford, G. (2006). *Ethical reasoning for mental health professionals.* Thousand Oaks, CA: Sage.

Fosha, D. (2000). *The transforming power of affect.* New York: Basic Books.

Fosha, D. (2002). The activation of affective change processes in AEDP (Accelerated Experiential-Dynamic Psychotherapy). In J. J. Magnavita (Ed.), *Comprehensive handbook of psychotherapy. Vol. 1: Psychodynamic and object relations psychotherapies* (pp. 309–344). New York: John Wiley & Sons.

Fosha, D. (2005). Emotion, true self, true other, core state: Toward a clinical theory of affective change process. *Psychoanalytic Review, 92,* 513–552.

Freeny, M. (2003, March–April). No hiding place: Will patient privacy become a thing of the past? *Psychotherapy Networker,* 42–45.

Gale, A. U. & Austin, B. D. (2003). Professionalism's challenges to professional counselors' collective identity. *Journal of Counseling and Development, 81,* 3–10.

Gibbs, L. (2003). *Evidence-based practice for social workers.* Pacific Grove, CA: Brooks/Cole.

Gilbert, L. A. & Scher, M. (1999). *Gender and sex in counseling and psychotherapy.* Boston: Allyn & Bacon.

Gilligan, S. (1997). *The courage to love: Principles and practices of self-relations psychotherapy.* New York: Norton.

Glosoff, H. L., Herlihy, B. & Spence, E. B. (2000). Privileged communication in the counselor–client relationship. *Journal of Counseling and Development, 78,* 454–462.

Goodheart, C., Kazdin, A. & Sternberg, R. (Eds.). (2006). *Evidence-based practice in psychotherapy: Where practice and research meet.* Washington, DC: American Psychological Association.

Greenberg, L. (2002). *Emotion-focused therapy: Coaching clients to work through their feelings.* Washington, DC: American Psychological Association.

Grepmair, L., Metterlehner, F., Lowe, T., Bachler, E., Rother, W. & Nickel, M. (2007). Promoting mindfulness in psychotherapists in training influences the treatment results of their patients: A randomized, double-blind, controlled study. *Psychotherapy and Psychosomatics, 76,* 332–338.

Haas, L. J. & Malouf, J. L. (2005). *Keeping up the good work: A practitioner's guide to mental health ethics, 4th edition.* Sarasota, FL: Professional Resource Exchange.

Hackney, H. & Cormier, L. S. (2009). *The professional counselor, 6th edition.* Upper Saddle River, NJ: Pearson.

Haeffel, G. (2010). When self-help is no help: Traditional cognitive skills training does not prevent depressive symptoms in people who ruminate. *Behaviour Research and Therapy, 48,* 152–157.

Haley, J. (1997). *Leaving home, 2nd edition.* New York: Brunner-Mazel.

Halpern, J. & Tramontin, M. (2007). *Disaster mental health.* Belmont, CA: Brooks/Cole, Thomson.

Hansen, N. D., Randazzo, K. V., Schwartz, A., Marshall, M., Kalis, D., Frazier, R., Burke, C., Kershner-Rice, K., & Norvig, G. (2006). Do we practice what we preach? An exploratory study of multicultural psychotherapy competencies. *Journal of Counseling Psychology, 37,* 66–74.

Hardy, K. V. & Laszloffy, T. (1995). The cultural genogram: Key to training culturally competent family therapists. *Journal of Marital and Family Therapy, 21,* 227–237.

Harris, A. H. S. (2009). Carl Thoresen: The evolving pioneer. *The Counseling Psychologist, 37,* 275–295.

Hayes, S. C. (2004). Acceptance and commitment therapy, relational frame theory, and the third-wave of behavioral and cognitive therapies. *Behavior Therapy, 35,* 639–665.

Hayes, S. C., Luoma, J., Bond, F., Masuda, A. & Lillis, J. (2006). Acceptance and commitment therapy: Model, processes, and outcomes. *Behaviour Research and Therapy, 44,* 1–25.

Hayes, S. C. & Smith, S. (2005). *Get out of your mind and into your life.* Oakland, CA: New Harbinger.

Hayes, S. C., Strosahl, K. & Wilson, K. G. (1999). *Acceptance and commitment therapy: An experiential approach to behavior change.* New York: Guilford Press.

Haynes, R., Corey, G. & Moulton, P. (2003). *Clinical supervision in the helping professions: A practical guide.* Pacific Grove, CA: Wadsworth.

Hays, P. A. & Iwamasa, G. (2006). *Culturally responsive cognitive-behavioral therapy.* Washington, DC: American Psychological Association.

Hazler, R. J. & Kottler, J. A. (2005). *The emerging counseling profession.* Alexandria, VA: American Counseling Association.

Heinlen, K. T., Welfel, E. R., Richmond, E. N. & Rak, C. F. (2003). The scope of webcounseling: A survey of service and compliance with NBCC Standards for the Ethical Practice of WebCounseling. *Journal of Counseling and Development, 81,* 61–69.

Helms, J. & Cook, D. (1999). *Using race and culture in counseling and psychotherapy.* Boston: Allyn & Bacon.

Hepworth, D. H., Rooney, R. H., Rooney, D. G., Strom-Gottfried, K. & Larsen, J. A. (2010). *Direct social work practice: Theory and skills, 8th edition.* Belmont, CA: Brooks/Cole, Cengage.

Hess, T. H. & Hess, A. K. (2008). On being supervised. In A. K. Hess, K. D. Hess & T. H. Hess (Eds.), *Psychotherapy supervision* (pp. 55–69). Hoboken, NJ: John Wiley & Sons.

Hewlett, K. (2001). Can low self-esteem and self-blame on the job make you sick? *Monitor on Psychology, 32*(7), 58.

Hill, C. & Knox, S. (2002). Self-disclosure. In J. C. Norcross (Ed.), *Psychotherapy relationships that work* (pp. 255–266). New York: Oxford University Press.

Hoffman, R. M. (2001). The measurement of masculinity and femininity: Historical perspective and implications for counseling. *Journal of Counseling and Development, 79,* 472–485.

Horney, K. (1970). *Neurosis and human growth.* New York: Norton.

Houser, R., Wilczenski, F. & Ham, M. (2006). *Culturally relevant ethical decision-making in counseling.* Thousand Oaks, CA: Sage.

Hutchins, D. & Cole-Vaught, C. (1997). *Helping relationships and strategies, 3rd edition.* Pacific Grove, CA: Brooks/Cole.

Ivey, A. E. (1995, April). *The community genogram: A strategy to assess culture and community resources.* The annual meeting of the American Counseling Association, Denver, CO.

Ivey, A. E., D'Andrea, M., Ivey, M. B. & Simek-Morgan, L. (2007). *Theories of counseling and psychotherapy: A multicultural perspective, 6th edition.* Upper Saddle River, NJ: Pearson.

Ivey, A. E., Gluckstern, N. & Ivey, M. B. (1993). *Basic attending skills.* North Amherst, MA: Microtraining Associates.

Ivey, A. E., Ivey, M. B. & Zalaquett, C. P. (2010). *Intentional interviewing and counseling, 7th edition.* Belmont, CA: Brooks/Cole, Cengage.

Jencius, M. & Finnerty, P. (August 2009). Counselors and social networking. *Counseling today,* 26–27.

Jenkins, A. H. (1997). The empathic context in psychotherapy with people of color. In A. Bohart & L. Greenberg (Eds.), *Empathy reconsidered* (pp. 321–342). Washington, DC: American Psychological Association.

Johnson, D. W. (2009). *Reaching out: Interpersonal effectiveness and self actualization, 10th edition.* Upper Saddle River, NJ: Pearson.

Joormann, J. & Gotlib, I. (2008). Updating the contents of working memory in depression: Interference from irrelevant negative material. *Journal of Abnormal Psychology, 117,* 182–192.

Jordan, J. (1997). Relational development through mutual empathy. In A. Bohart & L. Greenberg (Eds.), *Empathy reconsidered* (pp. 343–352). Washington, DC: American Psychological Association.

Jourard, S. M. (1963). *Personal adjustment.* New York: Macmillan.

Joyce, P. & Sills, C. (2010). *Skills in Gestalt counselling and psychotherapy, 2nd edition.* Thousand Oaks, CA: Sage.

Kabat-Zinn, J. (2003). Mindfulness-based interventions in context: Past, present, and future. *Clinical Psychology: Science and Practice, 10,* 144–156.

Kabat-Zinn, J. (2005). *Coming to our senses: Healing ourselves and the world through mindfulness.* New York: Hyperion.

Karasu, T. B. (1992). *Wisdom in the practice of psychotherapy.* New York: Basic Books.

Karen, R. (1992). Shame. *Atlantic Monthly, 269,* 40–70.

Kelley, C. (1974). *Education in feeling and purpose.* Vancouver, WA: The Radix Institute, c/o C. Kelley, 13715 Southeast 36th St., Vancouver, WA 98684.

Kelley, C. R. (1979). Freeing blocked anger. *The Radix Journal, 1,* 19–33.

Kennedy, A. (2004, September). College counseling center extends reach through technology. *Counseling Today,* 10–11.

Klein, M. H., Kolden, G. G., Michels, J. L. & Chisholm-Stockard, S. (2002). Congruence. In J. C. Norcross (Ed.), *Psychotherapy relationships that work* (pp. 195–215). New York: Oxford University Press.

Kleist, D. & Bitter, J. (2009). Virtue, ethics, and legality in family practice. In J. Bitter, *Theories and practice of family therapy* (pp. 43–66). Belmont, CA: Brooks/Cole, Cengage.

Klerman, G. & Weissman, M. (1992). Interpersonal psychotherapy: Efficacy and adaptations. In E. S. Paykel (Ed.). *Handbook of affective disorders* (pp. 501–510). Edinburgh: Churchill Livingstone.

Knapp, M. L. & Hall, J. (2006). *Nonverbal communication in human interaction, 6th edition.* Belmont, CA: Brooks/Cole, Thomson.

Kottler, J. (1991). *The compleat therapist.* San Francisco: Jossey-Bass.

Kottler, J. (2010). *On being a therapist, 4th edition.* San Francisco: Jossey-Bass.

Kramer, P. D. (1993). *Listening to Prozac.* New York: Viking.

Lanning, W. (1997). Ethical codes and responsive decision-making. In J. A. Kottler (Ed.), *Finding your way as a counselor* (pp. 111–113). Alexandria, VA: American Counseling Association.

Lee, C. C. (1996). MCT theory and implications for indigenous healing. In D. W. Sue, A. E. Ivey & P. B. Pedersen (Eds.), *A theory of multicultural counseling and therapy* (pp. 86–98). Pacific Grove, CA: Brooks/Cole.

Lewis, J. B. (1971). *Shame and guilt in neurosis.* Lido Beach, NY: International Universities Press.

Liddle, B. J. (1986). Resistance in supervision: A response to perceived threat. *Counselor Education and Supervision, 26,* 117–127.

Lilliengren, P. & Werbart, A. J. (2005). A model of therapeutic action grounded in the patients' view of curative and hindering factors in psychoanalytic psychotherapy. *Psychotherapy: Theory, Research, Training, Practice, 42,* 32–39.

Linehan, M. (1993). *Cognitive-behavioral treatment of borderline personality disorder.* New York: Guilford Press.

Lott, B. (2002). Cognitive and behavioral distancing from the poor. *American Psychologist, 57,* 100–110.

Lowen, A. (1965). *Breathing, movement, and feeling.* New York: Institute for Bioenergetic Analysis.

Luoma, J. B., Hayes, S. C. & Walser, R. D. (2007). *Learning ACT: An acceptance and commitment therapy skills-training manual for therapists.* Oakland, CA: New Harbinger.

Marra, T. (2004). *Depressed and anxious: The dialectical behavior therapy workbook for overcoming depression and anxiety.* Oakland, CA: New Harbinger.

McMullin, R. E. (2000). *The new handbook of cognitive therapy techniques.* New York: Norton.

McNeil, D. W. & Kyle, B. N. (2009). Exposure strategies. In S. Cormier, P. S. Nurius & C. J. Osborn, *Interviewing and change strategies for helpers, 6th edition* (pp. 486–516). Belmont, Ca: Brooks/Cole, Cengage.

Meichenbaum, D. (2007). Stress inoculation training: A preventive and treatment approach. In P. M. Lehrer, R. L. Woolfork, & W. Sime, (Eds.), *Principles and practice of stress management, 3rd edition* (pp. 497–518). New York: Guilford.

Mellody, P. (1989). *Facing codependence.* New York: Harper and Row.

Mesquita, B. & Frijda, N. (1992). Cultural variations in emotions: A review. *Psychological Bulletin, 112,* 179–204.

Miller, A. (1981). *The drama of the gifted child.* New York: Basic Books.

Miller, D. (1999). *Principles of social justice.* Cambridge, MA: Harvard University Press.

Miller, G. (2006, May 12). Probing the social brain. *Science, 312* (5775), 838–839.

Miller, S. (1985). *The shame experience.* Haberford, PA: Analytic Press.

Minuchin, S. (1974). *Families and family therapy.* Cambridge, MA: Harvard University Press.

Morrison, J. (2008). *The first interview: A guide for clinicians, 3rd edition.* New York: Guilford.

Morrissette, P. J. (2001). *Self-supervision: A primer for counselors and helping professionals.* Lillington, NC: Edwards Brothers.

Murdin, L. (2000). *How much is enough: Endings in psychotherapy and counseling.* London: Routledge.

Murphy, B. & Dillon, C. (2008). *Interviewing in action, 3rd edition.* Belmont, CA: Brooks/Cole, Cengage.

Myers, J. E., Sweeney, T. J. & White, V. E. (2002). Advocacy for counseling and counselors: A professional imperative. *Journal of Counseling and Development, 80,* 394–402.

Nathan, P. & Gorman, J. (Eds.). (2007). *A guide to treatments that work.* New York: Oxford University Press.

National Association of Social Workers. (1999). *Code of ethics.* Washington, DC: Author.

Newman, C. F. (2003). Cognitive restructuring: Identifying and modifying maladaptive schemas. In W. O'Donohue, J. E. Fisher & S. C. Hayes (Eds.), *Cognitive-behavior therapy: Applying empirically supported techniques in your practice* (pp. 89–95). New York: John Wiley & Sons.

Norcross, J. C. (2001). Empirically supported therapy relationships: Summary report of the Division 29 Task Force. *Psychotherapy, 38*(4).

Norcross, J. C. (Ed.). (2002). *Psychotherapy relationships that work.* New York: Oxford University Press.

Ogrodniczuk, J. S., Joyce, A. S. & Piper, W. E. (2005). Strategies for reducing patient-initiated premature termination of psychotherapy. *Harvard Review of Psychiatry, 13,* 57–70.

O'Hara, M. (1997). Relational empathy: Beyond modernist egocentrism to postmodern holistic contextualism. In A. Bohart & L. Greenberg (Eds.), *Empathy reconsidered* (pp. 295–320). Washington, DC: American Psychological Association.

O'Neill, T. D. (1993). "Feeling worthless": An ethnographic investigation of depression and problem drinking at the Flathead Reservation. *Culture, Medicine, and Psychiatry, 16,* 447–469.

Osborn, C. J. (2004). Seven salutary suggestions for counselor stamina. *Journal of Counseling and Development, 82,* 319–328.

Pedersen, P., Crethar, H. C. & Carlson, J. (2008). *Inclusive cultural empathy.* Washington DC: American Psychological Association.

Pedersen, P. & Ivey, A. (1993). *Culture-centered counseling and interviewing skills.* Westport, CT: Praeger.

Pennebaker, J. W. (1990). *Opening up: The healing power of confiding in others.* New York: Morrow.

Perls, F. (1969). *Ego, hunger, and aggression.* New York: Vintage.

Perls, F. (1973). *The gestalt approach and eyewitness to therapy.* Palo Alto, CA: Science and Behavior Books.

Pittman, F. (1985). Gender myths: When does gender become pathology? *Family Therapy Networker, 9,* 25–33.

Ponton, R. F. & Duba, J. D. (2009). The ACA *Code of Ethics:* Articulating counseling's professional covenant. *Journal of Counseling and Development, 87,* 117–121.

Pope, K. & Vasquez, M. (2007). *Ethics in psychotherapy and counseling, 3rd edition.* San Francisco: Jossey-Bass.

Power, S. J. & Rothausen, T. J. (2003). The work-oriented midcareer development model: An extension of Super's maintenance stage. *The Counseling Psychologist, 31,* 157–197.

Pressman, S. D. & Cohen, S. (2005). Does positive affect influence health? *Psychological Bulletin, 131,* 925–971.

Prochaska, J.O., DiClemente, C. & Norcross, J. C. (1992). In search of how people change. *American Psychologist, 47,* 1102–1114.

Prochaska, J. O. & Norcross, J. C. (2010). *Systems of psychotherapy: A transtheoretical analysis, 7th edition.* Belmont, CA: Brooks/Cole, Cengage.

Quintana, S. & Atkinson, D. R. (2002). A multicultural perspective on principles of empirically supported interventions. *The Counseling Psychologist, 30,* 281–290.

Ratts, M. J., Toporek, R. L. & Lewis, J. A. (2010). *ACA advocacy competencies: A social justice framework for counselors.* Washington DC: American Counseling Association.

Reiser, M. (2008). Five tips for mindful living. *Counseling Today, 9,* 14–15.

Robinson, T. (1997). Insurmountable opportunities. *Journal of Counseling and Development, 76,* 6–7.

Robinson, T. & Howard-Hamilton, M. (2000). *The convergence of race, ethnicity, and gender.* Upper Saddle River, NJ: Prentice Hall.

Rochlen, A. B. (2007). *Applying counseling theories: An online, case-based approach.* Upper Saddle River, NJ: Pearson Education.

Rogers, C. (1957). The necessary and sufficient conditions of therapeutic personality change. *Journal of Counseling Psychology, 21,* 95–103.

Rollins, J. (2005, September). The need to reach across campus: Strategies for engaging special student populations. *Counseling Today,* 10–13.

Ronnestad, M. H. & Skovholt, T. M. (2003). The journey of the counselor and therapist: Research findings and perspectives on professional development. *Journal of Career Development, 30.* 5–44.

Rosado Jr., J. W. & Elias, M. J. (1993). Ecological and psychocultural mediators in the delivery of services for urban, culturally diverse Hispanic clients. *Professional Psychology: Research and Practice, 24,* 450–459.

Roysircar, G., Arredondo, P., Fuertes, J., Ponterotto, J., Coleman, H., Israel, T. & Toporek, R. (2002). *Updated operationalization of the multicultural competencies.* Washington, DC: American Counseling Association.

Roysircar, G., Sandju, D. S. & Bibbins, V. (2003). *Multicultural competencies: A guidebook of practices.* Washington, DC: American Counseling Association.

Sanchez-Hucles, J. & Jones, N. (2005). Breaking the silence around race in training, practice, and research. *The Counseling Psychologist, 33,* 547–558.

Savickas, M. L. (1993). Career counseling in the postmodern era. *Journal of Cognitive Psychotherapy, 7,* 205–215.

Sedney, M., Baker, J. & Gross, E. (1994). "The story" of a death: Therapeutic considerations with bereaved families. *Journal of Marital and Family Therapy, 20,* 287–296.

Segal, Z. V., Williams Jr., J. M. & Teasdale, J. D. (2001). *Mindfulness-based cognitive therapy for depression: A new approach to preventing relapse.* New York: Guilford Press.

Seligman, M. (2000). Positive psychology: An introduction. *American Psychologist, 55,* 5–14.

Sharf, R. S. (2007). *Theories of psychotherapy and counseling: Concepts and cases, 4th edition.* Belmont, CA: Wadsworth.

Sharpley, C. F., Munro, D. M. & Elly, M. J. (2005). Silence and rapport during initial interviews. *Counseling Psychology Quarterly, 18,* 149–159.

Shaw, H. E. & Shaw, S. F. (2006). Critical ethical issues in online counseling: Assessing current practices with an ethical intent checklist. *Journal of Counseling and Development, 84,* 41–53.

Siegel, D. (1999). *The developing mind: Toward a neurobiology of interpersonal experience.* New York: Guilford.

Siegel, D. (2006). An interpersonal neurobiology approach to psychotherapy: Awareness, mirror neurons, and neural plasticity in the development of well-being. *Psychiatric Annals, 36,* 248–256.

Siegel, D. (2007). *The mindful brain.* New York: Norton.

Siegel, D. & Hartzell, M. (2003). *Parenting from the inside out.* New York: Tarcher Penguin.

Siegle, G., Carter, C. & Thase, M. (2006). Use of fMRI to predict recovery from unipolar depression with cognitive behavior therapy. *American Journal of Psychiatry, 163,* 735–738.

Smith, D. & Fitzpatrick, M. (1995). Patient-therapist boundary issues. *Professional Psychology, 26,* 499–506.

Smith, E. (1985). *The body in psychotherapy.* Jefferson, NC: McFarland.

Smith, E. (2006). The strength-based counseling model. *The Counseling Psychologist, 34,* 13–79.

Smyth, L. (1999). *Overcoming post-traumatic stress disorder: A cognitive-behavioral exposure-based protocol for the treatment of PTSD and the other anxiety disorders.* Oakland, CA: New Harbinger.

Sommers-Flanagan, J. & Sommers-Flanagan, R. (2003). *Clinical interviewing, 3rd edition.* New York: John Wiley & Sons.

Sperry, L., Carlson, J. & Kjos, D. (2003). *Becoming an effective therapist.* Boston: Allyn & Bacon.

Spiegler, M. D. & Guevremont, D. C. (2010). *Contemporary behavior therapy, 5th edition.* Belmont, CA: Wadsworth, Cengage.

Steinem, G. (1992). *Revolution from within: A book of self-esteem.* Boston: Little, Brown.

Stevenson, H. & Renard, G. (1993). Trusting ol' wise owls: Therapeutic rise of cultural strengths in African-American families. *Professional Psychology: Research and Practice, 24,* 433–442.

Stoltenberg, C. D. & McNeill, B. W. (2010). *IDM Supervision: An integrative developmental model for supervising counselors and therapists.* New York: Taylor and Francis.

Sue, D. W. (1992). The challenge of multiculturalism: The road less traveled. *American Counselor, 1,* 6–15.

Sue, D. W., Arredondo, P. & McDavis, R. J. (1992). Multicultural competencies/standards: A call to the profession. *Journal of Counseling and Development, 70,* 477–486.

Sue, D. W., Capodilupo, C. M., Torino, G. C., Bucceri, J. M., Holder, M. B., Nadal, K. L. & Esquilin, M. (2007). Racial microaggressions in everyday life: Implications for clinical practice. *The American Psychologist, 62,* 271–286.

Sue, D. W. & Sue, D. (2008). *Counseling the culturally diverse.* New York: John Wiley & Sons.

Sue, S. & Lam, A. (2002). Cultural and demographic diversity. In J. C. Norcross (Ed.), *Psychotherapy relationships that work* (pp. 401–422). New York: Oxford University Press.

Sullivan, J. G. (2004). *Living large: Transformative work at the intersection of ethics and spirituality.* Laurel, MD: Tai Sophia Press.

Tannen, D. (1990). *You just don't understand.* New York: Random House.

Teyber, E. (2006). *Interpersonal processes in psychotherapy, 5th edition.* Belmont, CA: Wadsworth.

Thompson, A. (August, 2008). Counselors' right to privacy: Potential boundary crossings through membership in online communities. *Counseling Today,* pp. 44–45.

Toporek, R. L, Lewis, J. A. & Crethar, H. C. (2009). Promoting systemic change through the ACA Advocacy competencies. *Journal of Counseling and Development, 87,* 260–268.

Vacc, N. A. & Loesch, L. C. (2000). *Professional orientation to counseling, 3rd edition.* Philadelphia: Brunner-Routledge.

Vailant, G. (2000). The mature defenses: Antecedents of joy. *American Psychologist, 55,* 89–98.

Vasquez, M. (2005, November/December). How to terminate psychotherapy. *The National Psychologist, 21.*

Vera, E. M. & Speight, S. L. (2003). Multicultural competence, social justice, and counseling psychology: Expanding our roles. *The Counseling Psychologist, 31,* 253–272.

Vogel, D. L., Epting, F. & Wester, S. B. (2003). Counselors' perceptions of female and male clients. *Journal of Counseling and Development, 81,* 131–140.

Walen, S. R., DiGiuseppe, R. & Wessler, R. L. (1992). *A practitioner's guide to rational-emotive therapy, 2nd edition.* New York: Oxford University Press.

Wampold, B., Lichtenberg, J. & Waehler, C. (2002). Principles of empirically supported interventions in counseling psychology. *The Counseling Psychologist, 30,* 197–217.

Warwar, N. & Greenberg, L. S. (2000, June). Emotional processing and therapeutic change. Paper presented at the annual meeting of the International Society for Psychotherapy Research, Indian Hills, IL.

Watson, D. & Tharp, R. (2007). *Self-directed behavior, 9th edition.* Belmont, CA: Wadsworth, Thomson.

Watson, J. C. (2002). Revisioning empathy. In D. Cain & J. Seeman (Eds.), *Humanistic psychotherapies handbook of research and practice* (pp. 445–472). Washington, DC: American Psychological Association.

Watson, O. M. (1970). *Proxemic behavior: A cross-cultural study.* The Hague: Mouton.

Watts-Jones, D. (2004, March–April). Social justice or political correctness? *Psychotherapy Networker,* 27–28.

Watzlawick, P., Beavin, J. H. & Jackson, D. D. (1967). *Pragmatics of human communication.* New York: Norton.

Wehrly, B. (1995). *Pathways to multicultural counseling competence.* Pacific Grove, CA: Brooks/Cole.

Weissman, M., Markowitz, J. & Klerman, G. (2007). *Clinician's quick guide to interpersonal psychotherapy.* New York: Oxford University Press.

Welfel, E. (2010). *Ethics in counseling and psychotherapy, 4th edition.* Belmont, CA: Brooks/Cole, Cengage.

White, M. & Epston, D. (1990). *Narrative means to therapeutic ends.* New York: Norton.

White, M. (2007). *Maps of narrative practice.* New York: Norton.

Williams, L. E. & Bargh, J. A. Experiencing physical warmth promotes interpersonal warmth. *Science, 322,* no. 5901.

Williams, M., Teasdale, J., Segal, Z. & Kabat Zinn, J. (2007). *The mindful way through depression.* New York: Guilford.

Wilson, G. T. (2010). Behavior therapy. In R. J. Corsini & D. Wedding (Eds.), *Current psychotherapies, 8th edition* (pp. 235–275). Belmont, CA Brooks/Cole, Cengage.

Wolpe, J. (1958). *Psychotherapy by reciprocal inhibition.* Stanford, CA: Stanford University Press.

Woolams, S. & Brown, M. (1979). *TA: The total handbook of transactional analysis.* Englewood Cliffs, NJ: Prentice Hall.

Worden, M. & Worden, B. (1998). *The gender dance in couples therapy.* Pacific Grove, CA: Brooks/Cole.

Younggren, J. N. & Gottlieb, M.C. (2008). Termination and abandonment: History, risk, and risk management. *Professional Psychology, 39,* 498–504.

Zuckerman, E. (2003). *HIPAA help: A compliance manual for psychotherapists.* Armbrust, PA: Three Wishes Press.

Zur, O., Williams, M., Lehavot, K. & Knapp, S. (2009). Psychotherapist self-disclosure and transparency in the Internet age. *Professional Psychology, 40,* 22–30.

INDEX